BLOCKED

JENNIFER LANE

PSYCHED PUBLISHING

Published by Psyched Publishing

First published, October 2014

The characters and events in this book are fictitious.
Any similarity to real persons, living or dead,
is coincidental and not intended by the author.

Library of Congress Cataloguing-in-Publication Data

Lane, Jennifer.
Blocked / Jennifer Lane – 1st ed.
ISBN: 978-0-692-30310-8
1. Volleyball — Fiction. 2. New Adult Romance — Fiction.
3. Politics — Fiction. 4. Psychology — Fiction. I. Title

10 9 8 7 6 5 4 3 2 1

Book Design by Coreen Montagna

Printed in the United States of America

To student-athletes and future leaders of America:
May you find balance and grace.

1
Lucia

As I plopped down on the bleachers and scanned my new teammates around me, one word came to mind: *heaven*. I wasn't the tallest girl in the gym for the first time in my eighteen years on earth.

The teammate on my right studied me, and I checked her out too. She was about my height—she probably blocked the ball like a wall of concrete—but she was way thinner than me. Her long blond hair glimmered in the overhead lights, and her unflinching stare just about guaranteed she was a junior or senior. She looked a little like the supermodel Gisele Bundchen. Was she the best hitter on the team I'd read about: Madison Brooks? No, Madison had appeared Black in the action shot I saw in the volleyball team media guide.

When the Gisele-lookalike turned to talk to another teammate, I scanned back over the rest of the twelve or so girls sprawled on the bleachers. It was easy to find the one who must have been Madison… her big smile and little wave from the front row were hard to miss. I lifted my hand to wave back, then panicked. *Is she smiling at me?*

I peeked over my shoulder to make sure, then looked back down to find her smirking as she pointed and mouthed, "Yes, you." *Great, the team captain thinks I'm an idiot before our first practice has even started.* I was acting every bit the stupid freshman I didn't want to be.

Madison wore a sleeveless shirt, which drew attention to her shoulder muscles and long, lean arms. *Hijole, she's fit.* With a growing sense of alarm, I realized I likely outweighed every girl on the team. *Awesome.* I pursed my lips. *Thanks, Mom and Dad. Gracias for your fat Mexican genes.*

The squeak of a door interrupted my inner diatribe. Coach Holter crossed the shiny gym floor with long strides, followed by his two assistants—Brian and Kara. Kara had sounded really kind during our phone conversation last week, and I hoped she was as nice in person because *somebody* had to balance out Wyatt Holter's scary intensity. I noticed my teammates sitting up straighter as Coach approached. The same gruff voice that had made me tremble on the phone a week ago now addressed the team.

"Welcome back, and I hope you had a relaxing time off," Coach said.

Blond Supermodel quietly grumbled, "A whole week off, *wow*."

"Because we're getting right into it this August," he continued. "If you aren't fit now, you will be soon—we'll make sure of that. We'll take advantage of our time before classes start in a couple of weeks. Our first order of business is some compliance paperwork over at Griffin. Let's—" He frowned as Kara leaned in to whisper in his ear. He glanced at his watch then nodded. "Right. We should have the freshmen introduce themselves before we head over."

My cheeks flamed when all eyes turned to me. Surely I wasn't the only first-year student on the team. *But everyone must know who I am, right? Should I say my name?*

When nobody said anything, Kara glanced at me before she spoke up. "The upperclassmen already know most of the freshmen from their recruiting visits, but why don't we refresh everyone's memory? Kaitlyn, would you introduce yourself?"

Right—everyone else already knew each other. I hadn't visited this Midwestern university because I was all set to play down south for my home state at the University of Texas...until that situation crashed and burned ten days ago.

A girl with spiky black hair said, "I'm Kaitlyn Thomas, and I'm from San Diego." On the short side, she was probably a setter or a defensive specialist. "I'm a libero." *Bingo*—she played defense. I hoped those spindly legs of hers were quick.

"Thanks, Kaitlyn," Kara said, then nodded to a long-legged girl. "Brianna?"

Brianna sat up a little straighter, but I heard nothing from my perch on a higher row.

"Speak up," Coach Holter demanded.

When she turned to face the bleachers, the poor girl looked terrified. "I'm Brianna?" Her voice trembled, and she forced a swallow. "I'm from Pittsburgh."

There was a pause, then Coach said, "She's a powerful outside hitter, if you can believe that." He emitted a little chuckle.

Was that supposed to be a joke? I shifted a bit, feeling uncomfortable as Brianna stared at her shoes. I did *not* want to get on Coach's bad side.

Oh, crap...now he stared straight at me. "Our last freshman was a recent addition." As he gestured my direction, all eyes zoomed up toward me. I gulped. "I think Lucia Ramirez needs no introduction," he continued. "But, Lucia, I want you to tell everyone how you joined us so late in the game."

My heart thrummed, and I sat on my hands to hide their shaking. Dad would be angry that the public speaking lessons hadn't helped one bit. "I had a scholarship at UT, uh, University of Texas," I managed. It seemed like everyone looked at my midsection, so I wrapped my arms around my muffin top. "I'm from Houston. But the head coach at Texas just resigned..." I wasn't sure if I should mention the scandal leading to his resignation. Coach's hard stare made me decide to drop it. "So, um, I was looking for another top-five program, and we called Coach Holter, and..."

He actually smiled at me. "And we were lucky we had some scholarship money available at the last minute. Welcome, Lucia." When his eyes drifted above me, his smile faded. "I don't recall inviting Secret Service to this meeting."

I'd forgotten about my new companions, Frank and Allison, and I glanced back to find them sitting in the top row of the bleachers. My face lit on fire.

"Sir," Frank boomed as he nodded at Coach. "We haven't had time to brief you yet, but you can be assured we'll be attending all volleyball team functions. Where Ms. Ramirez goes, we go."

I swiveled back around to catch Coach's scowl. *Great.* I'd already angered him, five minutes after meeting him. So much for my hope that life would be more normal here than in Texas, where the media had hounded my family non-stop.

The Gisele-lookalike nudged me and whispered, "Adolfo Ramirez is your *dad?*"

"Yeah." I smiled.

Her perfect little nose wrinkled with distaste. "So you're against abortion."

Here we go. Dad had warned me that universities were "bastions of liberal orthodoxy," and here was my first induction into the faith. "Why do you want to know?" I whispered.

Her blue eyes narrowed. "You're pro-life—I can tell. No one messes with *my* body." She tossed her hair. "But I don't have to worry—your dad won't win anyway."

My dad will *win*, I silently countered, even as I smiled sweetly. I couldn't wait to spike the ball right through her block, no matter how tall she was. In health class we'd learned that if Barbie were human, she'd be six feet tall and weigh one hundred pounds, and Gisele seemed pretty close to those dimensions. By contrast, *my* doll representation would be more like Barbie's Fat Mexican-American Republican sidekick.

"Nina," Coach barked, zooming my attention back on him. He glared at the supermodel formerly known as Gisele. "Time to head to the compliance meeting. Lead the way."

Nina popped to her feet and hustled down the bleachers. The rest of the team followed suit, and I found myself pulled along in a stream of tall, built women on a brisk walk out of the gym. I looked over my shoulder and saw Secret Service Agent Allison wink at me before she slid on her aviator sunglasses. Hot, stagnant air greeted us as we filed out the door, but it was nothing like the blanketing humidity of Houston. I bet Allison and Frank were more comfortable in their constant suit jackets here in the north.

I stiffened as Coach Holter and his assistants approached me. We maintained our quick pace as they each shook my hand. "When did you get into town?" Brian asked. He was tall and lanky—I bet he'd played college ball.

"Last night," I answered.

"That's not much time to get settled." Kara smiled.

Self-consciously, I played with the tip of my braided ponytail. I'd mastered the sporty do years ago. "My dad asked me to attend his speech in Detroit yesterday."

"Must be tough to be the daughter of the Republican nominee for president."

You have no freaking idea.

"I saw that speech on TV," Coach said. "Governor Ramirez made a big deal about you playing for Highbanks University when he introduced you to the crowd."

I grinned, thinking Coach would be proud to have his volleyball program highlighted on a national stage.

But Coach maintained his stony expression. "It's interesting you came all the way here…with this being a swing state and all."

Wait a minute—was he implying my choice of school was a *political* decision? I scrunched my forehead. Dad wouldn't have manipulated me into choosing this university simply to win votes, would he? No, that didn't sound like him. "But…my club coach in Houston—"

"Brian, Kara," Coach interrupted. "Let's talk to Secret Service. I don't like the idea of them breathing down our necks every second."

I watched them drop back to match stride with Allison and Frank. I turned around and clenched my teeth. Coach Holter hadn't let me explain that my club coach Susie had been the one to recommend Highbanks. Susie had played for Coach Holter almost twenty years ago. "*He's tough,*" she'd said. "*But he's one of the best coaches in the country.*"

I sighed. I'd seen the tough part already. Still waiting to see the best part.

"Hey, Ramirez," a friendly voice said, and I turned to find a welcoming smile. "I'm Maddie Brooks."

"The team captain?"

"That's me." We were about the same height—six-foot-two—and she studied me for a moment. "You're obviously a strong side hitter."

I cocked my head. "How'd you know?"

"You look strong as hell, girl." She rubbed my right shoulder.

I felt twenty pounds lighter all of a sudden. The awesome team captain said something nice about me! "Actually, I'm a lefty."

"Even better!" Maddie's eyes lit up. "Bridgetown won't know what hit them when you slam the ball down the line."

I laughed. The Ramirez-Monroe presidential rivalry had just begun, but the storied Highbanks-Bridgetown sports rivalry had been around for years. When things had gone south at Texas, I'd considered playing at Bridgetown until my club coach Susie had squashed that idea like a tiny bug.

"So, what happened to the Texas coach?" asked Maddie.

I peeked back at Coach Holter, who appeared engrossed in lecturing Allison and Frank. Frank's jaw looked pretty tight but Allison maintained her serene smile. *Good luck fighting US Government regulations, Coach.*

Noting my hesitation, Maddie asked, "Or maybe that was a nosy question?"

"It's okay." I shrugged. "Apparently the Texas coach had an affair with one of the players."

Maddie's jaw dropped.

"When he got caught, the athletic director made him resign."

"Whoa."

I nodded. "He seemed like a cool guy on my recruiting trip, and I had a full ride. But my dad freaked—he told me I couldn't go to UT anymore, even after the coach resigned."

Maddie blinked. "Why?"

"My dad was concerned that the affair had gone on for two years before anyone found out." To mimic my father, I tucked in my chin and deepened my voice, allowing a subtle version of Grandpa's Mexican accent to creep in. "*My daughter will* not *play for such a morally reprehensible program.*"

"My God!" She snickered. "You sound just like him. It's so cool to have somebody famous on our team."

As we approached Griffin Athletic Complex, I heard the throng of reporters a moment before I saw them. "You might not think so in a second."

"Lucia Ramirez!" a female reporter called as she jogged toward me in heels and awakened the ten or so ambulance chasers behind her.

My chest tightened as I braced myself. I immediately felt the presence of Frank on one side and Allison on the other, hustling me forward and pushing Maddie to the side. "Sorry," I said, and she nodded.

The breathless reporter neared me. "How do you like Highbanks, Lucia?"

"Dammit, how'd they know we'd be here?" Allison whispered as her eyes darted right and left.

Frank tapped his left ear—he must have been getting something on his earpiece. "Jansen just told me they were already here for Monroe."

My knees almost buckled—I'd thought it would be at least a couple of days before I ran into Dane Monroe. Maybe it wasn't such a great idea to attend Highbanks. "Is the men's team's inside?" I cried.

Questions hurled toward me like whizzing volleyballs.

"Why aren't you at University of Texas?"

"Are you living in the dorms, like normal freshmen?"

"Why'd you choose the same school as Dane Monroe?"

I closed my eyes. *Why, indeed? Why attend the same university as the son of the Democratic nominee for president—my dad's opponent in the election?* When my eyes opened, we were almost at the door.

"Back off, people!" Coach hollered from behind me. He gestured to the sign posted to the right of the entrance: *No Media and No Autographs Allowed.* I felt certain the sign was for the benefit of the wildly popular football team. This was probably the first time a lowly sport like volleyball had received the media's invasive attention.

As I'd been instructed, I didn't respond to any of the questions zinged at me. Allison and Frank jostled me inside, and my teammates followed, with the coaches bringing up the rear. Coach clanged the door shut on the reporters, and I felt the familiar squeeze of pressure in my chest that followed every media encounter. *Don't panic.* I closed my eyes and forced a breath down my narrowing windpipe.

"You're okay," Allison whispered.

I saw her reassuring smile a moment before I noticed Coach's frown. I knew I'd better get my anxiety in check if I wanted a chance to play for him sometime in the next four years.

"Head to the athletic training classroom," Coach ordered, and we filed down the hall. My muscles tingled from oxygen deprivation. When I snuck a glance over my shoulder to confirm the reporters were still safely outside, I exhaled. With the election still three months away, it wasn't a good sign that media attention already initiated such panic.

I didn't realize Madison had stopped ahead of me until I almost plowed into her. Allison caught my elbow with her left hand.

"Go on in!" Coach barked from behind me.

From the front of the line, Blond Nina frowned at him. "There's another team in the classroom."

Coach bustled past me as he checked his watch. "They should be done by now. It's our turn."

"Hey, Frank," a deep, male voice called.

I looked down the hall to find a muscled Secret Service agent approaching us. That must mean Dane Monroe was nearby. *Oh, no.*

Frank left my side and walked toward the behemoth with his hand extended. "How ya doin', Brad?" he asked as he pumped his hand.

The button of Brad's suit jacket strained across his expansive pectorals, and he wore his mirrored sunglasses even though we were inside. "Good, buddy, good. Welcome."

Frank gestured toward us. "Let me introduce you to my partner, Allison."

Brad's heft shifted side to side as he hulked over. Could he run fast with all that bulk?

"Ms. Ramirez." Brad nodded at me.

"Lucia is fine," I corrected.

Brad shook Allison's hand. "I've heard good things about you from my partner."

"Really?" Allison seemed pleased. "Who's that?"

"She's inside with the men's team," Brad said. "China Halloway."

Allison's hold on my elbow tightened as her face froze. She must have noticed my wiggle because she let go of my arm. "I thought China was on the VP's detail?"

"Once the committee decided Mr. Monroe and Ms. Ramirez would be protected before the election, she got reassigned," Brad said.

"Wow," Allison gushed. "That's great. I mean, uh, good for her, I guess."

What was *up* with Allison? She wouldn't meet my questioning eyes. I'd have to ask her about that agent, China, later.

Brad looked at Frank. "Where're you putting up Ms. Ramirez?"

"For now we're at the campus hotel. An advance team is scoping out a secure location."

Brad shook his head. "Good luck finding a place—it took us a week to identify our current living quarters. The campus area's crime central, but Mr. Monroe didn't want to be too far off campus because of all of his practices and games."

Frank shrugged. "We've got a good team on it."

"Okay!" Coach hollered, drawing our attention. "They're finally done. Once the men's team exits, get in there."

Brad thumped Frank on the back. "Catch you guys later."

A gray-haired man emerged into the hallway—*he must be the men's volleyball head coach*—followed by a few more tall guys. When the next player stepped out, I held my breath. Dane Monroe now stood ten yards away.

He searched the hallway for a moment before he found me. Deep blue eyes narrowed into slits as he moved toward me.

His tan face and broad shoulders would make any girl swoon, but what I liked best about him was that he towered over me—all six-foot-eight of him. It wasn't often I had the pleasure of looking up at a man, but I definitely had to aim high to see his tousled blond hair.

Why had I chosen this university? Sure, the volleyball team was top-ranked, they had a good business school, and Susie had recommended it. But the real reason? The reason I hadn't shared with anyone, *especially* my die-hard Republican family?

I was in love with Dane Monroe.

2

Dane

I can't fucking believe it. I thought for sure Brad was shitting me when he said Lucia Ramirez was coming to play volleyball here. No way Hitler's daughter would crash my world like that. But there she stood, behind Nina, Maddie, and a few other girls' players I knew. Secret Service agents flanked her. Her big, brown eyes widened as I approached.

"What're you doing here?" I hissed. "It's bad enough you play my sport, but now you go to my school, too? Couldn't you choose another program?"

It seemed like it took a moment for my words to register. *Is she as mentally retarded as her dad?* Then her eyes turned down as she took a step back. *Crap, is that a look of…hurt?* For a second I felt a twinge of guilt in my gut, but then I remembered all the things her father had said on the campaign trail. Accusing the disabled of mooching off the government? Calling women who got abortions *murderers?* The guy was a piece of work.

"And now I won't be able to *move* without the media hounding me," I continued. "They're all jizzed up about Adolf's daughter."

A storm brewed in those shiny eyes as her tawny skin flushed. "My father's name is *Adolfo*."

Her voice was higher than I'd expected from such a tall, muscular girl. Higher, and sort of breathy. *Sort of sexy.*

I felt Brad come up behind me. "Dane, it's time for practice, buddy."

I stared at her. "Why *did* you come here? Besides trying to torture me?"

"This isn't about you at all." Her arms laced in front of her chest. "I had a full ride at Texas— "

"Why didn't you stay there, then?"

"The coach resigned! My father wanted me to find a new school."

I shook my head. "This is *my* territory. I grew up here. You can tell Adolf he won't win this state no matter how many of his kids attend Highbanks."

Her mouth popped open. She looked about to deliver a salty retort when Coach Holter called to her from the doorway of the classroom.

"Lucia! Let's go!"

She jumped and gave a little squeak. She sucked in a breath through her teeth and glared at me, then jogged to the classroom as she muttered in Spanish.

"Did you just call me a *bitch?*" I challenged.

She spun around with a flaming blush on her cheeks and tugged on the hem of her shorts.

"Mr. Monroe, it's time to leave," China ordered. She patted the shoulder of Lucia's female agent and walked my direction. *Shit.* I could ignore Brad, but China tended to get her way. And now *I* was the one noticing my team had vanished. But I never backed down from a battle.

I gave Lucia a smug smile. "Yeah, I speak Spanish. You got something to say, you say it to my face."

"Lucia!" Coach Holter barked.

Ignoring him, she took a step toward me. Her long braid whipped behind her shoulder. "I have my reasons for being here, and it's not about the election."

"What reasons?"

"C'mon," said the agent with blond curly hair as she put her arm around Lucia's shoulders. Her voice lowered. "Your coach is having a cow."

"Oh, no." Lucia closed her eyes, turned, and made a beeline for the classroom. At the door, Coach Holter grabbed her shoulder and jabbed his finger toward her chest. I couldn't hear his words, but he was pissed. Lucia's head lowered as she nodded, and I couldn't take my eyes off her.

Her thick, black hair shone. She wore modest dresses on the campaign trail, but her volleyball practice uniform—a form-fitting gray T-shirt and black Spandex shorts—was far superior. The toned muscles of her arms and long-ass legs left no doubt she was a scholarship athlete. Whether or not she could really play—to *earn* that scholarship—was yet to be seen. She didn't have much of a chest, but the luscious curve of her butt more than compensated. Talk about junk in the trunk. *Damn.* Why'd all of that have to belong to *her?*

Coach Holter's lecture appeared to gain momentum and his voice rose loud enough for me to hear. "Do you think you deserve special treatment!?"

Lucia shook her head as she continued staring at her shoes.

"Look at me when I talk to you!"

When her head snapped up, I could see tears in her eyes. As she stared wide-eyed at her coach, her clenched fists shook at her side. *La chica* looked on the verge of meltdown, and I didn't envy her. I'd been on the receiving end of my club coach's ass-chewing too many times to count. Thank God my college coach, Phil, was as chill as they came.

China's stern face filled my line of vision. "Time to *go*, Mr. Monroe." Her short brown hair, gelled into place, didn't move an inch as she shook her head. "I know it must be a pleasure for you to watch Ms. Ramirez get reamed by her coach—"

"Not really." Sure, it was kind of fun to see Miss-Conservative-Know-it-All get her comeuppance, but I wasn't made of stone.

"But if we don't leave now, you'll be late for practice."

By the time I was able to step around China to check out the doorway again, Lucia and Holter had disappeared into the classroom. "Fine. Let's go."

"This way." Brad pointed to the opposite end of the hallway. "If ya want to avoid the media."

I was all for that, especially now that Lucia's arrival had spawned a mutinous star-fucker population. "Make sure you keep those Fox News asshats away from me," I muttered.

"No problem." China grinned as we climbed into our vehicle. She cranked the A/C from the driver's seat.

Next to me in the back seat of the stifling-hot Hummer, Brad remained silent. He'd been a Marine, and I was pretty sure he would embrace the whole hoo-rah guns thing and vote for Adolf come election time. I tried not to hold that against him, but *really?* How could a badass like Brad want that egomaniac Ramirez as leader of the free world? My mom would be so much better. *She* will *be much better*, I corrected myself. Damn Lucia for giving me Adolf on the brain.

Ten minutes later, I warmed up for practice with my teammate and best friend, Josh Williams. Amidst our game of pepper—back and forth volleyball bumps, sets, and spikes—he peppered me with questions.

"Why didn't she go to Texas like she was supposed to?"

I felt a bead of sweat slide down my forehead as I spiked the ball to his left. It was a solid hit but he dug the ball with ease. "To make my life miserable."

Josh frowned. "That's rough, bra." His slow, southern-California dialect made me smile every time. He sounded stoned twenty-four-seven. "What'd your mom say about it?"

"Haven't talked to her." I dug his spike and passed the ball to him in a perfect arch.

When he set the ball back to me with stiff fingers, I stifled a laugh. "Good thing you're not the setter." The set was so bad I had to improvise with a roll-off hit that he dove forward to retrieve.

"We can't *all* have your pillow-soft hands," he grunted after peeling himself off the floor in time to zing a spike at my face. My defensive maneuver didn't go quite as planned, and the ball dribbled to the gym floor, rolling toward our coach. *Damn, Phil saw my screw-up.*

Josh grinned at Phil as he scooped up the ball.

Phil rolled his eyes with a look that seemed to say, *Touché.*

"So," I conceded, "playing sand all summer *did* elevate your game, like you promised Phil it would."

Josh bounced the ball. "Dude, I just couldn't take another humid summer here. The beach—she called to me. She wanted me back in her cool clutches, and we danced together in sandy synchrony."

Huh? I guess I'd have to take his word for it. When I glanced at Phil, he arched one gray eyebrow. After a year with him, I knew that look. It meant *Less talking, more working.* "C'mon," I said as I wiped my elbow across my forehead, "let's see if you can handle the moves *I* learned this summer."

"Bring it, Mr. Setter Man." The ball floated my way, and I cradled it with my "pillow-soft" hands to launch the perfect set.

About midway through our three-hour practice, Phil called me over. By now sweat had drenched my shirt, but it felt amazing to get back to work with the entire team. My individual sessions with the coaches and pick-up games with the guys had been somewhat satisfying this summer, but full-on team practice really scratched my itch. With that thought, I snuck a scratch as I adjusted my jockstrap.

"Get your hands off your junk," Phil said.

My hand stilled.

"You're the setter," he continued as he nodded toward the rolling cart of volleyballs. "Don't want our balls to get sticky."

I rested my hands on my hips as I waited for him to get to his real point. He was old, so sometimes that took a while. His pale eyes observed the practice drill with detachment, but I knew how passionate he was about the game he'd played for more than forty years. And how wise he was, too. At first I thought he'd coached for so long that he didn't truly have his finger on the pulse of the team. But after what happened last year with Nina from the girls' team, I learned never to underestimate Phil again.

"What do you see out there?" he asked.

I swallowed and honed in on the drill. Jason, Phil's long-time assistant coach, stood atop a platform on one side of the net and spiked balls at my teammates. The poor saps played defense, attempting to field Jason's heat-seeking missiles. Jason was probably in his forties, but his spikes were just as strong as those from guys my age. Add a height advantage with the platform, and my teammates were toast. About one in five passes hit their target, and the rest shanked all over the gym. Phil and I had to duck as one ball careened off a guy's arm.

"Not a great passing game right now," I said.

The furry eyebrow twitched, and I knew he wanted more than a statement of the obvious.

"Uh, Pete needs to get lower in his stance."

Phil nodded. "Tell him."

I gave my coach a questioning look. Pete the junior wouldn't take too kindly to Dane the sophomore giving him tips. When Phil looked at me with a challenging stare, I remembered his advice all summer long: *You're the starting setter. You're the leader on this team. This is your team.*

"Pete." My voice halted the drill, and he straightened up to stare me down. "You need to get down in your stance."

As expected, he glared at me.

"It's interesting how much more you see on the sidelines," I added, trying to diffuse the anger likely building after a snot-nosed underclassman had told him what to do. "Now I know why Phil keeps telling me my technique's shit."

With Josh's low chuckle off-court, Pete's glare faded. He turned back to the net and squatted down so low his butt almost grazed the ground. His next pass wasn't straight to target, but it was much better than the projectile shank that had almost beheaded us moments ago.

When Pete rotated out of defense, he looked over at me and gave a slight nod. It was probably the most acknowledgment he'd given me since I started on the team.

The drill continued, and Phil said, "That was diplomatic." He turned to me. "Smooth and political. 'Course, it's probably in the genes."

Where is he going with this?

"Lot of stress this fall. Come November, your mother could be president."

Ah. We'd arrived at the real reason for this conversation. "She *will* be president." I nodded. "And I'm handling the stress just fine."

He stayed quiet beside me, but I sensed there was more to come.

"*How* are you handling the stress, then?" he finally asked.

"Vodka. Bruce and China set me up with my own mini-bar." My grin faded when he didn't seem to appreciate my joke. "C'mon, Phil. My mom's been Senate Majority Leader. This isn't all that different."

His hard stare told me he didn't believe me. I guess *I* didn't really believe me either. I wished my mother's political ambition didn't have to fuck up my life, but that was a pipe dream.

"You could meet with the sport psychologist," he said.

I laughed. "Good one." When he didn't crack a smile, my eyes bugged. "*Seriously*, Phil? I don't need to see a shrink. Only the crazy athletes see her."

His mouth turned down, and I sighed. "Okay, I know I should be more open to the idea, with my mom being a psychologist and me majoring in psychology. But I don't need to go. I'm very self-aware, and I'm doing fine, all right?"

"Just think about it," he said.

Fuckballs. He'd planted the psychotherapy seed, and now he'd wear me down with his Jedi mind tricks until I caved. Sometimes I hated having such an intuitive coach. He could read me like he was my father. Actually, much better than any father I knew.

"And stay away from Lucia Ramirez," he added.

I clenched my jaw. I thought Phil had left the hallway before I'd exchanged words with her. "Why? It's not *my* fault she's invading my space."

"You know the media's wet dream is conflict between you. They pick up on any of that, and you'll get *hounded* all year. Your tenuous focus will flush down the toilet."

"My focus is fine."

A blur of white caught my eye a second before Phil's fist zoomed in front of my nose to bat down the errant volleyball. I flinched, then glanced at the teammate who must've shanked the ball in our direction. He winced. That one could've broken my nose.

"You were saying?" Phil asked.

Just then my assistant coach's screams filled the air. "You guys *suck!"* Jason jumped off the platform, ducked under the net, and got in my teammate's face. "If we were still in the arena, I'd have you running stairs for the next hour!"

That threat elicited a silent prayer of thanks to the demolition gods. The school was tearing down our old arena, and we had to share this smaller gym with the girls' team until the new one was finished—hopefully by the time our season began in January. Running stairs in the old arena was my least favorite memory from freshman year.

"On the line," Jason said, and my stomach clenched.

When Phil's nod dismissed me from our powwow, I sprinted to the baseline along with the rest of the team. I hadn't screwed up on the passing drill, but I would have to endure the running punishment anyway. That group mentality was what defined our team. There was no "I" in team, but there *was* meat in team. And we were all dead meat.

A shrill whistle launched me on a crusade to reach the ten-foot line first. My fingertips grazed the line, then I shot back to the baseline and reached down to touch the gym floor. I spun around and sprinted to the centerline, lunged to touch it under the net, then returned to baseline. I set off for the ten-foot line on the other side of the net, tilting my body forward to shimmy under the net before touching the gym floor. Next was the far baseline—the longest sprint yet.

Sharp gasps for air filled my consciousness as the suicide drill continued. *Suicides*...what an appropriate name for this inane fitness sprint. My racing heart and burning chest would surely give me a heart attack one of these days. But when I realized I was ahead of my teammates, I felt a zing of energy propel me forward. Phil was right. Because the previous starting setter graduated a few months ago, I was now the leader of this team.

Josh was a little behind me, and as I passed him on the start of my second suicide, I managed, "Let's go!"

He was too winded to respond but grinned at me the next time we passed each other. Though my lungs were on fire, I bore down and refused to let Josh or Pete catch up.

Jason was freaking merciless today, and I think I was on my seventh suicide when his whistle finally blew. My chest heaving, sweat splashed from my forehead onto the gym floor as I bent over and sucked in air. The trickle of perspiration had morphed into a downpour—now I'd have to wipe the floor down to prevent an ankle injury.

I heard a female voice say "Gross," and I looked up to find Nina wearing a look of disgust as she stared at me from across the gym. I could see her teammates hanging out on the bleachers. When the hell had the girls' team arrived? My gaze landed on the girl at the far end of one row, whose face turned away from me.

I know you saw me look at you, Lucia. The wall seemed to fascinate her.

Phil walked up to Coach Holter and his assistants—there must've been some screw-up with scheduling the temporary gym for our practices—and I looked back at Lucia, who still avoided my eyes. Besides Nina, she was about the tallest girl on the team, and her height combined with her fidgeting drew my attention. Had she seen me beat all my teammates on the suicides? Did she know I was the fastest on the team?

Wait a minute. Why did I give a flying fuck what Hitler's spawn thought about me?

"Grab some water," Jason told us as the dialogue between the head coaches seemed to heat up. Well, actually only one side intensified, I noticed as I headed toward my water bottle. Coach Holter appeared tense, but Phil maintained his relaxed stance. Nothing could ruffle my cool coach.

Jason patted my shoulder as I passed him. "Good job, GD."

"Thanks." The cool water slid down my hot throat. I felt Lucia looking at me as I grabbed a towel and wiped my forehead, and I tried to stand a little taller. For some reason, I liked her staring at me.

3

Lucia

Sweat poured off Dane in a steady stream, but he didn't even look like he was breathing hard. *I* started sweating just watching him. His muscular forearm glistened as he clutched his water bottle. I couldn't believe a man that tall could run so fast. I hoped he wouldn't be around to witness *me* sprinting at practice, because my jiggling butt would probably repulse him.

When Maddie came to sit on my left, I pried my gaze away from Dane and strived for nonchalance. "So, uh, why did the coach call him GD?"

"It's his nickname," she answered as she tugged kneepads over her shoes. "Great Dane."

"Oh." I lifted my arm overhead and stretched my triceps muscle, simply to have something to do. *Great* was certainly *one* word for him.

A teammate I didn't know yet chuckled from the other side of Maddie. "Or God *Damn*, as some of us call him. As in *goddamn, he's fine*."

Maddie grinned as she tilted her head toward the end of the bleachers. "Better not let Nina hear you say that."

"Why not?" I asked.

The other teammate shrugged. "Last year— "

"Ladies!" Coach boomed as he stormed away from the men's coach. "We're taking over the gym. We've got priority here. Madison, get us started on warm-up."

Maddie ran to the net, and when my teammates followed her, I jogged over too. I snuck a glance at Dane to find him positively murdering me with those eyes. *Oops*. He was mad at me again? How was it *my* fault our practice times got messed up?

A male voice boomed, "Hold it!" and I halted mid-step. I turned to see Dane point at the gym floor in front of me a second before he loped over, clutching his towel. Would he strangle me with it? My eyes darted to Allison at the sideline, but my Secret Service agent didn't seem to be on alert. I braced myself as he neared, but my fear turned to surprise when he dropped to the floor and wiped it with his towel.

"Close your mouth, Ramirez," he said as he popped back up and stood inches from me. *How does he smell so yummy despite his soaked shirt?* It was a manly scent, tinged with some sort of aftershave. "I sweat like a cow." His angular body towered over me. *Not a bovine in sight.*

His eyebrows knitted together as I stared up at him. His eyes were so pretty, so deep. "I didn't want you to fall and break your ankle," he continued. "At least not because of me." His insult barely registered over the blood rushing in my ears. When I continued to stand mute in his presence, his head tilted. "I know you can speak…" One corner of his mouth perked up. "You're not going to call me *bitch* again, are you?"

When I finally wrestled my gaze from his face, I noticed everyone in the gym watching us. I tried to swallow, but my throat was dry.

"Thanks, Dane," Maddie said as she gestured for me to join the team for warm-ups. She turned around, jumped to block at one end of the net, shuffled over a few steps, and jumped again. She had an awesome vertical leap, and I watched Nina and the other teammates follow her lead.

I looked back at Dane. *Say something, idiota.* "I don't know…do you *deserve* to be called bitch again?" I backpedaled toward the net so he wouldn't get me in trouble with Coach this time.

"I deserve only kindness and affection." He smirked.

Above one of his mischievous eyes I noticed a scar. *Where'd he get that?* "We'll see, GD." I spun around and hustled to join my teammates. My heart pounded and my face flushed before I even took my first jump, and I hoped he didn't look at my big butt. *Focus, Ramirez.* I couldn't let him distract me. I had too much to prove.

I panicked when my fingertips barely cleared the top of the net as I jumped. Were my legs shaking so bad that I couldn't jump anymore? But then I noticed Kara at one end of the net and Brian at the other, lowering the net to women's height. *Phew.* Once the net was shorter, I lunged for the ceiling as I leaped, then sidestepped over to the next spot on the net. Blocking was my specialty, requiring strong legs and impeccable timing.

My quick breaths and hammering heart somehow soothed me, bringing peace in the midst of this tumultuous transition. So much was happening right as Dad ran for president, and I had to endure it all under the hateful gaze of his opponent's son. But no matter how bad the rest of my life became, the gym was my home. Volleyball was my clarity.

When Maddie introduced the next running and shuffling drill, I grinned. My club coach, Susie, used to lead us through the exact same sequence of movements for warm-up—apparently having learned them from Coach Holter. The other freshmen fumbled with the intricate footwork, but I skated through. When I looked up to see if Coach had noticed my smooth moves, I saw Dane watching me from across the gym. His arms laced across his chest as he studied me with an appraising eye…

And then I was on the floor. What the hell? Apparently I'd just tripped over my feet. *Real smooth, estúpida.* I peeked up to see Dane duck through a door off the gym, and flames of mortification licked at my face.

"Anything hurt?" Kara had kneeled beside me before I could peel myself off the floor, and our athletic trainer, Tina, headed over.

Just my ego. "I'm fine." I jogged to the basket of volleyballs and grabbed one for the serving drill. I hoped my coordination would improve for the jump serve.

Three hours later, we were in the weight room, and my arms shook violently as I strained to raise the bar off my chest.

"Only three more, Lucia," fellow freshman Kaitlyn said from above as she spotted me on the bench press. Three more? *Kill me now.* I squeezed my eyes shut as I somehow lifted the bar twice more, then a tsunami of trembles ripped through my arms on the last rep. I would've never made that last one if Kaitlyn hadn't helped me guide the bar back to its home. *Thank God for spotters.*

As I wiped my sweat off the bench with a towel, Kaitlyn slid my weights off the bar, and we traded places. "One-forty-five," Brian said, nodding at the twenty-five pound plates Kaitlyn had removed. "Nice."

"Thanks." But I didn't feel proud. The way I see it, if you're as big as I am, you'd *better* lift the most on the team.

Finally I made it to my hotel room, happily showered and fed, and sprawled on my bed. It wasn't a good sign that I already ached from practice, because I knew muscle soreness wouldn't peak until tomorrow. Frank and Allison had joined another agent in scoping out apartments for me, and I relished some time alone. I'd just opened my laptop when Lady Gaga sang "Alejandro" from my cell phone—my older brother's ring tone.

"Hey, Alex." My wet hair fanned out as I sank back into the assortment of fluffy pillows.

"*Hermanita.*" His deep, warm voice made me smile. "How's my lil' sis?"

"Tired. Our first practice was almost four hours long."

He hissed in a breath. "Ouch. And you have another one this afternoon?"

I groaned. "Don't remind me. Susie's practices seem *easy* by comparison. I think I'll send her some hate texts for recommending this program."

"So your new coach is as tough as advertised?"

"Worse, I think." Coach Holter's cruel comment came back to me, and I seized the opportunity to share it with someone who would understand exactly how insulting it was. "He...he asked me if I came to Highbanks just because it was in a swing state."

"He said *what?*" My brother wasn't known for his anger-management skills. "What a bastard."

"So he's dead wrong, right? Dad didn't want me to attend Highbanks just to get votes."

Alejandro exhaled. "Lucia, get a grip. Mom didn't want you to go to school so far away from Texas, and Dad didn't want you to have to deal with all the media crap. But Susie convinced them Highbanks would be your best chance to make the national team one day. If your coach needs someone to blame for your last-minute decision, it's your club coach, not Dad."

I sighed. I already knew that was true, but it helped to hear him say it. *Screw* you, *Coach Holter. You don't know me. You don't know my family.*

"Besides," he continued, "Dad doesn't need extra votes. He'll win this thing no problem."

I wished *I* felt as confident. "How's Mom?"

He was quiet for a moment.

"You flew back to Houston with her and Mateo, right? And you're still there?"

"Yeah," he said. "I have a couple more days before I go back to school."

My *inteligente* brother was about to start his second year of medical school at Johns Hopkins. "So..." I prompted. "Mom?"

"She's stressed. She said the photos of her at the Detroit rally made her look huge, and she won't leave the house until she loses fifteen pounds."

I frowned. My mother had been overweight her entire life, but it never was a big deal to me—she gave great hugs, made the best taquitos I'd ever eaten, and never seemed to get sick. I admired her strength. Her weight didn't seem to bother *her* that much, either, until the Republican primaries hit this year. My dad's closest opponent had a wife who was a stick, and Mom had felt intimidated by the national scrutiny. MSNBC had been merciless.

Alex continued, "I can handle her crazy diets, but when I caught her smoking—"

"No!" I cringed. "Not that again." My mother had quit cigarettes approximately sixty-seven times in the past eighteen years.

"I know. It's so nasty."

"Alex? I wonder if we should just let her smoke until the election is over. It's gotta be tough on her."

"And let her set a bad example for Mateo?" he huffed. "No way. He could *die* if he started smoking, you know."

I knew my younger brother Mateo picking up cigarettes certainly wouldn't *help* his diabetes, but it's not like it would kill him on the spot, right? Alex had a flair for the dramatic. And a flair for the overprotective, which started when Dad hadn't been around much after he'd been elected governor of Texas more than three years ago. "How're Matty's sugars?"

"Okay, I guess. He won't tell me the numbers."

I grinned. Mateo had already complained to me about our brother hovering over him at every turn, with texts like: *Why can't he play doctor with ANOTHER patient?* Alejandro's one year of medical school had added to his already elevated sense of authority over us.

"Maybe you could give Matty some space?" I suggested. "He's *sixteen*. He won't act civilized for at least a couple of years."

"Maybe. Wait a minute…are you implying that *you* behave in a civilized manner, Ms. Eighteen-Year-Old?"

"Girls mature faster than boys." When I found myself sticking my tongue out at him—a useless gesture over the phone—I considered retracting that statement.

"Speaking of immature…" He paused, like we'd arrived at the crux of the conversation. "Have you run into Douchebag yet?"

My heart rate sped up. If Alejandro ever found out how I truly felt about Dane Monroe, he'd fly here immediately and lock me in a convent. He'd threatened about as much when the nerdiest boy in school had taken me to senior prom last year. And *that* boy had been a Republican.

"Yep, ran into him twice already—at a compliance meeting and at practice. Unfortunately we have to share the same gym while they renovate the arena."

"But isn't the guys' season in the spring? Why're they practicing already?"

"Welcome to Division One athletics. There *is* no off-season."

"Sounds almost as bad as med school. Will you have time to study if you're practicing all the time?"

I was starting to have the same worries. *Will I be able to get* anything *done if I'm too sore to walk?* I dreaded having every minute of my day scheduled for me, including forced study time for the freshmen once school started. "Well, we have mandated study tables every night, to 'help' us study."

"Right." He caught my sarcasm and chuckled. "So did Douchebag dare to say anything to you?"

I hesitated. Alejandro already hated Dane, simply because he was a liberal. To add fuel to the *fuego* by sharing his aggressive introduction hardly seemed wise. "He, um, he didn't seem happy I came to school here." Remembering those deep blue eyes made my breath hitch.

"Probably doesn't want anyone nearby to catch him in his lies and manipulation. The whole administration's corrupt. Can you believe Cannell refused to answer the special committee's questions about Yemen?"

He droned on about the latest scandal involving the Secretary of State, and all I could think about was Dane's sturdy body next to me on the gym floor, so close, emitting heat and strength. He'd stared down at me with a playful smirk as he clutched the towel in his hand—the towel he'd used to wipe the floor and keep me safe, despite what he'd said. Tingles had crept up my spine from his mere presence.

"Lucia!"

"Huh?" My brother's voice snapped me back to the empty hotel room. No sweaty muscles in sight. *Bummer.*

"Are you listening? I asked if you could stay away from Dane. I don't trust him or his family."

Could I stay away from Dane Monroe? Probably not. *Would* I stay away from him? Definitely not. "I don't trust him either," I said, to placate my brother. But I definitely wanted to see him again. Soon.

There was a knock on the door. "I think Secret Service is here."

"Good," he said. "I'm glad they decided to protect you."

"*I'm* not." I tossed my legs over the side of the mattress and headed to the door. "Will you have to be under protection in Baltimore?"

"Last thing I heard was no, not all the time. Apparently I'm not as high profile as a Highbanks student-athlete." His tone was teasing. "They'll just catch up with me for public appearances, and Mateo has Mom's detail, so we're all good."

I peeked out the peephole and saw my two constant companions there. "Gotta go, okay? *Te amo*."

"Love you too, Lucy."

As soon as I opened the door, Frank asked, "Did you get some rest?"

"A little." I stepped aside to let them in. "Any luck finding an apartment for me?"

"We found the perfect place!" Allison gushed.

I sensed some tension between them, and Frank looked away. I frowned. "When can I see it?"

Allison glanced at her watch. "How about tonight, after you're done with all your practices?"

"You sure that's okay with the other party?" Frank asked her. "Maybe we should wait until tomorrow."

I looked back and forth between them. "*What* other party?" Frank went back to averting his gaze, which made me tense. *Why won't Frank make eye contact?*

4

Dane

That evening, after Lucia Ramirez dropped a bomb on my day, I finally had some time to chillax. I sank back onto the sofa, and the black leather made a satisfying crunch as it absorbed my freakishly tall body. Good thing my grandfather was loaded. His money had furnished this sweet house in style, turning it into my tricked-out bachelor pad. After I unleashed a monster, burrito-flavored burp, I patted my gut.

I scooped up the remote and flipped through my recorded programs on the DVR. *What?* My thumb locked in place over the remote as my chin retracted into my neck. Why the fuck was *that* on the list?

"Braaaad!" I hollered.

Silence.

"China?"

More silence.

Awesome. The fuckers were all over my case when I wanted privacy, and now when I needed help, they'd entered stealth mode. Was the stupid TV broken? I blew out a heavy breath and clenched my teeth, but I was too tired to move my ass off the sofa to call the cable company. Instead, I scrolled down and clicked on my favorite show.

Once the familiar music played, I eased into a smile and propped my feet up on the ottoman. Damn, my feet were huge—I could barely see the screen over the top of my toes. And you know what they say about guys with big feet...Oh, *yeah.* I sure was proud of my pocket rocket.

My grin faded as my little sister Jessica's words echoed in my mind. "*You're such a nympho,*" she'd said when she found a porn magazine in my backpack a month ago.

"*And* you're *a prude,*" I'd replied. "*It's normal for men my age to think about sex.*" I'd learned that fact in psych class. But when her mouth had contorted to convey her shock, I'd ripped the magazine from her grasp. Thinking about it now, maybe I didn't mind her prudish nature. She was only sixteen, after all.

There was a teenage character on my favorite TV show, too, only the actress playing her looked about twenty-five. No way those tits were real, but did I care? She was *hawt.* Josh would give me shit for the rest of our volleyball career if he ever discovered I watched this inane crap, but I couldn't stop. Not only was the actress smokin', but I *had* to find out what happened with the teenage pregnancy storyline. Damn Jessica for getting me addicted!

I was so engrossed in Marlena and Roman's argument that I barely noticed when Brad breezed into the room. "Dane, buddy, we gotta talk."

Fast as a quick-set, I stopped my show so he couldn't see it and glared at him. "Why the hell is Bill O'Reilly on my DVR?" I demanded.

He took a step back and paused. Then he gave an innocent shrug.

"It was *you!*" I gasped. "You programmed that show."

"No, I didn't."

"Dude, you suck at lying."

He shook his head. "It wasn't me. That's your DVR."

"Okay." My eyes narrowed. "You won't mind if I delete it, then."

When his attempt at nonchalance epically failed, I struggled not to laugh. I clicked on the button to bring up the list of recorded programs, but inadvertently hit play instead.

Shit! I shut it down in an instant but I could tell the damage was done.

Brad grinned. "Relax, little girl. I already saw that soap opera on the recorded list."

"Stay out of my DVR," I growled.

He laughed, and I folded my arms across my chest. This faux pas did *not* earn me a good score on the cool meter. "Don't tell China," I said.

"Why do you care if China knows you watch *Days of Our Lives*?"

Because she'd mock the hell out of me. "Because I don't want her lusting over the same chicks on the show as I do."

He rolled his eyes. "You got something against gay people?"

"What? My mother freaking *led* the crusade for gay marriage! You're the one who should answer that question—not me."

"And why's that?" A huge neck muscle bulged over his collar, and I hoped he wouldn't stroke out on me.

"You tell me, Semper Fi."

Brad studied me for a moment and finally said, "China's my partner now. Therefore, she's cool. I don't care about her personal life." He cleared his throat. "*Your* personal life, however, is my concern. And I got some news about that."

"News?" I got the niggling sense something bad was about to go down. Maybe it was Brad's uncharacteristic fidgeting. But before he had the chance to lay it on me, a buzzing sound filled the room. *Somebody at the security gate.*

"The news has arrived." Brad shuffled from one foot to the other, and I heard China's voice from the hallway, likely speaking to the arriving guest over the intercom. She sounded eerily friendly.

I stood and felt my shoulders tense. "China let the media in?"

"Nope. Listen, Dane, this may take some getting used to, but it was the only place they could find for her—"

The Chipotle burrito I'd just scarfed down for dinner turned to a brick in my gut as I realized who the mystery guest was. "No." My face got hot. "No!" I raced past him to the foyer and saw China head for the front door. Though I didn't want confirmation of my fears, my eyes flew to the bank of video monitors on the wall and got it anyway. Pulling up to the entrance of the house were two SUVs with Secret Service written all over them. "Nooo!" My pathetic cry echoed in the empty hallway.

Brad's bulky body came up behind me. "Breathe, Dane."

"*You* fucking breathe!" I whirled and glared at him. "You're telling me in a city of over two million people they couldn't find another house—"

"Here we are." I heard China reenter and wheeled back around to see the blond curly-haired agent also come in, followed by Hitler's Spawn: *Ramirez*. Lucia took one look at me and froze in the doorway.

Good. She can see how pissed off I am. "No can do, Ramirez—we don't want any. Just turn around. You aren't staying here. Find your own damn house."

"Mr. Monroe." China's sharp tone cut into me. "Ms. Ramirez *is* staying here. Get used to it."

The male agent came up behind Lucia, and she squeaked when he nudged her forward. "Go on in, Lucia," he said, and she moved a step inside without taking her big eyes off mine.

"My grandfather pays for this place!" I yelled once the door had closed.

"The *government* pays for this place," China corrected. "They're footing the cost due to the special security requirements."

My heart pounded as I searched for another reason this wouldn't work. "There's not enough room for everyone."

China's mouth tightened. "There are six bedrooms in this palace. More than enough space."

"Six bedrooms?" Lucia's eyes lit up, and she didn't look quite so miserable anymore. "This has to be better than the dorms."

"It *used* to be better the dorms, that's for sure," I shot back. My eyes drifted down to her neon-green T-shirt, which had volleyballs replacing the "o" letters in:

You Just Got Served.

Fucking A I did. And I wanted to spike the serve back in her face.

"Mr. Monroe," the blond agent said as she stuck out her hand. "I'm Allison Largent."

Though I didn't want to, I shook her hand. My mother had raised me to be a gentleman.

"And that's Frank Vanderberg," Allison continued, tilting her head over her shoulder in the older agent's direction. Frank stayed planted behind Lucia, so we merely nodded at each other. "I know this isn't what you were expecting, and I'm so sorry to barge in here unannounced."

She actually did look somewhat contrite, and I tried to relax a little. Mom always told me I got scary intense when I was angry.

"But we've been all over town, and there literally isn't one place with our protection specifications near the university. You know the crime statistics for off-campus housing, right? And when China told me how much space this house has..."

At that point I didn't care how intense my death stare was—China would get the full brunt of it. As expected, she didn't flinch. Instead, she stared right back at me with such heat that eventually I looked away. *Damn it!* I hated when she bested me like that.

I swallowed and retracted my shoulders. "This house belongs to my mother's friend, Dr. James Thompson. He's on leave from the university, working for the Department of Energy." I tried to steady my voice. "The government may be paying the rent, but my mother set this whole thing up. And she wouldn't want a Ramirez under this roof, I can guarantee it."

"Then you don't know your mother very well," China said. "Senator Monroe has already approved of Ms. Ramirez staying here."

Her self-righteous smile made my heart stop. How the fuck did *that* happen? I glanced at Lucia, and she seemed just as surprised as me. I tried to make sense of this clusterfuck. "Why would she do that without talking to me first?"

China shrugged. "She has her reasons—call her yourself."

You bet I will.

"So my dad's okay with this?" Lucia asked.

I watched Allison exchange a glance with China before she said, "We haven't been able to reach Governor Ramirez's team yet. There must be problems with the comm system on his jet." When Lucia took a step back, Allison added, "But I'm sure he'd want you in a secure location. And the hotel wasn't it."

Lucia tucked a strand of hair behind her ear, which drew my attention to the fact that her hair was free of its tight braid. The way her thick, black waves curled over her shoulders looked really pretty, actually. And her T-shirt hugged her curves just right. *Holy crap*—was that a nipple faintly visible under her sports bra?

"I...don't think this is a good idea," she said as she retreated another step and almost backed into Frank. She wouldn't look at me. "Dane obviously doesn't want me here, and my dad probably won't go for it, anyway. Maybe we should go back to the hotel until we find another place."

It seemed Allison was about to speak, but I beat her to it. "I see how it is." I waited for Lucia to meet my eyes, which took a while. How could a girl so tall and strong appear so skittish? "You always do everything Daddy tells you to." I snapped my fingers. "You're like his bitch."

Her mouth popped open as she drew in a sharp breath. Her cheeks colored and her eyes flared. "Ohh!" she cried. "I can't *believe* you said that." In a flash, her indignant reaction ignited some hot stirrings down below. It felt warm. It felt good. And I knew I wanted more of that, so I kept going.

"He rules your family like he wants to rule the country, huh? Mr. Iron Fist. Change this democracy into a dictatorship, Adolf-Hitler-style. Outlaw gay marriage, outlaw abortion, defund Social Security—"

"You know *nothing* about my father!" She had advanced with impressive speed and now stood right in front of me. A light, floral scent wafted off her hair, which I could see was still a bit wet, and the smell intoxicated me. Good thing I wore baggy shorts. "He knows what's best for me, and he knows what's best for the country."

I snorted. "Is throwing millions of Americans off food stamps best for the country?"

"Yes, it is!" *She actually said that?* "There are some people who legitimately need government assistance, of course, but for those who can work, they don't need food stamps. They need jobs!"

"Then why did his company just lay off so many workers?" Adolfo Ramirez had started an engineering firm that exploded when they'd perfected a new technique for extracting oil from underground. But its stock value had fallen recently, as reported in the news.

When her eyes blazed, I knew I'd hit a soft spot, and that knowledge made me push even harder. "Because of the Democrats' regulations forbidding drilling on US soil! Don't you understand we have enough American oil to fuel our economy for the next hundred years?" *That can't be right. She sure seemed confident in her delivery, though.* When she started speaking again, I honed in on her glossy, plump lips. "We'd stop our dependency on the Middle East if they'd just let us drill."

Let us drill, I chanted silently, still studying those lips. *Let me drill!*

"Are you even listening to me?"

My mouth stretched in a gargantuan yawn. "Sorry, were you saying something?" I looked over my shoulder in the direction of the TV room. "Did someone leave Fox News on? I think Adolf's spouting off another campaign speech."

Lucia's eyes narrowed.

"Just go ask Daddy if it's okay to live here." I jammed my hands into the pockets of my shorts and rocked back on my feet. "I'll wait."

"Don't say another word about my father," she fumed.

Damn, she was mad! And so cute, all worked up like that. I'd never derived so much satisfaction from riling someone up like this before.

"Dane," China barked, and I looked over. I'd almost forgotten she was there. The other three agents frowned at me. "You're not being a considerate host."

"I never *asked* to be a host!"

The Frank dude stepped out from behind Lucia. "That's no way to treat a lady, Mr. Monroe. You're hurting Ms. Ramirez's feelings."

"Better call the waahmbulance then." I glanced at Lucia to see if that comment produced the desired reaction, but she stared down at her running shoes now, looking more defeated than angry.

Frank's pale face reddened. "Listen, young man, I don't care who your mother is—you need to learn some manners!"

"Senator Monroe will be your boss in a few months, Agent. *You* don't tell me what to do."

Brad tugged my elbow. "Dane, buddy. How 'bout you go call your mom?"

"No. I don't want to speak to her—this is *her* fault." I shrugged him off.

Frank shot me the evil eye while Allison and China surrounded Lucia, murmuring soothing words to her. *This is bullshit.* I was the one getting my home crashed, and *she* was being consoled by three fucking agents?

"C'mon, Dane. See why Senator Monroe agreed to this. Give her a call. She must have her reasons."

Brad's suggestion did sound somewhat reasonable. And when China reached down to pick up the gym bag Frank had carried in, I knew I couldn't stand here and watch Lucia move in and invade my space. "Fine," I said through clenched teeth and went to my bedroom. When I arrived, it took all my restraint not to slam the door shut.

I had Mom's campaign manager, Steve, dialed up in seconds, and I paced my room while waiting for the call to connect. "I need to talk to my mother," I told him.

"She's autographing photos," he replied.

"I don't fucking care, Steve. Get her on the phone."

He sighed like the little bitch he was, but soon my mom's voice came on the line. "How are you, Apple Danish?" I hated that fake lilt to her voice that crept in when campaign appearances flooded her schedule.

"I seriously hope no one overheard you call me that."

"Just Steve, dear."

I took a deep breath. "Why'd you allow a *Ramirez* live with me?"

"Oh." She exhaled. "She already arrived, then?"

"Yes, she arrived. Thanks for the advance notice, by the way. And don't evade the question."

"I know this is a surprise for you—*I* was shocked when her security team contacted me." Her voice now sounded more natural, thankfully. "But, Dane, when I started thinking about it, this girl has been through hell. She was all set to attend the University of Texas when a scandal hit—"

"*What* scandal?" I stopped pacing.

"That's really not important, honey."

Grr. My mother undoubtedly knew exactly what had happened at Texas but wouldn't share it with me. The woman was a crypt-keeper of secrets. When I was a kid, she wouldn't talk about the psychotherapy clients she saw out of her office in our home. Since she'd become senator eleven years ago, her secrets had expanded to include matters of national security—though the reason Lucia had bailed from UT probably had nothing to do with America's safety.

"What *is* important," she droned on, "is that we help that poor girl. Her agents told us she literally has nowhere to live that's safe, and my heart went out to her, knowing you're in James's huge house, all alone..."

The creepy lilt was back, and I knew my mother wasn't telling me the whole story. She hadn't given the thumbs up just out of the goodness of her heart. "So you agreed to this inane plan simply to help out Lucia?"

"Exactly, honey."

"Mom, did you ever think to ask if this was okay with *me?*"

She paused. "You're angry I didn't consult with you first."

"Damn right I am!"

Another pause, then, "I'm sorry. You're right. I should've asked your opinion first, of course. I've just been so busy with the campaign, and Secret Service called me right before a CNN interview, and I just wanted to help..."

Now I felt like a heel. My mother was vying to become leader of the free world and here I was bitching about my new roommate. My new...*sexy*...roommate. *Gah!* She wasn't that attractive, was she? Probably any guy my age would salivate to have a girl like her live with him. But her father's politics drove me *nuts.* He was such a tool.

"Would you like me to call this off?" Mom asked. "I mean, I don't know where Lucia will stay, and I know you want to do the kind, caring thing, but if it makes you uncomfortable..."

"It's fine," I managed to say through the guilt tightening my throat. I'd have to deal with the tool's daughter for a while longer. "I'll just avoid her."

"Oh, really?" Her voice elevated on the last syllable, and became breathier. "Thank you so much, dear. I knew you'd make the right choice."

Yuck. Plastic Mom had returned. "I gotta go."

"Bye bye, sweetie!"

When I tossed my phone to the bed, I heard soft murmurs through the wall behind my headboard. I grimaced as my finger traced a jagged line on the light green wallpaper—naturally China had given Lucia the room next to mine. I heard the scrape of furniture on the floor and scowled. The home invasion had begun.

Remnants of my burrito clumped once again like a rock in my belly. I often felt uneasy after conversations with my mother—almost like she'd played me or something. Too bad I didn't know the rules of the game. Technically I'd just agreed to this living arrangement, but it still didn't feel right. Class, practice, and dodging the media kicked my ass, and I wanted to feel safe and easy in my home. I just wanted to relax.

My palm smacked the wall. How the hell would I relax with Satan's spawn taking up residence right next door?

5

Lucia

I'm so stupid. Tears welled up, and I was too tired to fight them. I just let my weakness seep out the corners of my eyes and onto the pillow. One hand wiped away a dribble of snot leaking from my nose while the other clutched the sheets.

When I found out Allison and Frank had picked Dane's house for my new living quarters, a spark of excitement had bloomed up my spine. Sure, Dane had been belligerent earlier today at practice, but I thought he'd lighten up once he got to know me…once he discovered the good volleyball player I was…once I was able to speak like a normal person in his presence…As soon as he saw past our political differences, I hoped he might eventually start treating me like I wasn't some Republican leper. But the way he'd just looked at me—the way he'd talked about my dad…It was clear: *He hates me.*

The thought made me cry harder, and now that we were practically bunkmates, I had to stifle a sob to make sure he wouldn't overhear and know he'd gotten to me. I wished his opinion didn't matter so much. I wished I didn't care that I repulsed him.

But ever since I'd seen Dane on TV a year ago, I'd been infatuated. His mother had spoken at a Highbanks rally, and she'd invited him and his little sister up on stage at the end of her speech. Tall, fit, and tan, his blond hair shining in the stage lights, he'd grinned and waved to the crowd. *"I love this state so much my son Dane is a scholarship volleyball player here!"* Senator Monroe had crowed. I'd leaned closer to the TV and felt my heart flutter. *That Adonis plays my sport?* He couldn't have been more perfect, and I'd devoured media coverage of him ever since.

Now that I'd met him in person, my dream of being his girl had shattered.

Boxes and gym bags littered the thick carpet of the bedroom, and I knew I should get up to unpack. When Allison and China had offered to help me set up my room, I'd waved them off, citing fatigue. But really, I'd known I was seconds from a meltdown, and I couldn't let them see me cry.

When a growl gurgled in my stomach, I realized I hadn't eaten dinner yet. More tears fell—I had no clue where the kitchen was in this place. And it wasn't like Dane would graciously give me the grand tour. Not to mention I wanted to avoid having him see me eat. He probably already thought I ate like a pig, given my size.

With a sigh, I covered my eyes with my forearm. I was even too tired to dig out my mp3 player and listen to some Neil Diamond. It wasn't quite eight p.m., but maybe I should crash early and put this awful first day at Highbanks behind me. At least I knew the next day couldn't get any worse.

Or so I thought. The next morning, I felt chilled sitting in Coach Holter's air-conditioned office in my sweaty uniform. Or maybe it was his frosty stare.

"That was a solid practice, Lucia."

Not what I'd expected him to say, and I let out a breath. "Thanks."

"Susie wasn't kidding when she said you're a skilled hitter. I'm excited to have the Lone Star Player of the Year in the lineup."

Why is he being so nice to me?

"But there are definitely some areas of your game you need to improve."

Ah. *This* was what I'd expected. "I know. My passes aren't very good."

"You're right. We'll work with you on your technique. What I was talking about needing improvement, though, was your blocking."

"My…blocking?" My forehead wrinkled. *I thought that was my forte.*

"Yes. You're not getting to the double block quickly enough. You need to get fitter."

Like more muscular? I blinked several times, trying to discern what he was telling me. I already killed it in the weight room…

"I want you to meet with the sports nutritionist."

Oh, Dios! The realization knocked into my substantial belly with a thud: he thought I was fat. *I am fat.*

"Now where *is* that nutritionist's card?" He dug around his immaculate desk as my throat tightened with imminent tears.

Don't cry. Don't cry.

"Brian!" he hollered, and I flinched in my chair.

The assistant coach stuck his head into the office. "What do you need?"

Oh, no. My breaths were coming quick and shallow, and I braced myself against the panic I knew would follow.

"Do you have Whitney's card? I want Lucia to see her."

Brian squinted at me. "You okay?"

Now Coach stared at me too. I nodded, too freaked to speak. *Don't cry.*

"Lucia, calm down," Coach said. "Whitney will help you get lighter and faster, so you'll block more effectively. She'll improve your chances of actually getting some playing time."

My heart raced. Was he saying if I don't lose weight, I'd ride the bench all season? That would be so humiliating, especially with all of America watching!

Brian came back in the office—I hadn't noticed him leave—and handed me a business card.

"Call her today," Coach ordered. "I want you working on your fitness as soon as possible."

I nodded, feeling nausea climb up my throat. Trembling overtook my body, and I knew I'd lose it any second. "Can I go shower?"

Coach stared at me like he was about to call the psych hospital. Finally, he said, "You can go."

I bolted past Brian and ran to the locker room, praying my teammates had already left.

"Lucia!" Allison called from the hallway. "What happened?"

I ignored her. Tears streamed down my face as I launched myself into a bathroom stall. My shaking hands took ten years to lock the door. *I'm fat. I'm fat. I'm not fit enough to play on this team. I'm fat.* I yanked some toilet paper off the roll to blow my nose. *No guy will ever love me…especially Dane. I'm fat.* My chest was so tight it was hard to breathe, and I turned to the toilet in case I had to throw up. But I'd only eaten a banana for breakfast, so there probably wasn't anything left to vomit. *I'm fat. I'm fat.* I would never eat again if that would be my only shot to play for that bastard.

Besides my internal fat mantra, it was quiet, and I gave silent thanks that Allison hadn't followed me in. Then I heard footsteps from the locker area and braced myself against the bathroom stall, but that person walked out the door. I exhaled as I closed my eyes—and realized how tired I was. Morning practice had been grueling, but I thought I'd done well. Coach devised the toughest, most ingenious drills, and it had actually been fun to challenge myself.

I sighed. It wouldn't be fun anymore, knowing he thought I was too fat to play for him. I grabbed a bulge of inner thigh and shuddered in disgust.

"Lucia?"

Oh, crap—that was Maddie's voice. I heard the door shut behind her as her footsteps neared.

"Lucia?" She was close to my stall now. "Did you just get sick?"

When I looked down at my feet facing the toilet, I understood her question. "No, I'm fine." My shaking voice betrayed me. I slowly turned around but didn't open the door. I couldn't let anyone see me like this.

"Allison sent me in here to check on you."

I narrowed my eyes. *Damn Secret Service!*

"Are you feeling okay?"

I drew in a breath. "Yeah."

"Are you crying?"

"No." *Liar.*

"Wait a minute." Maddie's voice sharpened. "Coach wanted to meet with you after practice." I saw her feet inch closer to the stall. "What'd he say?"

Hijole. How could I admit to the team captain that Coach thought I was too ginormous to block effectively? Maddie probably thought the same thing.

"Don't listen to him, Lucia. He plays mind games, especially with the freshmen. Don't take him seriously."

Mind games? His words seemed pretty straightforward to me: *You're fat.* Well, he'd used the code words "You need to get fitter," but I'd caught their meaning. Loud and clear.

"Hey, I'm going to grab some lunch…want to come?"

That certainly wouldn't fit with my never-eat-again plan. "No… thanks. I don't think Secret Service would let me."

"That sucks. It's like your parents are here with you, hovering every second."

I'd never thought of it that way, but she was kind of right. Except Allison and Frank were nowhere near as comforting as my parents, because they barely knew me. I still hadn't heard from my dad about my new residence.

"So, will you *ever* come out of that bathroom stall?"

I pressed my palms against the cool, safe walls. "No."

She laughed. "Okaaay, then."

She probably thought I was way cray.

"I'll come back and fetch you for afternoon practice at two-thirty."

"Thanks, Maddie." My voice trembled.

"Hang in there. Freshman year was tough for me, too. Things will get better."

As her footsteps faded, I let out a breath. *Would* things improve? What if they didn't, once classes started? I'd be stuck at this stupid school for at least a few months because it would reflect badly on my dad if I left before the election. If I bailed, I could just picture the headlines:

`Another Ramirez Can't Handle the Pressure`

My traitorous stomach picked that moment to emit a deep growl. I glared at my round Buddha belly. "Shut up. You're the one making my coach mad at me." It answered me with another rumble. Stupid thing wouldn't listen.

After a few more minutes in my stall-haven, I tiptoed into the locker room and found it empty. *Thank God.* Sweaty clothes fell into a heap at my feet, and I grabbed my towel. The steamy pulse of water pounding my aching muscles had never felt better, and by the time I emerged from the locker room, I felt marginally calmer. Then I saw my new "mom." Allison hadn't moved from her spot, but at least she hadn't come in after me.

"Maddie told me to give you some space," she explained.

My team captain was a total gem. I had to remember to thank her later for being so cool. Between Dane and Coach, I *needed* someone as nice as her in my life.

"But I couldn't wait much longer. We finally touched base with Governor Ramirez, and he wants to talk to you."

I inhaled my first full breath of the morning. I wanted to talk to him, too.

"He's only got a few minutes till his next speech." She dialed a number on her secure cell phone, then handed it to me.

"Where is he?" I asked as I waited for the call to connect.

Allison glanced at her watch. "Des Moines."

"Aldolfo Ramirez."

His voice almost made me start crying again. What was my problem? I tried to steady my voice. "Hey, Dad."

"*¡Mija!*"

I smiled, hearing the affection in his voice.

"I've missed you so much. How's it going at Highbanks?"

"It's great."

He paused. "Lucia?"

Crap. I wasn't fooling him. "It's…tough." I took a shaky breath. "But I'll be okay."

"That coach of yours—he's giving you a hard time?"

"Well, Susie did tell me what to expect."

"What's his number? I want to speak to him."

My eyes widened. "Dad, no! You can't call him. That would be so embarrassing. Please."

I could picture his forehead creasing as he considered my words. Then he probably patted his thigh like he always did when he was deep in thought. "We'll table this discussion for later, because I don't have the time right now. But I do want to discuss your living situation."

I tensed. Would he make me move out? Dane would have a freaking field day.

"The agents told me you're in Dane Monroe's house."

"Well, it's not *his* house, technically. It's some professor's house they're renting."

"Jim Thompson," my dad railed. "The inept leader of the green energy movement that's wasted *billions* in taxpayer money."

Uh-oh. Nothing could fire up my dad like government waste.

"How dare they put you in that environment without consulting me first. It must be awful for you, *mija.* I'm sorry my choice to run for president has made your life so difficult. You can't live in the dorm like normal freshmen—instead you have to live with my opponent's *son.* What's he like, by the way?"

"Um..."

"And I hear Senator Monroe has approved of this?" He exhaled. "I don't trust her, Lucy. I don't trust *them.* There's got to be some angle they're working here."

Angle? My stomach twisted. I hated the underhanded manipulation my dad had learned to deal with since entering politics. He said all the handshakes and hidden meanings weren't any different from big business, but he'd seemed way more relaxed running his company than running the state of Texas. And the stress of running an entire country...I worried that overwhelming responsibility would change him even more—and not in a good way.

"Frank and Allison said it was the only place they could find," I offered.

"So you *want* to live there?"

"Uh...They said they'll keep looking for another place, but for now...you shouldn't worry about it. I'll be fine."

"Oh, *mija.* I don't deserve you—always so sacrificial for the family. I *do* worry about you. Listen, I'll tell them..." His voice faded off, and I heard some background noise. "I have to run, Lucy. Listen, I'll tell your agents to find you another place, and I'll come there and help you move, okay?"

"Dad. You don't have time for that, and I don't have time to move again. We practice, like, all day long." I stifled a groan, thinking about another long practice ahead of me in a few hours. "I'll be okay. I will."

More voices in the background. "I wish we had more time to discuss this!" My dad sighed. "You tell me the second you feel uncomfortable there—the second you want to move out, okay? I'll make it happen."

I nodded. "Okay."

"Love you, Lucia. Bye!"

He'd hung up before I had the chance to tell him I loved him too. It was a typical ending to our phone calls, with his aides swooping in to whoosh him off to another campaign appearance. I was tortured by the cozy warmth of a memory: my dad hugging me after my high-school team had competed in the state championship last fall. Even though we'd lost, he'd said, "I'm so proud of you, *mija.*"

I wondered how proud he'd feel now if he knew I was too fat to play in college.

"So I take it we're staying at the greenhouse for now?" Allison asked as she took back her phone.

I stared at her. "The greenhouse?"

"Thompson's house. You know, Mr. Green Energy?"

Why did the Secret Service have to use so many code words? "I guess." I followed her as we headed to the parking lot, where Frank waited for us in the air-conditioned SUV. Thankfully there were no reporters in sight. As Allison scooted in next to me in the backseat, she glanced over.

"Dane will come around, you know."

My breath hitched, and I wouldn't look at her. Was my attraction to him so obvious?

"If that cocky bastard doesn't start behaving," Frank growled as he pulled out of the lot, "I'll *make* him."

Yikes. I glanced at Allison and found her grinning. "*Men*," she whispered. In her regular voice she said, "Let's get some lunch back at the greenhouse—you must be famished. I'm hungry, and *I* just stood around for three hours."

My empty belly lurched with hope at her words, but I scowled and silently told it to pipe down. I hadn't been too keen about eating in front of Dane in the first place, and now Coach's threat would be just the motivation I needed to stay away from the kitchen.

I stared out the window as campus buildings whizzed by. Classes wouldn't start for another two weeks, but when they did, they'd add a whole new layer of stress to my life. Right now there wasn't much action in the hazy sunlight, other than a few students strolling the sidewalks. I wished I didn't feel so lonely here. Maddie had a bunch of senior friends and probably wouldn't want to hang out with a freshman like me. I didn't know Kaitlyn or my other teammates very well. And even if I did, it seemed like a hassle for Secret Service to approve spending time with them outside of practice.

We continued our journey to my new home, where hopefully Dane would leave me alone. I couldn't handle his attacks after the morning I'd just endured. My conversation with Coach looped in my mind, and I grimaced, knowing what I had to do this afternoon: schedule an appointment with Whitney the sports nutritionist. *Yay.*

6

Dane

Kaitlyn rubbed her spiky black hair as she frowned at the cards in her hand. "The jack of clubs is a *spade?* But it's a club."

I wondered if the freshman would ever understand the rules of the game.

"You Californians," I scoffed as I crunched a chip coated with salsa. "Such a crime you don't play euchre in your state. You're seriously deprived."

Josh rolled his eyes and stretched his arms overhead as he leaned back on his kitchen chair. We were at his apartment for an impromptu euchre showdown since Lucia had crashed my house yesterday. Though it was fantastic to get out of there, the euchre game hardly felt as lively as it had last year when Nina and I had partnered against Josh and Amy. Sometimes our games had lasted until the wee morning hours—one of the few times I'd actually had fun with Nina. But Amy, a player on the girls' team, had graduated in May, and Nina... well, Nina wanted nothing to do with me now.

"The jack of clubs is considered a spade when spades are trump," Pete explained, sounding bored. "It's the left bower—the second-most-powerful card."

At least Pete, my current euchre partner, knew the rules. Josh and Kaitlyn didn't have a chance against us.

"Dude, that, like, makes no sense," Kaitlyn pouted.

I sighed, annoyed. "Josh, tell me you have some beer in that fridge."

"Don't think so, Danester," Secret Service man Brad boomed from across the room. Josh had shoved aside clothes, papers, books, and other crap so that Brad could sit on the sofa to watch TV, and the burly agent looked totally out of place surrounded by mountains of college apartment rubble.

"I *do* think so, Brad," I countered. "You can't stop me from drinking."

"You're nineteen. It's against the law."

Josh and I only had to look at each other for a second before we both cracked up. "It never stopped us before," he said. I knew my partner in crime preferred weed over alcohol, but the athletic department's drug tests squelched that idea. Josh stood and headed to the kitchen. "I'll see if I can hook you up."

Pete grinned as he pointed at his chest. "Oh, yeah. This adult here will have to show the kids how to drink."

"Stop gloating." I rolled my eyes. Pete had turned twenty-one in July and hadn't shut up about it since.

"Score!" Kaitlyn said. "I knew you guys were partiers."

I shook my head. "No way. You're a freshman, and you're in season. We're not supplying you with alcohol."

"Well, that's ruuude." She pouted again. "You invite me to play cards and don't even serve me a beverage?"

Josh had only invited her because he'd run into her at the gym, after our stint in the weight room for the day. The girls had just finished afternoon practice. I'd wanted to invite Maddie, but she was going out with her boyfriend, and there was no way in hell I'd invite Lucia.

"Relax," Josh said as he set three bottles of beer on the table and farmed one out to each of us. Kaitlyn's face lit up as she downed a big swig.

"Dane, don't touch that beer," Brad said. I took a sip.

When Josh returned to the table with his own bottle, I tilted my head toward the freshman. "Coach Holter will kill us if he finds out."

"*You're* not supposed to drink, either, Mr. Sophomoric." Kaitlyn glared at me.

"Yeah, but *our* coach isn't a control-freak fuckbag. And our season doesn't start until January. If I'm a little slower in practice, I'll have no one to blame but myself."

I heard the sofa shift as Brad heaved himself up. "I can't be here while you girls break the law." He pressed a button on the remote. "I'll be outside with China." It wasn't until he was at the door that I realized he'd increased the volume on the TV as a parting gift. *Jerk.*

I sniffed and pretended to wipe away a tear. "I'll miss you, Braddy Boy."

When he slammed the door on the way out, I grinned. If all it took to get rid of him was alcohol, I would drink *lots* this fall. But following Brad's departure, I looked up at three sets of wary eyes. I guessed I wasn't the only one still getting used to the Secret Service supervising my every move.

The TV volume was epic. "*Secretary of State Bob Cannell appeared in front of the congressional special committee, but he might as well have stayed home,*" the reporter said. "*I've never seen an official of the state dodge and deflect questions about Americans getting killed.*"

My stomach clenched. That bitch sounded like somebody on Fox News. I popped off my chair and stormed over to the couch. Sure enough, the Fox reporter droned on, "*When will this administration stop hiding behind its mistakes? What exactly happened in Yemen? You can be sure we'll get to the bottom of this mess.*"

"Shut this shit off." I grabbed the remote and turned off the TV, then stalked over to the table and seized my beer, knocking back half of it in one gulp.

Josh studied me as I sat back down. "Your mom's going to win. Don't worry."

"I know." I sighed. "Then I'll have even more agents crawling up my ass."

"Are you sure it's okay he saw us drinking?" Kaitlyn asked. "I mean, like, will he tell my coach?"

"Not so confident anymore, freshman, huh?" I teased. "Scared about losing your scholarship?" When she paled, I took pity on her. "The agents aren't supposed to interfere with my life, and they're sworn to secrecy. So we're cool."

Her second sip conveyed that I'd convinced her. "That blows that you and Lucia have to be protected," she said. "I heard she's stuck living in a hotel for preseason." Kaitlyn grimaced. "That would get old real fast."

Josh and I glanced at each other. I'd told him about Lucia crashing my place—hence our presence at his apartment, not mine—but apparently that wasn't public knowledge yet.

"I'm sure she'll be fine. Daddy Adolf will take care of her."

Pete shifted in his chair. "Are we gonna play this game or not, children?"

"Yeah, we are." Josh shuffled the deck and grinned across the table at Kaitlyn. "The Golden State will win the gold."

I snorted. *Nobody* was better at euchre than I was.

Five beers, three victorious games, and countless fist pumps later, I strolled out of the apartment toward the SUV. I jumped when Brad fell into step next to me—he must have been standing right outside the apartment, waiting. "Jesus! You mind warning me next time you set up an ambush?"

"Give me a break—that was hardly an ambush." We climbed into the backseat.

China ended her phone call and straightened in the driver's seat. Our eyes met in the rearview mirror as she turned the ignition. "Awareness of your surroundings goes into the shitter when you're drunk, Mr. Monroe. It makes it harder for us to protect you."

"I'm not drunk." *Happily buzzed, yes. Drunk, no.*

"How many beers did you have?"

I looked away from the mirror. "None of your damn business."

"You *are* my business." China pulled our oversized vehicle into traffic. "Everything about you. How would it look if the media discovered you drinking? That would hurt your mother's campaign, you know."

"Every college student drinks."

Brad chimed in. "Yeah, but *you're* not every college student. You're the son of the Democratic nominee for president."

Brad could be cool, but not when he was around China. It was like she rode the crimson wave every day of the month, and her bitchy hormones seemed to affect everyone around her.

"Look, I didn't ask for this, okay? I didn't ask for freaking chaperones. I already have parents."

"Well, your mother's kind of busy right now," China said, "and I've never even met your father."

My face got hot. "What's *that* supposed to mean?"

She looked up in the mirror, and her forehead creased. "Uh, it means I've never met your father. What do *you* think I meant?"

I wouldn't give her the satisfaction of admitting anything. I kept my mouth shut and looked out the window, pleased to see the convenience store on the corner. We were close to home.

"I know this situation sucks for you," Brad said, and I unclenched my fists a little. "Nobody wants supervision round the clock. But we got no choice here. Congress ordered us to protect you, and *we* follow orders."

I sighed. He didn't know I'd already followed coaches' orders all my life. I could certainly comply with orders from those I respected. But, like many adults I'd encountered, these two simply hadn't earned my respect. They were giant pains in my ass.

"What the hell?" As China slowed down, my buzz vanished. Reporters swarmed the gate of the greenhouse, hovering like angry hornets. Why the fuck were *they* here? After China's warning about me hurting my mom's campaign, I straightened up, then looked down at my shirt to make sure there weren't any beer stains. I would've killed for a breath mint.

"Shit, they saw us." Brad blew out a breath, and I realized the SUV had come to a stop. "Go ahead, China. Let's face the music."

"But they'll come inside the gate if we go in now."

Brad grunted. "What choice do we have? If we turn around, they'll follow us."

That sounded pretty good to me—I could stay hidden in the vehicle until I sobered up. "Why don't we do that?"

"Because the president of Highbanks University told us to keep a low profile," China answered. "He threatened to complain to our supervisor if we—" She performed air quotes. "—'make a scene' in town."

She eased the car forward, much to my unease. A few intrepid reporters jogged toward us.

"I bet this is about the Yemen thing." Brad gave me an evil smile. "Maybe they want your opinion."

My heart lurched.

He snickered. "Your *drunk-ass* opinion."

If he weren't so muscular, I would've clocked him.

"*Dane!*" one yelled, easily heard through the bulletproof glass.

"*Mr. Monroe! How do you like living with Lucia Ramirez?*"

My stomach clenched, and Brad's eyebrows shot up.

"That was fast," China muttered as she pressed the remote to open the gate. "Who'd you tell about Lucia moving in?"

"Just Josh! He wouldn't tell anyone, I swear."

One female reporter kept pace with the vehicle, right next to me, and I tried not to stare at her breasts bopping up and down as she jogged. "*Is it true Dr. Thompson invited Lucia to live with you?*"

"*Or was it your mother who invited her to stay here?*" a male reporter shouted from behind me.

I tried to make sense of the questions hurled at me. Had Mom invited Lucia? Not really—more like she'd *allowed* her to live with me. We drove through the gate, and I frowned when reporters followed us inside.

The questions kept coming. "*Do you and Lucia work out together?*"

I smirked. As if she could keep up with me.

China pulled up to the entrance and turned around to glare at me. "Brad and I will hustle you in there. Not one word, Mr. Monroe—got it?"

"You tell me that every time. I'm not stupid."

"No, but you're under the influence, and I'm not losing my job just because you wanted to tie one on with your buddies."

She could lose her job over me having a few beers? I tried to adopt a serious expression, but it was tough amidst the nonstop media questions.

"*What's it like living with Governor Ramirez's daughter?*"

I wished I could answer that: *Fucking awful.*

"*Do you two talk politics?*"

Not unless she wants to show how dumb and wrong she is.

China opened the driver-side door and dodged some reporters to zoom around the hood of the vehicle just as Brad stepped out. I scooted over to Brad's side to emerge between the agents—*see, I can follow orders*—and they marched me toward the front door.

Above the cacophony I heard one question: "*Dane! Are you and Lucia sleeping in the same bedroom?*"

What the fuck? I couldn't help it—I started laughing. How I wished I could respond to that asinine question! *Yeah, we share a bed. We make love every night after practice, for extra cardio.*

China clenched my arm tighter as I chuckled. "Not one word," she hissed.

As we passed through the front door, a surprising image flashed in my mind: Lucia's long hair fanned out on the pillow beneath me, her shining eyes watching me as my hands massaged her breasts. I'd bet a crap-ton of money that her nipples were dark. I could hear her soft moans and picture her smooth, caramel skin responding to my touch, her hips bucking as my hands drifted down the centerline of her stomach—

"Is he *drunk?*"

I looked up to see Frank's ugly scowl. Brad and China let go of me, and I rubbed my scalp, trying to orient myself away from the sexy-time images in my head. The reporters kept yelling stuff beyond the closed door, but thankfully their voices had become fainter.

"For the last time," I roared, "I'm not drunk!"

The object of the reporters' interest—the one who'd had a starring role in my imagery moments ago—appeared in the hallway. Lucia wore black yoga pants and a fuchsia compression shirt, and dammit if her nipples didn't strain against the tight fabric.

"He had some beers, yes," China told Frank.

Lucia gasped.

"Seriously?" I gaped at her. "You've never had alcohol?"

She blinked quickly and her face flushed, but she didn't answer me. *How dare she try to judge me! Will she blab about this?*

"You better not tell my coach I was drinking!"

She took a step back. "I, I wouldn't do that."

I noticed that she was trembling. "What's your problem?"

"Are the reporters gone?" She gulped.

I walked past Frank to look at the monitors on the wall. "Nope. The bloodsuckers are still out there." I frowned at her. "Like I told you, now that *you're* here, they won't leave us alone. Thanks for bringing them into our lives."

"I didn't choose to live here!" Her voice shook. "I hate them! I just want to live my life—I hate them watching me every second."

I felt the exact same way, and it was only August. I knew it would get much worse as the election neared. "How'd they find out you were here so fast? Who'd you tell?"

"Nobody!"

"Are you sure?"

She paused. "I talked to my dad today, but he wouldn't say anything. He doesn't like me living here, so it's not like he'd advertise it."

Why'd she have to bring Adolf into the conversation? I hated talking about him. Except for the times I could rile her up by insulting him—those could be fun, as I recalled. "Aw, he doesn't like it. Will Big Daddy still let you stay with me?" I suppressed the smile threatening to cut loose.

When her eyes narrowed into slits, my dick expanded into a tree trunk.

Frank cleared his throat, and his glare before he walked away let me know how he felt about me.

Brad took that opportunity to bail as well. "C'mon, China, let's hit the weights."

"I thought you'd never ask. I need to rage after dealing with those reporters." She followed him to the stocked gym in the basement. This house had everything.

Now that we were alone in the hallway, my eyes swept up Lucia's firm body, and I decided to play with her a bit. "Did you hear what one of those reporters said?"

She studied me with nervous eyes, then shook her head.

"They asked if we slept in the same bedroom."

Her lips parted as she drew a breath, and her face turned a delicious shade of pink. I watched one hand smooth down her thigh, then dart up to the back of her neck. The other hand fidgeted at her side. It looked like she had to force a swallow.

Sweet Jesus. Her embarrassment totally turned me on.

"So, um…what did you tell them?" she finally asked.

Almost painful at this point, my erection pulled me toward her. Her eyes widened as I approached, but she seemed more excited than frightened.

Her breezy, floral scent mingled with the liquid courage in my veins, and before I knew it I was running my fingers into her thick, damp hair. *What the hell am I doing?* God, it felt good, and she tilted her ear toward me like she enjoyed it too. There was a cute little dimple on her right cheek that winked at me. I found myself leaning closer to her face, and considering her impressive height, I didn't have far to go. Her shiny eyes turned back to me, and she gazed up with such yearning, such depth.

My heart thundered. *Stop seducing me, Devil Spawn!*

Those sensuous lips opened for me, their sweetness luring me forward. I held my face over hers, breathing in her smell, and her eyes fluttered shut as she surrendered to me. I stared at her soft features for too long, shocking myself with an insane desire to kiss those sweet lips. Before I totally freaked myself out, I shifted an inch to press a kiss onto her warm cheek, right on her dimple. I could feel her tremble beneath my touch.

My hand still tangled in her hair, I pulled back to gaze into her mesmerized eyes. "I told them I never kiss and tell."

When I let her go, I heard a little squawk of protest. That adorable noise reminded me of the pressure down below—pressure I needed to do something about. I turned and took swift strides down the hall.

"Where are you going?" Her breathy voice was tinged with desperation.

I grinned. She was just too easy to mess with.

After I relieved my little problem, I emerged from my bedroom and followed the sound of the TV to find Allison, one of Lucia's agents, hunkered down on the sofa watching CNN. When she saw me come in, she bolted upright. "I was just leaving."

"No, it's okay." I held out my hand. "Stay." I plopped down next to her. "I need to see if it was obvious I'd been drinking."

Allison gestured toward the screen. "I'm expecting them to show video from our front yard any second. Two confrontations in one evening—it's a banner day for them."

"*Two* confrontations?"

"They were waiting for us when we got home from practice," she explained. "Lucia freaked out."

I took that in. "It seemed like she was shaking when I saw her. Why?"

Allison tapped her chin. "She…gets panicked around the media. They've said some pretty mean things about her family."

"Well-deserved things."

Allison shrugged.

I tilted my head. "Don't tell me you agree with the jacked-up things her father stands for."

"I'm a Democrat, and I'm voting for your mother. I just...I like Lucia. I've only known her for a couple of days now, but she's a sweet girl. She works hard. And it's tough to see her go through all this just because her dad wants to be president."

I stared at the commercial for antidepressant medication. The list of side effects went on forever...just like the side effects of our parents vying to be leader of the free world.

Allison's voice lowered. "You haven't exactly been kind to her, you know. It's not *her* fault she had to bail on Texas. It's not her fault we moved her here."

I felt like a limp, deflated volleyball, and I looked away as I chewed the inside of my mouth. My buzz was all but gone now, and I was hungry again.

The anchorman's voice drew my attention back to CNN. "*An interesting development in the presidential race today, as we show you the home of green energy specialist Dr. James Thompson near the campus of Highbanks University.*" I watched an image of Lucia's SUV inching toward the cameras in the fading light of early evening. "*We've learned that the son of Democratic nominee Senator Lois Monroe—Dane Monroe—has chosen this location as living quarters for his sophomore year of college.*"

I braced myself as the SUV stopped in front of my house. "*But in an amazing show of bipartisan welcome, Senator Monroe invited her opponent's daughter to share the home when Secret Service had trouble finding secure living quarters for Ms. Ramirez. That's right, Governor Ramirez's daughter Lucia will start soon as a freshman at Highbanks and will live in the same home as Dane Monroe, thanks to the generosity of his mother.*"

Lucia emerged from the vehicle with Allison and Frank flanking her. She seemed to flinch at each shouted question.

"*Amazingly, both candidates' offspring are scholarship volleyball players at the university. Not only do they share a sport, but now they share a home.*"

They cut to my shuffle through a sea of reporters en route to our front door. I leaned forward to scrutinize my TV self, and thankfully it appeared I was sober. The stupid female reporter hollered the question about us sharing a bedroom, and—*oh, crap*—my massive grin was totally obvious.

"*It appears Senator Monroe's son is happy about the living arrangement.*"

I cringed and glanced at Allison, who laughed at me.

The video ended, and the anchorman's face filled the screen. "*With our country bitterly divided on issues, it's wonderful to see Dane and Lucia putting aside their differences to live together. Perhaps the candidates can learn from their children and treat each other more civilly. Bravo, Senator Monroe.*"

When the reporter moved on to another story, Allison shook her head. "If only he knew how contentious it's been in this house."

I thought back to brushing my lips on Lucia's soft cheek. Things hadn't seemed so contentious then.

Probably mistaking my far-off gaze as me feeling upset. Allison patted my arm. "At least that story knocked the attention off of Yemen."

I nodded, then froze. I now had a good idea who had leaked the story about Lucia and me living together.

7

Lucia

Days later, my hand zoomed from my face to my lap once I realized I was touching my cheek, *again*. I took a sideways glance at Allison, but thankfully she didn't seem to have noticed my caress of the spot Dane's lips had graced. Though the kiss had been a few days ago, I could still feel his warm breath tickle my skin. I could still see his cocky grin as he lingered above me for a moment, gazing into my eyes. My heartbeat had rushed in my ears as I wondered if he would kiss me for real, on the lips this time, aggressive, hot and spicy…

Then he'd just walked away. *He just walked away!* And he hadn't talked to me for three days. His jagged journey from hate, to kiss, back to hate had given me whiplash. Talk about mind games. Apparently Coach Holter had nowhere near the psychological manipulation skills of Dane Monroe.

"Loosha?"

A feminine voice brought me back to the sports medicine waiting room, and I looked up to find a tiny, blond woman holding the door open. In Texas, nobody would mispronounce my name like that.

Speaking of mind games, now I had to deal with Coach's mandated nutrition referral. I stood and blinked for a second to slough off my lightheadedness, then approached the nutritionist. "It's Loo-see-uh."

"Oh." She blushed. "Botched that one. Sorry. I'm Whitney Randall."

Doesn't she know who I am? When she reached out to shake my hand, her iron grip surprised me.

I felt Allison's presence behind me before she spoke. "I need to do a sweep of your office."

Whitney's elfin nose wrinkled as she looked up at both of us. Though Allison was a few inches shorter than me, she was still close to six feet, and we towered over the Lilliputian Whitney.

"I'm with Secret Service," Allison offered.

"Oh!" Whitney nodded, though she still seemed confused. "Well, if Lucia's okay with it, you can come back with us."

It *wasn't* okay with me—being forced to see a nutritionist was embarrassing enough without a chaperone—but I didn't have a choice. I managed a thin smile (the only thin part of me), and we headed to her office.

As Allison's shrewd gaze scanned the small space, I took in the clean desk, athletic posters on the wall, and food boxes on the bookshelf. But what held my gaze and twisted my stomach was the scale in one corner. I did *not* want to get on that thing.

"I can pull in another chair for you," Whitney said.

"No, I won't be staying," Allison replied, and I let out a breath. Maybe this wouldn't be as humiliating as I'd imagined. "I'll be right outside, though."

"Uh, okay." Whitney seemed out of her depth.

After Allison left and Whitney had invited me to sit in the chair across from her desk, I asked, "You don't know who I am?"

"I know you're a Highbanks athlete." She grabbed a notebook and sat in her desk chair. "I'm guessing basketball?"

She didn't know my dad! I loved her all of a sudden. "Volleyball."

"Got it. Why do you have a Secret Service agent with you?" When I paused, she added, "I probably should already know this, sorry. I don't watch the news, though—too depressing."

I certainly could understand. Sometimes I wished *I* could be oblivious to national news, but my dad always ranted about low-information voters. "Is it, um, is it okay if I don't answer that question?"

"Absolutely! No pressure here."

Her warm smile helped me relax into the chair. I liked being Lucia, the volleyball player, instead of always being Lucia, daughter of a presidential nominee.

"So, like I said, I'm Whitney, the sports dietitian for Highbanks. I was a diver here a while ago. Did someone refer you to me?"

"I guess my coach did."

"Wyatt Holter?"

The sound of his name made me twitch. "That's the one."

She grinned. "He's kind of intense, huh?"

"You know him well."

"Yes, he's sent me several athletes over the years." She scribbled on her notepad. "So why does he want you to see me?"

I broke eye contact and looked around the room. My gaze landed on that damn scale. "He thinks I'm fat."

"He *said* that?" Her blue eyes widened.

"Well, not exactly." My fingertips brushed my cheek for a few seconds, then I yanked my hand down. A guy as handsome as Dane would never want a girl with a weight problem. "He says I need to get fitter."

"Are you sure? You look quite muscular already."

I dropped my head. Highbanks paid her to work with athletes, so she must have felt obligated to say something nice like that.

"What do *you* think, Lucia?"

I looked up. "About what?"

"Do you want to get fitter?"

"Yes. Coach says I need to get to the double block faster."

"Do you agree with him?"

I paused. "I thought I was a good blocker, but…" I felt my face warm as she continued starting at me. Did she want me to admit that I sucked at my sport? "I'll be better once I lose weight."

"Hmm. I want to gather some data first, approach this scientifically. I'm sending you to get a bone scan, to assess your body composition, before we make any changes to your diet." She picked up the phone and dialed while I receded into my chair and sulked.

She wasn't going to help me with my diet? Then why was I fricking meeting with her?

"One o'clock next Thursday," she said as she hung up the phone. "You can make that, right? It's between morning and afternoon practices, and that's still a few days before you start classes."

"We start competing soon, though. I'm not sure we'll be in town."

She turned to her computer and brought up the Highbanks University Athletics website. A few clicks and she had the women's volleyball schedule on the screen. "You're right—your first games start next weekend. But they're home matches, so you should be fine."

Nausea stirred in my gut as I thought about my first college match. *If* I got any playing time, would I make a complete fool of myself out there?

"I'd like to get to know you better." Whitney had picked up her notepad again. "Are you having regular menses?"

What the heck are menses?

When I didn't answer, she chuckled. "Sorry to confuse you with the medical jargon. Are you having regular periods?"

¡Híjole! She didn't beat around the bush. "Uh, yes?"

"Good. That's a sign you're eating enough to support all the exercise you do."

I was pretty sure one look at me would tell her I ate enough.

"What are some of your favorite foods?"

"Um, salads, and bananas, and apples, and..." I trailed off when she glared at me. "What?"

"*Nobody* lists those as their favorite foods. Stop telling me what you think I want to hear, and start answering my questions honestly."

She was half my size, but the fierceness in her eyes made me realize her pixie power. I sat up a bit. "But the foods I like are fattening."

"Fat makes food taste better, but it doesn't mean the food itself will make you gain weight. What do you like to eat?"

"Fajitas." My mouth watered just thinking about my favorite Houston restaurant's sizzling chicken and steak.

"Fajitas are a well-balanced choice with all three macronutrients. Tortillas and rice have carbohydrates, meat and beans have protein, and cheese and guacamole have fat. Plus, there are vegetables. What else do you like?"

She was saying fajitas were *healthy?* My head spun, and I said the first thing that came to mind: "Sopaipillas." When she tilted her head, I cringed. *Way to tell a nutritionist that you like to eat the most fattening food ever.*

"I've never had those before." She turned to her computer and pulled up a link. "Oh! Fried Mexican dough. Yeah, I've heard of these."

I waited for her to tell me I could never eat them again.

"So, this is a nutrient-dense food that the average person should eat sparingly. Athletes might get by with eating sopapillas more frequently. How often do you eat them?"

"I don't think I've had any since my birthday."

"And when was that?"

"September twentieth."

"Almost a *year* ago?" Whitney shook her head. "But it's one of your favorite foods."

I shrugged. "My mom said I shouldn't eat it."

Whitney kept writing, and I wondered how hopeless she thought I was. She glanced at the clock on the wall. "Let's see, it's one fifteen. What have you eaten today?"

Ah. This was an easier question, since all morning I had calmed myself by repeating the small number of calories I'd consumed: eighty. "I had a banana."

"What size banana?"

"Medium." *Eighty calories, eighty calories.*

"Okay, what else?" She smiled at me.

"That's it." If I could've gotten by with eating nothing, I would have, but Allison and had been in the kitchen this morning and had shoved a banana at me when I'd gotten my coffee. "Oh! I had coffee too."

"Any cream and sugar?"

"Black." *Disgusting.* I missed my favorite flavored creamer.

Whitney frowned. "Lucia. That's not enough. You need to eat more."

I pulled back, deeper into my chair. She was *mad* at me? I'd thought she'd be pleased with my self-restraint!

"If you like bananas, then add some peanut butter, maybe some milk. You need more to keep you going for a three-hour practice."

Peanut butter? That would go straight to my butt. No way I'd eat peanut butter.

"Did you drink any water today?"

"Of course."

"How much?"

"Uh, about one and a half water bottles."

She jotted that down.

"Part of my assessment is to take your height and weight." Whitney stood and stepped toward the evil scale.

Here it comes. As my heart raced, I wished I hadn't consumed any water at practice. "Can I go to the bathroom real quick?"

She studied me. "No need. We're almost done here, once I take your weight."

I slowly got to my feet and approached the gallows.

She extended a bar on the back of the scale toward the ceiling. "Let's measure your height first."

"I'm six-two."

She laughed as she looked up at me. "I can see that. Just want to get the most accurate measurement. Please back onto the scale."

I. Hate. This. I turned around and stepped backward onto the instrument of doom.

"Yep, seventy-four inches. Okay, stay right there, and I'll get your weight."

My chest squeezed around my galloping heart. "I don't get to *see* it?"

"It's just a number, Lucia. It doesn't define you."

Right. If only it didn't define me. I heard the slide of metal across the scale, and when the sound continued, ticking up the pounds, I stopped breathing.

"Okay, you can step off."

I whipped around as I stepped down, but she'd zoomed the metal piece back to the left before I could see the massive number.

"Schedule with me in two weeks," she said, handing me one of her business cards. "We'll review the results of the bone scan."

Yippee. "Thanks." I bolted from her office, and for once I was actually happy to see Allison.

Nina's wilting set floated far to my right, and I had to sprint from the left corner of the net to reach the ball in time. There was no way I could make it to spike that ball with my left hand, so I made a split-second decision to dink it over the net with my right. Rolling off my fingertips with a light touch, the ball dribbled to the gym floor before Kaitlyn could dig it on the opposite side of the net. In a game, that would be our point. In a practice drill in which I was supposed to spike the ball down the line, it was our undoing.

"So many screw-ups with that play, I don't know where to begin," Coach Holter said in a tight voice.

I didn't want to look at him, but I knew he'd get on my case if I didn't make eye contact. The veins on his neck bulged, and I braced myself for his tirade.

"Nina, is Lucia right-handed?"

Once I saw her fearful expression, I actually felt sympathy for our team setter. Holding the most important position on the team, Nina had been forced to absorb much of our coach's wrath. "No," she finally said.

"Then why aren't you pushing the ball out to her left side?"

She looked down. I chewed on my lip as I wiped the back of my hand across my forehead. It had taken my high-school setter a couple of years to perfect setting to a left-hander, and Nina had only been working on it for a week. Not that those details mattered to Coach.

"And Ramirez," he said, his stony face turning toward me. "This is exactly what I mean about your weight holding you back. A faster hitter would've made it to that ball. But you—you lumber over to the set..." He made a big show of stomping one heavy foot in front of another, waddling forward as he puffed his cheeks out.

Oh my God. Did I actually look like that when I spiked the ball? I wanted to melt into the floor like a massive marshmallow. *Eighty calories, eighty calories, eighty calories.*

"And *Kaitlyn!*"

Phew. He'd moved on to his next prey. I clasped my hands together to stop their shaking.

"You asked me why you're on the practice team? Why you're not a starter?" He flung his arms in the air. "It's not such a damn mystery, is it?" He paced the sideline. "I thought you were a defensive specialist! Play some actual *defense* then."

I peeked at Kaitlyn, whose brown eyes blazed. She was a feisty one, and I bet she'd fly all over the court to get the next ball, just to prove Coach wrong. I wished I felt some of her fire inside. Right now all I felt was exhaustion.

"We'll get the next one." Maddie stood next to me as the middle blocker and smiled when I looked at her. How did she stay so positive in this hellish environment?

"Again." Coach crossed his arms over his chest. "Turn your brains on this time, you airheads."

I wanted to kill him. On the opposite side of the net, a sophomore teammate tossed up the ball to execute her jump serve, but the ball careened into the net. *Uh-oh.* I stole a glance at Coach, who appeared ready to stroke out.

"*Jesus!* You're so undependable, Murphy—no wonder you're not a starter. Serve the damn ball *in play*. Again."

I exhaled when her next serve made it over the net, and thankfully my teammate in the back row passed the ball perfectly to Nina. Maddie made a fast approach toward Nina, pretending she would execute a quick-hit to fake out the defense, while I waited for Nina to set the ball to me. Her set sailed to the left corner of the net—just where I liked it—and I took two steps then leaped up to snap the heel of my hand through the ball, slamming it down the line.

I heard Maddie's voice. "Good job, Lucia!"

I shook my head. That spike was nowhere near as powerful as it could've been. I tried to blink away the dizziness I felt.

"Madison—get over to block," Coach ordered, and Maddie hustled to face me from the opposing side of the net. Coach nodded at me. "Let's see you try that same hit through our best blocker."

Mierda.

8

Dane

I was just about to slurp the leftover milk from my second bowl of cereal when Lucia entered the kitchen. With my bowl suspended in midair, I watched her stop in place once she saw me.

Shit. So much for avoiding her after my beer-goggle kiss a week ago. The girl confused the hell out of me. I'd hoped some time away from her would clarify things, but given the uptick of my heartbeat when she strolled in the room, that obviously hadn't happened.

As I set my bowl back on the table, my eyes floated from her flushed face to the slogan on her hot-pink T-shirt:

Volleyball is my passion
and
Spandex is my fashion

I grinned. *Thank God guys don't have to wear Spandex.* When she turned to leave, I caught a glimpse of the luscious curve of her bottom. *And thank God girl players do.*

"Wait, don't go." *Why did I just say that?*

She pivoted and nailed me with her suspicious gaze. "What?"

Feeling unnerved, I gestured toward the open box of cereal on the table. "Want some dinner? You don't have to leave on my account."

She stared at the cereal for a few moments. At first she seemed to give the box a longing look, like she'd discovered a deep cache of oil on a barren stretch of land. Then her eyes tightened into the same hostile look I'd seen so many times on her father. Despite this, I noticed dark hollows beneath her eyes and felt a smidgen of concern for her. That level of exhaustion typically didn't occur until later in the season, when Holter's constant demands would inevitably wear down the girl's team.

"I'm not hungry," she finally said.

"But you haven't eaten anything."

She glanced up from the box of cereal with wide eyes. "Yes, yes, I have."

When she stepped away from me, I took my time getting to my feet in an effort to avoid scaring her away. "Then why'd you come to the kitchen?"

"I..." Her eyes darted around the modern appliances. She backed up until her butt brushed the counter, which one hand gripped with white knuckles. "I came to get a drink."

Why did she look so tortured? "Oh." I shrugged. "I'll get it for you."

"No—"

I made it to the fridge in two strides and opened the door. "What'd you want? We've got cranberry juice, orange juice, Coke...hey, there's even some beer hidden back here—"

"Water," she said. I backed out of the shelf and straightened, wondering if I'd heard her correctly. "Just ice water."

"*That's* kind of boring." I crossed over to the cabinet and snatched a glass from the shelf, then returned to the refrigerator door to fill it with crushed ice and filtered water. "Here ya go."

She hesitated as she studied the drink in my outstretched hand.

"Relax. It's not poisoned." I grinned at her.

She grasped the glass. Her hand trembled as she took a sip. "Why are you being nice to me?"

Man, she had trust issues. All I did was get her a freaking glass of water! I performed a little bow and adopted an English accent. "The setter is here to serve the hitter, milady."

Was that a hint of a smile? The subtle quirk of one corner of her mouth filled me with warmth, and I realized that was the first time

I'd seen her even come close to a smile. *Esa chica* needed to learn how to chill if she wanted to last as a Highbanks varsity athlete. She set down her glass and seemed to take a deep breath.

"Have you always been a setter?"

Her question made me pause. *Why does she want to know?* "Yep."

"Why?"

I need to be in charge. "I like being the leader of the team."

"Kind of tall for a setter, aren't you?"

Wow. Mute Girl actually engaged me in conversation? I watched her gaze linger at my feet and slowly sweep up my body. I stared right back at her, trying to figure out what she found so fascinating. When our eyes met, it took a second to register what was going on. *Damn!* She had just *ogled* me. Having her eyes roam over my body…I had to admit it felt pretty great. I winked at her, and a pretty, rose-colored blush crept up her neck a second before she looked away.

Huh. I already knew she elicited some puzzling turn-on inside of me, but was it possible I did the same thing to her? I'd chalked up her heated reaction to my alcohol-induced kiss as mere surprise, but maybe there'd been something more.

"Sure, I'm tall. Every *inch* helps." When her lips parted, I knew she'd understood my innuendo. "Besides, your setter's tall too."

She finally managed to look in my eyes. "Huh?"

"Nina. She's a tall setter."

I wasn't sure what happened, but something broke the spell between us. Lucia looked down as she wrapped her arms around her midsection. She seemed to stiffen and shuffled from one foot to another.

I took a step toward her. "Did I say something wrong?"

"No." She kept her head down.

"*Hey, China!*" Allison's voice drew my attention to the foyer. "*Are you guys expecting company?*" I looked at Lucia, but she seemed as confused as I was. The buzzer sounded.

"C'mon," I said and headed to the front hallway. I felt Lucia come up behind me as I stopped to see Allison frowning at the monitors. The buzzer beeped in staccato.

"Who is it?" China asked as she bustled around me to join Allison.

I felt my shoulders tense. More reporters?

"The guy's wearing shades," Allison said. "Don't know about him."

I circled around the agents to peer over their heads at the monitor showing the camera feed for the front gate. *Definitely shady.* The guy wore a baseball cap and sunglasses and leaned out the open car window with his arms up to the side, waving them like a madman.

China pressed the intercom button. "State your business, sir."

"*This is ridículo! You know who I am.*"

"Alex!" Lucia piped up with a clap. "I'd recognize that voice anywhere." She pointed at the monitor. "It's okay, it's my brother."

Oh, fuck. Alejandro Ramirez was even *more* opinionated than his father, if that was possible. And vitriol, racism, and classism fueled many of those opinions.

Allison turned to look at us. "Doesn't he have a security detail?"

"No." Lucia shrugged. "They think he'll be safe at Johns Hopkins. Only for public events."

Lucky bastard. "Well, *we're* safe at Highbanks, too," I pointed out. "We don't need protection either."

"But then we wouldn't have the pleasure of dealing with your scintillating personality every day, Mr. Monroe."

China was such a bitch. She reached for the button again. "Remove your hat and sunglasses, sir."

I watched Alejandro toss his hands up, appearing pissed off, but he did follow the agent's orders. A thick head of black, wavy hair emerged once he freed it from the Houston Texans baseball cap, and his dark eyes bored holes into the camera. He'd begun appearing on talk shows over the summer, spouting off about health care in America, pretending he had a fucking clue. It had been obvious he was simply a child masquerading as an adult—he was only twenty-three or something like that, for Christ's sake. But damn, today he looked more like his father than I'd ever seen him.

China shifted in front of me, and I noticed she'd patted the butt of her weapon in its holster. She tended to do that when she was nervous.

"Wait a minute—you're not thinking of letting him in, are you?"

China spun around to look at me. "Of course I am. He's Lucia's brother."

I ignored the hurt look in Lucia's eyes and scowled at China. "But did you know he was coming?"

"No." China squinted. "What difference does *that* make?"

"Security protocol!" I placed my hands on my hips. "You're not supposed to admit unplanned visitors."

"What's going on?" With a white towel slung around his neck, Frank arrived on the scene, with Brad lumbering behind him. They both wore boxing gloves and reeked from their workout in the basement.

"Alejandro Ramirez is outside," Allison answered. "And Dane was just voicing some concerns about our security protocol for visitors." She smiled sweetly at me. "But Mr. Ramirez is on our approved list of visitors, so China's going to buzz him in while I greet him outside."

All four agents looked at me with challenging stares, daring me to protest. Lucia watched me too, seeming to hold her breath. I sighed as I laced my arms across my chest. "Fine. Just admit the entire Ramirez clan while you're at it. *Mi casa es su casa.*"

My grumpy harrumph hung in the air a moment before Lucia grinned. "*Gracias, Señor* Monroe. Thanks for opening up your *casa* to us." She performed a little curtsy, and it was so damn cute I almost grinned too.

Wait a minute! I was supposed to be mad. Alejandro Asswipe was about to breach my territory.

China pressed the button to open the security gate, and Allison arched one eyebrow at me as she crossed between us.

"Here we go," I said to Lucia. "I get to meet your older brother—this should be good. Do you know why he's visiting you?"

Her smile vanished. "I think I have an idea." She rubbed the back of her neck as she trailed Allison toward the front door.

"Stay inside, Lucia," Allison said over her shoulder before she exited the house.

Lucia turned to face me. She opened her mouth to say something, but then shut it again. Her hands twisted together as she looked up at me. "Be nice?"

I frowned. Why was she so nervous? "This is my house. Will *he* be nice?"

She winced. "Probably not."

Fan-fucking-tastic. I braced myself for Adolf Junior.

As Alejandro walked in ahead of Allison, his face lit up. "*¡Hermanita!*" He gathered Lucia in a bear hug, and I noticed he was maybe a couple of inches taller than her. Still shorter than me. When his eyes found me over her shoulder, he quickly let her go.

His face darkened as he studied me, and I drew to my full height as I stared back at him. I imagined him as the starting setter for Bridgetown University—our biggest rival—and composed a stoic game face to match. From the corner of my eye, I saw Lucia look back and forth between us, her hands fidgeting at her side.

"Welcome, Mr. Ramirez," China said as she approached him with her hand extended. "I'm Agent Halloway."

He nodded as he shook her hand. "Alejandro. You're one of the agents protecting Lucy?"

I looked at "Lucy," who predictably blushed and ducked her head. She somehow seemed younger...*softer*...in her brother's commanding presence.

"I protect Mr. Monroe," China replied. She gestured to Allison. "You already met Agent Largent, and Agent Frank Vanderberg is also on Lucia's detail."

Alejandro grinned as he raised his fists in front of his chest, jabbing the air a few times while dancing and juking. "You guys don't mess around with security, huh? Are you always this prepared?"

Frank held up his gloved hands and nodded, while Brad gave a hearty laugh. "I'm Brad Jansen. Welcome to the compound." He bopped Frank's shoulder with his boxing glove. "This old man and I will leave you to it—we need to get back to work. Frank's got some catching up to do...what're you down by, Frank—six or seven bouts?"

Frank shoved the muscled agent toward the basement door. "Dream on, Steroid Boy."

Once the male agents left, silence descended on the remaining four of us. China cleared her throat, and her glare probably meant I should also welcome Adolf Junior to my house. *Fat chance.* Then I looked at Lucia, whose eyes pleaded with me. *Fuck.*

I squared my shoulders and met those cold, Nazi eyes. "I'm Dane Monroe." I made myself approach the guy to shake his hand, and the force of his grip almost broke a few bones in my fingers. *Dude, lighten up.*

"Your mother set this up?" Alejandro asked once he let go of my hand. He gestured around the foyer. "Lucia living here, with you?"

I hesitated. What was he implying? "My mother set this up for *me*. The agents are responsible for Lucia living here."

"And that's our cue to leave," Allison said. Her chuckle sounded nervous. "China and I will give you some privacy. Would you like to make yourselves comfortable in the living room?" She extended her arm to the left.

Awesome. Looks like Baby Hitler will stay for a while. But maybe I could prevent future visits by marking my territory. To let him know this was *my* house, I led the way to the sitting area. I plopped down on the big chair, forcing Lucia and her brother to share the sofa.

"How's Mom?" Lucia asked.

Alejandro looked at me like he was waiting for me to leave, but I didn't budge. He leaned in and spoke rapid Spanish to his sister, and I stifled a laugh.

Lucia pressed her lips together. "*Dane habla español también.*"

His narrowed eyes darted to me, displeased.

"It's okay, you can talk in front of the gringo." This time I didn't bother to stifle my chuckle. When he didn't speak, I asked, "Why are you here, Alejandro?"

"This is not good. Not good at all. I have to find out on the *news* that my little sister is living with you—"

"Sorry, we practice almost all day long," Lucia cut in. "I didn't have time to call."

I didn't like him getting on her case—she'd done nothing wrong. "That news story was days ago. You must not have been *that* concerned."

He refused to look at me, and his voice lowered with fury. "I had a *test* to study for. I'm in medical school."

As if I didn't know that. He'd shared that fact with every news outlet in America. Not that one year of med school made him the expert he purported to be on health care policy.

"I just..." He sighed. "Are you okay here, Lucy?" He cradled her elbow as he searched her eyes.

"I'm fine."

"Dad told me he offered to find you another place, but you didn't take him up on it."

I felt my eyebrows lift. That was news to me.

She snuck a glance at me, and that lovely blush spread across her face. "I don't have time to move, and the agents can't find another place, anyway. Like I said, I'm fine."

"I still don't like it."

And *I* didn't like him hounding her for something outside her control. "Dude, what do you think? That I'm going to force her to drink Democratic Kool-Aid or something if she lives here? This wasn't her choice."

"Stay out of this, *cabrón*. Why are you even here?"

"Classy. Call me bastard again and *you* won't be here for long."

He popped to his feet. "You're all about choices, *¿verdad?* I know how your mother loves choice. Abortions have killed fifty million babies. That's a great choice right there."

"You're such an assbag." I was on my feet before I knew it, and I loved the height advantage over Adolf Junior. "Just like your father."

"Our father has more honor than a hundred Democratic senators!"

"Oh, yeah, like the Republicans have so much honor. Kicking mentally ill people off disability? Does that make you proud?"

"Damn bleeding-heart liberals! You're *ruining* our country." His flaring eyes and clenched jaw made me wonder if he was going to take a swing at me.

Lucia cried, "Alex!"

We both turned to her. I'd almost forgotten she was there.

"*Cálmate, hermano. Tranquilo.*" She rubbed his shoulder.

Tranquilo. Her soothing voice echoed in my mind, instructing me to calm down. I inhaled a long breath, trying to remember what Phil would tell me when I freaked out in the huddle in the middle of a close game. But even the Bridgetown setter didn't have the audacity to label my mother a baby killer.

"It's okay, Alex," Lucia cooed. "It's okay to disagree on stuff." She kept murmuring soothing words in his ear, and his shoulders slumped as he nodded. How did she do that? She was the freaking Tea Party Whisperer or something.

The evaporation of his rage now complete, Alejandro returned to the sofa. Feeling calmer myself, I sat back down too. He gave me a sheepish look. "*Lo siento.* That wasn't my most mature moment. My dad always tells me I'll never get anywhere unless I learn to control my temper."

Huh. Mom had said the same thing to me.

"That wasn't right to say that stuff about your mother," Alejandro said.

But no way in hell I'm retracting my criticism of your father. "Especially since it was her generosity that allowed Lucia to live here."

"Generosity?" Alejandro's eyebrows rose.

Apparently *enfurecido* had replaced *tranquilo.*

He sucked in a breath. "You...You actually *believe* that? That she's *generous?*"

"Alex?" Lucia fidgeted next to him.

"*Lucy.*" He scoffed, then looked at her. "You can't let him get away with that."

"Get away with what?"

He knocked the heel of his hand on his forehead. "Jesus. Don't tell me you're so naïve!"

"Stop being a jerk, Alex—I'm not naïve."

"This is all a political ploy!" He threw his arms in the air. "This isn't about generosity. She has ulterior motives for everything she does!"

Shut the fuck up.

"What are you saying?" Lucia seemed baffled.

"She 'allowed' you to live here to distract the media from Yemen."

My heart thundered. "You son of a bitch."

"No, I'm afraid that honor is all yours, son of that bitch Monroe."

Now I was the one who sprang to my feet. My hands itched with the desire to smack the smug off his face.

"Dane." Lucia stood and shook her head.

"Bite me, bitch nugget! You don't know anything about my mother!"

He just kept sitting there, smirking. I wanted to spike his volleyball-shaped head right into the floor.

Lucia crossed over to me. "Dane." Her hand clasped my wrist. "Don't let him get to you."

I looked down at her hand cradling my wrist and noticed the femininity of her long fingers. I felt the warmth of her skin on mine, and my fists unfurled. But my heart skipped a beat when I felt a tremble flow from her hand to my wrist.

"Why are you shaking?"

She yanked back her hand. "You're...you two are stressing me out." She glanced at her brother. "Listen, whatever Senator Monroe's motives were, she did allow me to live here, which helps keep me safe. You want that, right? You want your *hermanita* to be protected?"

Alejandro grunted.

Then she looked at me. "And you should be more understanding, Mr. Psych Major."

How'd she know my major?

"You have a little sister, too. How would you feel if Jessica was forced to live with Alex at Johns Hopkins?"

My jaw unhinged. "That would never happen."

"Well, how would you handle it if it did? Probably a lot more aggressively than Alex is handling it, knowing *you*."

"What does *that* mean?"

"You seem to enjoy jumping in to stir the pot. You're just like our little brother Mateo, arguing with Alex all the time."

"You're comparing me to a sixteen-year-old?"

"Hey, if the shoe fits..." Alejandro chimed in.

I rolled my eyes at him.

Lucia's hands perched on her curvy hips. "Do I have to separate you two?"

My burst of laughter surprised me, and judging from Alejandro's expression, it surprised him too. Lucia was finally showing some spunk, which I had to admit was preferable to her flitting-bird persona. Maybe she'd needed the comfort of a family member to help coax that out. I studied her. "You're the middle child, right? I bet you play mediator a lot. You seem really good at it."

"¡Oh, *Dios!*" Alejandro said as he stood. "Don't try to psychoanalyze our family, Monroe. Even a psychologist like your mother couldn't help us."

Wow. That was about the longest olive branch ever extended. I wasn't sure how to respond. "My, my mother doesn't practice anymore."

"She'll be practicing again soon." Alejandro grinned. "Once our dad crushes her in the election."

I shook my head. *Aannnndd...olive branch yanked back.*

"Where's the *cocina* in this place, Lucy? I'm cooking you dinner before I fly out tomorrow."

"No, Alex!"

He took off in the wrong direction, muttering something about nutrition for athletes, and she began to follow him before turning back to me. Her dark eyes shone as she blinked at me, and I noticed some dimple action as she smiled. "Thank you," she whispered, then spun around to chase her brother.

I looked down at my wrist and could almost still feel her gentle touch on my skin. Then I pressed my hands to my face, massaging my closed eyelids, as I exhaled. What was this right-wing girl doing to me?

9

Lucia

I let Alex wander around the house for a while, refusing to show him the correct way to the kitchen, until he stumbled upon it himself. He whistled through his teeth as he entered the expansive space. "So this is how green-energy thieves live. Good thing the government pays so much to fools like him. This house is *so* worth digging into deeper debt with China." He poked his head into the fridge, then the pantry and eyed me. "I'm making you a sandwich."

Awesome. I clenched my jaw.

"Most freshmen eat at the dining hall," he said as he assembled fixings on the counter. "They're too clueless to cook for themselves. Are the agents at least cooking for you?"

"Sometimes." Brad made a mean flank steak. Of course, I'd only allowed myself a bite or two before rushing off to practice.

"Does *your roommate* make food for you?"

I studied my brother. His voice was missing the vitriol it had previously carried when discussing Dane. I wondered if meeting Mr. Stud Athlete in person—and throwing out some heated barbs—had calmed him down. Then another thought made me freeze. Had Alex caught on to my ill-advised crush?

I sidled up to him to try to discern if I was busted. "So, how's your second year going?"

When he slapped some mayonnaise on a piece of toasted bread, my heart thundered. *Way too much fat!*

"Got a ninety-five on my first test."

I gripped the counter when he proceeded to plop two pieces of cheese on my sandwich. *Oh, hell no.* "That's...great."

"When do classes start for you?" He cut the sandwich in half.

Good, I only have to eat half of it.

Then he slid the plate toward me and reached to the bread to pick out two more slices for his own sandwich. *Mierda!*

"Lucy?"

I peeled my gaze away from the offending hunk of calories. "What?"

"I asked you when your classes start."

"Oh." I swallowed. "Next week, after our first match."

"How're you feeling about your first game as a Highbanks Cougar?"

I gasped. "*Why* are you using so much mayo?" When Alex frowned at me, I realized I'd said that out loud.

"Relax, *hermanita*. You need some fat in your diet."

Like hell I do.

"In my neuro class we learned how your brain *needs* fat. You see, your brain has nerve cells called neurons. The axon of the neuron is coated in a myelin sheath, which basically consists of fat..."

He launched into one of his insufferable medical lectures, and all I could focus on was the chubby blob of white mayo oozing out of my sandwich.

"Have you heard a word I said?" His eyes darkened. "This is exactly why you need to eat more fat, to focus better."

"Huh?"

"If you don't eat enough fat, your brain doesn't concentrate well. C'mon." He picked up his plate and carried it over to the dining table, gesturing for me to do the same. He sat and took a ginormous bite of turkey and cheese.

I swallowed again. The sandwich looked delicious, but I knew it would slow me down on the court.

"Are you going to make me eat all by myself?" He patted the chair next to him. "That's not being a very gracious host."

I glared at him. Mom had always taught us the importance of caring for guests, even Aunt Maricela. My dad's sister had a way of getting under my mother's skin, but still, Mom would prepare Maricela's favorite dish and boot me out of my bedroom so *Tia* Mari would have a nice place to sleep.

I grabbed the plate and set it down with a clatter on the table.

Alex's eyes creased with amusement, and I realized I'd acted just like the child he thought I was. To spite him, I took a bite. *Oh*...tart tomato intertwined with creamy mayo and sharp cheddar cheese: a flavor profile that lingered on my tongue and sparked the flow of juices in my withering stomach. I looked down at the sandwich. *I've missed you, food.*

"Dad's poll numbers went down this week." Alex's fierce chomp told me what he thought of that.

I winced. *I should pay more attention to the election.* "Do they know why?"

"We have to get the focus back on Yemen. Somebody's got to be accountable for that cluster." Alex's gaze darted around, and he leaned in to whisper, "Do you think they've got this place bugged?"

I certainly hoped not. I didn't want Dane to know about my crying jag the night I'd moved in. I mimicked my brother's body language by holding still and listening, but all I could hear was faint music floating from Dane's bedroom.

"I've never heard that band before," Alex said.

"They're Dane's favorite," I said. They weren't as great as Neil Diamond, of course, but they were growing on me. I'd already studied the lyrics online, and the song "Attraction Infraction" was my favorite:

You turn your body away from me
Your eyes too dark, too blind to see
I want you, more than you can know
It's wrong, it's wrong, but oh-oh-oh...

If only Dane felt that way about *me!* My silent humming halted when I noticed Alex staring at me with a quizzical look. I attempted to swallow the bite I'd been chewing. "What?"

"You know his favorite band?"

I shrugged. "He plays them nonstop—how could I not know? The electric guitar's so obnoxious." When the tight lines around his eyes didn't relax, my heartbeat surged. A wad of turkey got stuck in my throat. "Drinks!" I shot out of my chair. "I forgot to get us drinks. Want some Coke?" I headed to the fridge. "They call it pop up here. Isn't that dumb?"

"Water's fine," he said, a hint of suspicion still lacing his voice.

I filled two glasses with ice water. "So, how can Dad's team get the focus back on Yemen?"

He accepted the glass. "It helps now that the story about you living with the enemy has died down." His skeptical eyes kept studying me, so I slid back into my chair and took another bite. "But what we really need is to put the heat on Secretary of State Cannell—what a *joke* he is. And the lamestream media definitely won't apply any pressure, so Dad will have to keep bringing it up on the campaign trail."

"But won't that make Dad look vindictive?" I asked.

My brother took the bait, went off on a diatribe about the best defense being offense, and just like that we had moved on from Dane.

The next morning, I waved goodbye to Alex as he climbed into his rental car. I closed the front door of the greenhouse and swiveled around to lean back against it. A long sigh deflated my lungs. I'd managed to diffuse the *caliente* argument between Alex and Dane last night, but keeping them apart since then had called upon all the skills I'd honed from years of living between two hothead brothers. Thank goodness Alex had a morning flight back to Baltimore.

I heard soft voices coming from the sitting area beside the foyer and knew Dane must be watching some sort of news show. Recalling his comment from last night, I smiled. He'd labeled me a *mediator* in my family, which was spot on. How had he read me so well?

Not only had Dane seemed to see right through me, he'd also been protective. I loved when he'd called Alex out for treating me like a child. I'd wanted to do that my whole life. I could still picture his smirk when he joked about forcing me to drink liberal Kool-Aid. When Dane wasn't busy insulting my father, his face seemed to relax—that sharp crease on his forehead smoothing out, his eyebrows lifting slightly—making him even more handsome.

I had it bad for my roommate, for sure. Hopefully Alex hadn't figured that out.

I was about to head to my room when an envelope on the small table near the front door caught my eye. "What's this?" I picked it up, realizing only after I'd spoken that I was snooping in Dane's outgoing mail.

"What?" he asked, apparently hearing my question from the other room.

Crap. I walked into the sitting room and read aloud the addressee. "African Children's Fund?"

He glanced up from his laptop, which looked tiny in his big lap. "Figured I'd do something good with my grandpa's money."

I felt my eyebrows arch. His grandfather owned scads of land across the Midwest, making him one of the richest men in the country.

"Why so surprised, Ramirez?" That beautiful smirk lifted half his mouth, mesmerizing me. "Feeling guilty you don't give to charity too?"

That preposterous question quickly un-mesmerized me. My dad's company donated a ton to charity—much more than Dane's mother had donated, according to her public tax records. "Hardly. Just surprised someone like you would give to charity at all." I waved the envelope at him.

"Nice. Thanks so much for judging me."

"Only stating the facts," I countered. *He is so infuriating!* I was determined to set him straight. "Conservatives donate way more to charity than liberals do."

He snapped his laptop shut. "That's a fantasy."

"It's true!" I gestured to his laptop. "Google it."

He popped to his feet, forcing me to look up to him. "No *way* that's true. My mother and I care about people. Conservatives care about things."

My jaw hung open for what felt like ten minutes before I finally closed my mouth, realizing I must have looked ridiculous. Hot blood pulsed through my veins and my chest tightened. "I...*you*...I..."

"You can't find the words to argue because you know it's true. You know your party doesn't care about the poor." He took a step closer to me. "Hell, your own Mexican father wants to throw undocumented workers into prison. How's that for hypocrisy?"

"He, he doesn't want to reward people who break the law!" I managed, my mind whirling. *Confrontation freaks me out.*

"Keep telling yourself that, sweetheart." He winked at me, then patted his taut abs. "Time for my second breakfast." He disappeared from the room, and I stared at the muscular V-shape of his back until he turned the corner.

I closed my eyes and tried to settle my surging heart. My face felt hot, and my hands trembled. *We* care *about people!* I wanted to shout. *Making citizens dependent on the government hurts them more than helps them. And my dad just wants to secure our borders, that's all.*

I clutched my forehead, feeling the stirrings of a headache. Why couldn't I have said those things to Dane in person? Why did I become a tongue-tied idiot in his presence? And the most important question of all: how could I be so attracted to such a *jerk?*

Cou, cou, cou, cou-gars!

The inane cheer pulsed through my head as I joined the huddle by our bench. I'd been reeling ever since the squad of Highbanks cheerleaders had run onto the court midway through our warm-up. *Cheerleaders!* At a *volleyball* match? If I hadn't known before that I'd arrived at big-time college sports, I now knew for certain.

Coach's voice drew my attention away from the pixie, miniskirted girl perched atop the male cheerleader's hands, holding steady above his head. There's no way a guy would ever be able to support *my* weight like that. "Ladies," Coach said.

The announcer boomed over the intercom, "Who wants a Cougar Pride T-shirt?" The cheerleaders bounded up to the university mascot, Banky—a guy in a light-brown cougar costume—and the fuzzy feline pumped a large water-gun-thingy before aiming it up into the stands. I realized it was a T-shirt launcher when teenage girls in the sizable crowd lunged for the grey blobs sailing toward them. A sizable crowd! At a *volleyball* match? Their roar of appreciation competed with the peppy tune played by the school band in the stands behind me.

"Eyes on me, Lucia," Coach barked.

I bobbed my head in a frantic nod, and my jittery energy must have been evident to Maddie because she placed a reassuring hand on my shoulder. She'd given me a pep talk in the locker room before the match. I still couldn't believe she'd said I was a much better player than she'd been as a freshman. No way that was true.

Coach frowned at me. "I know this environment is distracting, but I need your complete focus."

The band's drums made me jump, but I nodded again. Coach had picked me to start tonight—the only freshman in the starting six—and I didn't want to blow it.

"Okay, back row: remember to shift left when number seventeen serves, and to watch for the 'out' call when number twenty-two serves. Nina..." Coach turned to our setter. "When do we run the one?"

"Whenever number sixteen is their middle blocker."

Her look of complete boredom as she answered his question amazed me. How was she so chill in this charged environment?

"Good." Coach nodded. "And use your legs to get your sets out to Lucia's left hand. She looks like she's about to crap her Spandex, so she'll need all the help she can get tonight."

My mouth dropped open as everyone stared at me. Was my nervousness that obvious? But then Maddie laughed and said, "That's okay, I made her wear three pairs of Spandex tonight just in case." Soon most of my teammates giggled, and even Coach smiled. When I let out a laugh, I felt some of my tension release. Holter had just made a joke? Who would've predicted *that?*

"Madison," Coach said, his face all serious again, "I need you to carry the load tonight. Lots of twos and back row hits."

"You got it."

My implacable teammate's confidence impressed the hell out of me. I wondered if I would ever feel so secure in my ability. Maybe her confidence stemmed from her lean body? Coach probably never made her get a body scan like I'd had to do yesterday. *So humiliating.* Now I had to remember to schedule another appointment with the dietitian to find out the dreaded results.

The announcer's voice filled the gym. "Please join us in standing for the national anthem." I followed the unfurling of the huddle and stood shoulder-to-shoulder with the rest of my teammates on the baseline. I could see the blue-and-white uniforms of our opponent through the net. Like my father had taught me, I placed my hand over my heart just as the recorded music boomed over the sound system.

Dane would've probably made fun of my patriotic gesture, but he wasn't in the stands. He'd left after morning practice for his mother's campaign stop in Milwaukee. Even though I hadn't said much to him since he'd spewed that ridiculous comment about conservatives a week ago, the house had felt lonely today. No Dane or Brad or China. I hadn't known what to do with myself without two practices filling my day, especially with classes not starting until next week.

I snuck a glance into the stands, and I couldn't stop the press of sadness weighing down my heart. This would be my first game without at least one family member attending. My mom had always been there, and my dad had made it to as many matches as he could, even after becoming the governor of Texas. But Dad was in California campaigning, and Mom still hadn't emerged from our Houston home. She claimed she wanted to be there for Mateo, but I bet she was still trying to lose weight. I knew what that was like—to want to hide from the public because of feeling fat. But I had no choice about standing in the spotlight tonight.

As I scanned the crowd, I noticed *one* person I knew: Allison. Frank was undoubtedly around somewhere, too, along with a couple of other agents brought in for the match. Allison's hand covered her heart, but she wasn't looking at the flag. Instead, she glared at something across the gym floor. I followed her gaze and felt my stomach drop when I saw a guy with a zoom-lens camera kneeling close to the referee's stand. Even worse, he had the camera aimed straight at me. I kept my eyes glued on the flag for the remainder of the anthem, hoping to avoid giving the media any ammunition about my lack of patriotism.

When the anthem ended, the announcer launched into introductions for our opponent's starting squad. I was surprised how many Kentucky fans there were—probably parents of the players, mostly. Then a rumble of cheers began as the announcer boomed, "Your Highbanks Cougar starters!" Wow, it got loud in this gym. "Number twelve, the starting setter, at six-foot-three, junior Nina Dahlstrom!"

I watched Nina step forward and wave to both sides of the stands as the crowd roared. Thankfully, the announcer didn't share our weight—just our height.

"Number twenty-eight, outside hitter, six-foot-two freshman Lucia Ramirez!" My face blazed as I managed to wave to the crowd amidst ear-splitting cheers. The fans were probably intrigued by somebody famous playing on the team. I gulped, knowing I needed to live up to my hype.

Mr. Paparazzi waved wildly by the net as he tried to get my attention. "Lucia!" He kept shouting my name right through the introductions of the remaining four starters, making me blush even more. *How rude.* I refused to look his way.

Once introductions finally ended, Maddie approached the net to shake the hands of the University of Kentucky team captains. *Whoa.* One of the Wildcats towered over Maddie—what was she, six-six? I'd been too distracted during their introductions to listen to their heights. And I thought *I* was a freak of nature.

Five of us stepped forward, toward the middle of our side of the court, while the rest of the team returned to the bench. Maddie joined our smaller huddle with a serene smile. "Relax, Rez," she said to me. "That tall girl was on their team last year. She's not that great."

That's good to know. It was like Maddie could read my mind. And I liked how she'd borrowed one of my dad's campaign slogans—Rez for Pres—for my nickname. A nickname solidified my place on the team.

"Okay, let's get a W for our first game, guys. First play's a one-four-three."

We each raised one arm, touched hands above our heads, then swung our arms down together while shouting, "Go Cougs!" I settled in my familiar spot on the left side of the front row with a massive grin on my face.

My smile vanished when I heard the *click-click-click* of the camera. The guy had planted himself just to my left, crouched down by the lower step of the referee's ladder.

"Rez!" From the middle of the net, Maddie beckoned me forward, and I tried to forget the stupid camera dude as I hustled to the net on her left. Kentucky had won the coin toss and elected to receive the serve, so Nina was behind us, preparing her jump serve. I held my arms up and scanned the defense as the ref above me blew her whistle to get play started. *¡Ay, Dios Mío!* My first college game. Coach was so right that I was about to crap my Spandex.

Nina's serve screamed over the net, but Kentucky's back-row player passed the ball cleanly to their setter, who was across the net just to my right. She set the ball to their outside hitter farthest from me, and I shuffled back to crouch in defense. There was no need for me to dig the ball, though, because Maddie's steel block stuffed the hit. The ball dribbled to the floor on their side of the net. *Point, Highbanks!*

I gave Maddie a high-five and settled back into my position. Maddie called out their defense as Nina slammed the next serve down their gullet. This time their setter arched her back and set the ball behind her, to the Kentucky hitter right in front of me. Oh no, it was the uber-tall girl. I felt Maddie join me on the right as we jumped together for the block. *Crap!* The ball went right through my hands down the line, and our defensive specialist Lynette couldn't get to it. *Click, click* went the camera, unnerving me. Now it was a side-out, and Kentucky would get the ball. *Point, Kentucky.*

"Lucia!" Coach hissed. With trepidation, I looked toward the bench. He held his arms up in the strong blocking position I should have had a moment ago. "Firm up the block! Get your timing down!"

I nodded.

"Breathe, Rez," Maddie murmured as I joined her in the middle of the net for service reception. "We'll stuff her next time."

I exhaled and attempted a smile. *If there is a next time.* Any second now, Coach was going to yank me to the bench.

The Kentucky player served, and Lynette passed it perfectly to Nina. Maddie approached the net as the pass floated over her head, and Nina softly set the ball just above the net as Maddie slammed the quick-set down. Kentucky's back-row player dived for the ball, and their setter somehow got it to their middle hitter, who evaded Maddie's block and spiked it hard toward Nina. Since our setter had been forced to pass the ball, Maddie had to jump in to set the ball to me. *¡Hijole!* My first hit as a Cougar. It wasn't a bad set, and I executed my three-step approach then leaped in the air. *Click-click-click.* All of a sudden, the play was over.

"Way to go, Rez!" Maddie said as she thumped me on the back.

I was in a daze as we rotated to the right. "What happened?"

"You got a kill down the line!" She shook her head, chuckling.

I looked up to see Coach Holter storming onto the court. *Oh, no. What did I do?* But he brushed past me and marched right up to the referee.

"Sit down, Coach," the ref said as she leaned forward to peer down at him from her perch. "You're not supposed to be on the court."

"And *he's* not supposed to be snapping photos on the court." He pointed an accusing finger at Mr. Paparazzi. "He's distracting my players!"

The ref glanced at her male counterpart on the other sideline, and he nodded at her. "You're right." She looked at the photographer and pointed to the first row of bleachers. "Move back, sir."

A small seed of satisfaction grew in my belly as I watched him slink back.

The referee glared at Coach, who still stood near her. "Take a seat, sir."

Coach Holter surprised me by spinning on his heel and returning to the bench. Apparently the bully could be bullied. As he passed by me, he said, "Nice hit."

The explosion of happiness in my heart overwhelmed me. I guessed my shock showed on my face because Maddie started laughing again. "He can be a bastard," she whispered. "But he makes you a great player."

As one of my teammates prepared to serve, I watched Mr. Paparazzi continue taking shots, this time from about fifteen feet away. *Good riddance.* Then he lowered his camera and stared right at me, his face a mask of unbridled hatred that made my stomach flip.

10

Dane

The hotel bed bounced, and I didn't have to open my eyes to know the identity of the annoying bouncer. Her chlorine smell gave her away in an instant. "Go away, Jess." I slung a forearm over my eyes and snuggled deeper into the crisp bedding.

"You're, like, *still* asleep?" The teeny-bop inflection of my sister's voice grated on my eardrums. "I've already done four-thousand yards!"

"What'd you want—a medal?" I wondered where she'd gotten a morning swim in—probably some local club practice she'd crashed. Unlike me, who played a team sport, she could take her swimming show on the road and train wherever our mom campaigned.

More bouncing, then I heard her chewing something. "C'mon, wake up. I've got something hilarious to show you."

Groaning, I sat up and rubbed my eyes. My rib was bruised from a collision with Pete in yesterday's practice, but my fatigue was more the source for the groan. After Mom's rousing speech at Marquette University last night, she'd tucked Jessica into bed in the adjoining room, and I'd asked her why Dad hadn't joined us. Why he *never* joined us anymore. Then Mom had shocked me by starting to cry. I'd been up late into the night with her, trying to console her—trying to figure out what the fuck he'd done to her—but she'd refused to tell me anything. More of her damn secrets.

Jessica's tight blond curls were wet and her cheeks flushed. She was still young and innocent, and I was glad she hadn't seen Mom cry. I snatched the egg sandwich from her grasp and took a big bite.

"Hey!"

"I'm hungry," I explained once I swallowed the cheesy goodness. As I handed the sandwich back to her, I glanced down at the complimentary copy of *USA Today* by her knee. "You actually read the newspaper? *That's* a first."

She scoffed, "I hate the news. But when Johnnie showed me this picture, I cracked up. I knew you'd want to see it."

John was one of the younger secret service agents on Mom's detail, and I was pretty sure Jessica had a crush on him. I gestured for the paper, expecting to see a photo of my sister's favorite band members dressed in silly costumes or something. She flipped over the sports section and thrust the paper into my hands as she giggled.

Oh, no.

Instead of a boy band, I stared at a blown-up photo of Lucia spiking the volleyball, probably at last night's match. She looked *huge*. It seemed like the photographer had been right under her—a perspective that magnified her size—and she wore the fiercest, ugliest expression I'd ever seen on a girl. She appeared nothing like the shy, passionate athlete I'd gotten to know.

"She looks like she's about to *eat* the ball," Jessica said with a laugh.

Could they have used a *more* unflattering photo? Doubtful. I scanned the headline: *Ramirez Unleashes Cougar Fury.*

"Aren't you scared to live with that ogre?" Jessica asked. "She could totally poison you while you sleep."

"What?" I looked up from the paper to find my sister smirking. "You don't know what you're talking about." I glanced at the words beneath the photo. "They won, I assume." I skimmed down the article and learned they'd beaten Kentucky three games to zero. I let out a breath when I read that Lucia had chipped in ten kills. *Not bad for a freshman.*

But I frowned as I kept reading: *It seems Governor Ramirez's daughter has inherited his penchant for aggression. While Adolfo railed against undocumented workers in San Jose last night, claiming their presence has ruined California's economy, Lucia slammed the Kentucky women with her violent spikes. Woe to anyone who opposes the powerful Ramirez clan.*

I squinted. *Violent spikes... WTF?* Of course her hits were violent—smashing the ball through the defense was the entire purpose of a hit. And the comparison the reporter drew between Adolf and Lucia sounded really far-fetched to me.

Jessica nudged me. "She's a jerk like her dad, right?"

I paused as I looked at my sister.

"Dane?"

"Her dad's definitely a jerk. And she follows the same right-wing party line as him, near as I can tell. But...she's not an ogre—not at all. She's actually kind of sweet."

"*Sweet?*" Jessica grabbed the photo and studied it again. "No way. She looks like an über-bitch."

"*Don't* call her that."

Jessica looked at me more closely. *Uh-oh.* I'd seen that conniving grin on her face before.

"Do you...*like* her, Danish?" Her eyes filled with menace as she drew out the sentence.

Do I like her? No. No way. Right? Then why did I feel a jab to the gut from seeing her pictured so unfairly? Why did I need to defend her to my sister? A self-aware psych major should have more of a friggin' clue about his feelings, but until I figured them out, I wasn't about to share them with my family. I pegged Jessica with an unwavering glare. "Not that it's any of your business, but *no.* She's Adolf's spawn! No way I could like her."

"You sound kind of defensive, there, brother."

"And you sound totally judgmental. Don't believe everything you see in the news—things aren't always as they seem. This photo is completely unfair to Lucia. She's actually really pretty."

"You *do* like her."

"No, I don't!"

"Yes, you do."

"No, I...*arghhh!*" I swallowed. "You're infuriating. I'm not into Lucia, okay?" *I'm not into Lucia,* I repeated silently. If I said it enough times, maybe it would be true. "I just don't like it when people portray Highbanks athletes in a negative light."

She maintained eye contact for a few moments before she pointed at the paper. "It's not like the Ramirez family will care about this. Hell, they probably *like* being called aggressive. That Lucia girl will be happy she's in the national news, I bet."

Lucia will not *be happy*. An image of the greenhouse TV room flashed in my mind, when Agent Allison and I had watched coverage of the shitstorm surrounding Lucia living in the same house as me.

"Lucia gets panicked around the media," Allison had said. *"They've said some mean things about her."*

My gut twisted as I imagined how Lucia would react to *this* photo, which was about as mean as it could get. *No one deserves that.* "Where's Mom?" I blurted.

Jessica shrugged. "She wasn't in her room when I got back."

"Where are my agents?"

"*Your* agents?" Jessica laughed as she tilted her head toward the adjoining suite. "Wonder Woman and Meathead are in there, eating." She held up the last bite of egg sandwich and popped it in her mouth. "They tchold me to get you upph for shome breakfash."

"Don't talk with your mouth full." I cringed as I climbed out of bed. "And beat it—I want some privacy."

That same wicked look returned to her eyes. "You want me to beat it so you can *beat it?*"

I leaned out the doorway of the bathroom to retort, "You're disgusting. Go hang out with *Johnnie*, you little ho-bag."

"Great idea!"

She bounded out of the bedroom, taking her eau de chlorine scent with her, and I unplugged my phone from the charger near the bathroom sink. My stomach growled, but suddenly I had something to do before breakfast. I found Allison's number in my contacts and dialed her.

"Is everything okay?" was her greeting.

"Yeah, I'm fine." I realized I had no idea how to phrase my question. Maybe this was a dumb idea to call. "Uh, how are you?"

She paused. "I'm...great. You're still in Wisconsin?"

"Yeah. We have a day off practice, so I'm coming back tonight."

"Right."

Another awkward pause. *Pony up, Monroe.* "Did, um, did Lucia see *USA Today* by any chance?"

"Oh, God—you saw it too?"

"Yeah. It was...awful."

"I have the paper right here, but she hasn't emerged from her room yet this morning. Frank and I are debating showing it to her." Allison fell silent for a moment. "What do *you* think we should do?"

I chewed my lower lip.

"I mean," she continued, "if an unflattering photo of you hit the national news like this, would you want to know?"

Would I want to know? I wasn't sure. What I *did* know was that I'd bludgeon the photographer with his damn camera if anyone ever printed something like that of me. Considering how rumors spread like poisonous gas through a locker room, I clenched my teeth. "She's going to find out eventually."

Allison sighed. "I think you're right. We leave in about five minutes for practice, and she's gonna want to know how the media covered the game."

I heard a voice in the background that sounded like Lucia's.

When Allison whispered, "*Shit*," I knew it was Lucia next to her. "This paper?" Allison's voice rose. "Aren't you going to eat some breakfast before practice?"

Lucia said something in response that I couldn't hear. Apparently Allison hadn't distracted her with the breakfast question because I heard some background noise followed by Allison asking, "Didn't you read about the game online?"

"I just got up," Lucia said. She must have stepped closer to Allison, and I could hear the sleepiness in her voice. "I was too jacked up from the game to fall asleep. C'mon, let me see the paper."

In the ensuing silence, I guessed that Allison had relinquished the newspaper. I bet she held her breath just like I did. Then Lucia's wail obliterated that silence.

"*¡Ay, Dios mío!* No, no...*nooo*. I'm a *ballena*."

You're not *a whale!* I wanted to yell.

"Lucia, it's okay," Allison said. "Calm down."

"What's happening?" I demanded. *What are you doing?* I asked myself.

Allison paused a moment. "She's shaking, and she's breathing really fast. She's holding onto the wall like she might pass out."

"Ask her if her heart's racing."

Allison relayed my question, and I heard Lucia gasp, "Yes."

"Ask her if she feels like she's about to throw up."

"Yes," Lucia responded to Allison, then asked her, "Who…are you…talking to?"

Allison said, "Dane."

"Oh, God," Lucia moaned. "He…*saw* the photo? *Noooo.*"

When it sounded like she started crying, I clenched my fists. I wished I was there with her—I wished I could tell her to hang in there. I knew as well as anyone that freshman year could suck, but things did get better. This just wasn't fair.

Allison whispered to me, "She's on the floor now," and to Lucia, "You don't look so good. Maybe I should take you to the ER."

"Let me talk to her, Allison." *I have to try to help her.*

"I…I don't think that would be wise," she whispered.

"Give her the phone!"

There was a rustling, then all I could hear were sharp gasps for air. I tried to remember what my mother used to say over the phone to a psychotherapy client in crisis. "Breathe, Lucia. Let your breaths go deep in your belly. Allow your muscles to relax, let your fists unclench. Float through this—nothing worse will happen. That's right, c'mon Lucy, breathe…"

A whimper leaked out between her panting breaths. "I'm dizzy. Something's…wrong with…me."

"Nothing is wrong with you. You're just having a panic attack."

"How do…you know?"

"Because I've overheard my mom on crisis calls. You feel like you're going to die, right?"

"*Sí.*"

"Well, you're not. Nobody's ever died from a panic attack. It's just your sympathetic nervous system kicking into overdrive." *That fucking photographer…he made an innocent girl think she was dying!* "C'mon, let's count to three when you breathe in, and three when you breathe out. Just like your approach to hit the ball. One, two, three…"

I heard a staccato gasp of breath—she sounded close to hyperventilating. "Count with me, Lucy. I know you want to brace against it, but it's just a feeling. It's just anxiety…float through it, and it will go away. *Cálmate*. Exhale completely. Let your shoulders fall as you breathe out."

I felt myself grow calmer as I practiced the breathing with her, and miraculously, her breaths slowed and smoothed out too. As I listened to her breathing, gradually matching mine, a strange sort of intimacy reverberated between us. It was like I wanted to hold her in my arms. *Tranquilo. That's right, keep breathing, Luz.* I felt puzzled, listening to my silent urges for her to calm down. Where had Luz come from? And what would she think if I said it out loud?

"I, I feel better," she said. She exhaled. "*Gracias*."

My chest flooded with warmth as I heard her quiet thanks. I'd barely known what to say to her, but it had seemed to help. "I'm glad."

"I have to get to practice."

When a sob escaped her mouth, my throat tightened. "What's wrong?"

"They'll see the photo." Her voice trembled. "Coach will make fun of me."

Fucker. "He better not." I drummed my fingers on my thigh and slid my tongue over my lower lip. "Listen, I bet your teammates will love the photo."

"*What?*"

"You're their new weapon. Can you imagine what Bridgetown will think when they see that photo? You look like a freaking badass. They'll be scared shitless to block you!"

Her sudden giggle caught me by surprise. It was a lilting, girlish sound, and I couldn't help but laugh as well.

"So this photo will scare the other teams?"

"Dude, *I'm* scared of you in this photo. Bridgetown will be *terrified*."

When her giggles multiplied, my grin stretched wider. She had such an infectious laugh.

"Maybe we can get that guy to photograph my jump serve," she said. "Then my *serve* will intimidate the hell out of them, too."

"Excellent idea." *I can't believe I'm smiling like an idiot. Is this awesome feeling because I helped her?*

"Ahhh…" The humor seemed to fade from her voice. "Allison's telling me it's time to go. See you tonight?"

Wow. It almost sounded like she wanted to see me. And it seemed I kind of wanted to see her too. "Sure. Don't take out too many of your teammates with your 'violent spikes' before then."

I could hear the smile in her voice. "They better watch out for my vicious violence. I'm gonna get my stuff—here's Allison."

"That was the worst I've seen her, but you really got her through that panic attack," Allison said when she was back on the phone. "What'd you say to her?"

"I just tried to channel Dr. Lois Monroe." I shrugged.

"You did great. Thank you, Dane—you averted a crisis there. We owe you one." She cleared her throat. "Is China around?"

My stomach grumbled as I looked toward the door. "She's in the other room, want me to get her?"

"Um, no...I'll catch up with her later. Lucia's ready—we have to go."

Once I hung up, I scrounged through my duffle bag for some clothes, wincing at the bruise near my ribs when I bent over.

"Hey, China," I said as I entered the attached suite a few minutes later. "When are we headed back?"

11

Lucia

When I entered the locker room, I could have sworn that sixteen pairs of eyes landed directly on me. I eased off my headphones, and the ensuing silence was louder than Neil Diamond's "Forever in Blue Jeans" had been. *Forever in Spandex, more like it.*

"Hey, guys."

Silence. I headed to the adjoining laundry room to pick up my mesh bag full of clean practice clothes. When I plopped it on the bench below my locker, Maddie sidled up to me.

"So, Rez, uh, how ya doin' this morning?"

"Great."

Maddie tilted her head as she peered at me.

"That was an awesome game, everyone," I told the room. "Well done."

Defensive specialist Lynnette pumped her fist in the air. "Hells, yeah!" She grinned at me as she headed toward the door. "Gotta get treatment."

I nodded. Lynnette was rehabilitating an ankle sprain she'd sustained the second day of practice. The athletic trainer, Tina, was a no-nonsense woman who kind of scared me—I hoped I'd never get injured.

"Speaking of the game," Maddie said. She leaned in and lowered her voice. "Did you check out your stats?"

I chuckled. "Relax, everyone. I saw the scary spike-beast photo."

A collective exhale flowed through the locker room.

To my left, Nina's eyes widened. "How are you so cavalier about it?"

"Imagine how Bridgetown will feel once they see that photo." I shrugged as I pulled on Spandex shorts. "It will *totally* psyche them out."

Maddie started laughing, and Kaitlyn joined in, adding her distinctive, ear-splitting cackle.

"What a great reframe," Maddie said, still laughing. "You're right—*I'd* be freaked out if I had to block you, Ms. Spike Beast, so I can only imagine how our rivals will take it. You're so mentally tough, Rez."

My grin vanished. Dad was big on personal responsibility, and it wasn't fair for me to assume undue credit. "Well, Dane pointed that out, actually."

Nina glared at me. "He did?"

"Yeah." My heart thumped faster with her evil eye on me, and I stalled my undressing because I didn't want to change into my sports bra next to her thin self. "He, uh, he called me before practice. I was a basket case, but he helped calm me down. He got me to laugh about it."

Slam! Nina spun around and stormed out of the locker room, leaving behind only the echo of her locker door.

I tensed. *What was* that *about?* I looked at Maddie, who frowned.

"She's got a bit of a temper," she said.

"What *happened* between her and Dane last year?"

Maddie's eyes flitted around the room, and I realized all my teammates were staring at us. She shook her head. "Nina asked me not to tell anyone about it. And one thing I've learned—never cross your setter." She turned toward the gym and said over her shoulder, "Ten minutes, guys."

I stared into my locker, trying to make sense of what had just transpired. Why had Nina cared what Dane said? Did she have a crush on him? Then why did she seem to hate him? I heard a few more of my teammates leave the locker room as I slid my practice shirt over my head.

"Lucia?"

Fellow freshman Brianna stood next to me. I was pretty sure it was the first word she'd spoken to anyone on the team, so I smiled to encourage her to continue.

"Um, I think that photo was really...mean. It was so unfair. You don't look like that at all." She blinked at me and appeared to wait for me to say something.

"Aw, thank you, Brianna."

She smiled, seeming bolstered by my response. "You're so pretty."

What?

"And you're such a good hitter. I hope I can be as good as you one day."

"Whoa. I...I don't know what to say, Bree." My mind raced. How could she think that? "I'm *not* pretty—I need to lose weight. And Maddie's a way better hitter than me."

Her face fell, and my stomach clenched with guilt for refusing to accept her compliment. "But you're a great hitter yourself," I added.

Her eyes turned down. "Coach doesn't think so. He told me..." She paused and took a deep breath. "He said it's unlikely I'll ever be a starter for this team."

"He told me the same thing."

Brianna's eyebrows knitted together. "But you started last night."

"Exactly my point. Don't let him get you down. Maddie told me Coach can be cruel, but he's also a great motivator."

"Hmm." She seemed to take that in. "But how is telling me I *suck* supposed to motivate me?"

"Yeah, that makes zero sense. You're right." We both smiled. Maybe I would ask Dane to explain Coach's crazy methods later. "Hold on—I'm almost ready." I pulled kneepads over my socks, laced up my ankle-support braces, and tied my gym shoes. "We don't want to be late."

We jogged out to the court, where the absence of the men's team seemed strange. I felt jealous of them for having a day off. Maybe we'd get a day off next year if we were lucky.

When I noticed the TV set up near the bleachers, I cringed. *More video work.* We'd spent hours watching previous Kentucky games before our first match, and I now it looked like the post-mortem on last night's game would delay our physical practice today as well. Though I was a little tired from this morning's emotional freakazoid, I'd been anticipating hitting drills. My hand twitched with the desire to karate-chop endless spikes, each time imagining that paparazzo's face on the ball.

Four hours later, I was sorry for what I'd wished. Coach had made Nina and me stay at practice after everyone else left, and my left arm was about to fall off from the hundreds of hits. My legs shook, my vision blurred, and I hadn't ever sweated as much in my life.

Nina had been frosty to me all practice, but at this point I doubted she had any energy left to keep up the mean act. She was simply in survival mode, like me. We kept practicing the four set, which we'd botched the night before. Coach had rewound that embarrassing play so many times during video review that he'd etched it into my brain.

"Again!" Coach said as he nodded at Kara. *I hate that word.* Kara tossed the ball to Nina, who set it to me on the left side of the net. But the ball sailed too far to my left, and I had to scramble to lob it over the net. Brian had no trouble fielding the ball on the other side of the net, and he tossed it into the rolling cart.

As I returned to the ten-foot line, panting for air, Coach glared at Nina. "Do you think this half-assed effort will be enough for my starting setter?"

"I'm sorry." Her voice sounded as weak as my legs felt.

I glanced at Frank, who sat in the bleachers with a sour expression on his weathered face. He probably wanted to get out of here even more than I did.

"You're *sorry?* That's not going to cut it, Nina."

Her normally perfect blond hair now hung in sweaty wisps around her face after working itself partially out of her ponytail. There was a wild look in her eyes that alarmed me. "I'm doing my *best!"* she cried in a shaky voice.

"If that's your best, I need a new setter. Again."

Kara paused as she looked at Coach for a moment, but then, like a good assistant, she tossed another ball in the air. Nina hustled to get under it, and she set it to me in a perfect arch. I executed my approach and jumped on tired legs, only to have the ball trickle down to my feet. *Oops.* My vertical leap was so low that the ball hadn't cleared the net.

"Jesus!" Coach pointed at Nina. "*This* one finally does her job..." His accusing finger then jabbed in my direction. "And *that* one muffs it up!" He threw his hands in the air. "You two aren't connecting at all today. What's your problem?"

I glanced at Nina, who looked away from me. *Nina hates me, and I don't know why*, I wanted to say. Instead I said, "It's because I'm a lefty. It took months for my club setter to get the feel for setting my left hand."

I snuck another look at Nina, and this time she looked back. The ice in her blue eyes seemed to melt a bit.

"We don't *have* months!" Coach hollered, recapturing my attention. "In case neither of you has noticed, our season has started. Every match counts for our national ranking. You need to get it right, *now*. Again." He nodded at Kara, who held another torture-ball in her grasp. "We'll keep going until you two execute ten solid hits. In a row."

I closed my eyes. *Por favor, ayúdame. Help me, God.*

Nina and I stumbled into the locker room sometime later after finally giving Coach what he wanted. Lacking the energy to care about lingering fungi, I sank to the germy floor and sprawled out on my back, arms and legs akimbo. Nina did the same a second later.

I stared at the dirty popcorn ceiling and noticed some spider webs clinging to the corner. Our new arena couldn't come fast enough.

"I hate you and your left hand," Nina said.

I winced. "Sorry."

I don't know how long we both remained collapsed on the floor, too tired to move, before Nina sniffled. I sat up when I saw she was crying.

"I'm sorry Coach was so mean to you," I offered.

She rolled her head away from me and wiped her nose with the back of her hand. "That's not...why I'm crying."

"It's not?"

She sniffed again, and I somehow managed to get to my feet. I shuffled on tired legs into the bathroom area, unrolled some toilet paper, and returned to my teammate.

"Thanks." She grabbed the tissue and sat up. As I shakily lowered myself back to the floor, sitting with my back against a locker, I tried not to watch her wipe the mascara mess from under her eyes or blow her button nose. She took her time with the tissues, then stared at me. "Did you hear what happened between me and Dane last year?"

Here we go. My stomach tightened, but I tried to play it cool. "No. Well, I know you don't like him, but I don't know why."

"But *you* like him," she said.

I was so used to denying my feelings for Great Dane that my headshake was automatic.

"Yes, you do. I've seen how you look at him."

My heart skipped a beat, and I stared at my lap. "It doesn't really matter how I feel about him. Dane hates Republicans—and probably me too."

She scoffed through her tears. "He likes a challenge."

Was that all I was to him? A *challenge?*

"Maybe he isn't into you—maybe you're not his type," Nina said.

Tell me something I don't know. Even sweaty and disheveled, she still looked beautiful. I bet *she* was his type.

"But still, you should know what kind of guy he is, if you have to live with him."

She was making me uneasy. "What happened last year?"

Nina glued her glassy gaze to the opposite wall. A minute ticked by. "I started dating Dane in November last year. I'd just broken up with Shep..." She glanced at me. "He was a football player. He graduated this summer." Her eyes found the wall again. "And Dane was a hot-shot freshman. We're both setters, so it made sense."

And they were both freakishly tall, blond, and blue-eyed. *Masters of the Aryan Universe.* They had undoubtedly made a beautiful couple. When I looked at Nina's profile, I noticed more tears cascading down her face, which unnerved me. I braced myself for what came next.

"Then I got pregnant."

I froze. *Pregnant?* As a scholarship athlete? How the hell would I deal with that? My parents would be horrified. I'd have to drop out of school, live at home, hide out from the media..."What'd you do?"

She smiled through her tears, then angrily wiped the heel of her hand under her eye. "I did the only thing I could do."

I stopped breathing.

Oh, no. My heart ached. That miraculous itty-bitty baby growing inside of her, counting on her for survival...so helpless, so innocent...

And then she'd snuffed out that life. What would Dad say? What would *God* say?

"This is where Ms. Republican gets all judgmental on me, right?" At first her stare was hard, but then her eyes pooled with tears. She drew a hand to her mouth as her body racked with sobs. Her whimpers and gasps filled the empty locker room.

My nose burned and my eyes misted over as I watched her misery. I felt awful for what she'd believed she had to do. I had a sudden realization: *my* judgment wasn't what she feared. But *her* self-judgment was another matter.

Slowly, I crawled toward her. Red splotches marred her lightly tanned complexion, and a bead of snot leaked out her nose. She swiped her face with the balled up tissue she held in one hand. When I clasped her other hand, she looked up at me, her chest heaving.

"Who am I to judge you, Nina?" I stroked her hand. "God doesn't want us to judge or condemn."

She started crying harder, which confused me. I'd been trying to soothe her.

"I...thought you'd...hate me."

I felt myself frown. "Then why'd you tell me?"

"I...don't know."

She seemed to regret what she'd done. Maybe she felt like she deserved my hate.

"I probably shouldn't have told you...but I'm too tired to think straight right now. Maddie told me...you were asking what happened with Dane...I figured you'd find out eventually. And maybe I thought you should know what Dane did before you got in too deep with him."

My heart fluttered. "What was his part in this?" I inhaled. Had he *demanded* that she get an abortion?

"He certainly had a part in me getting pregnant," she muttered.

Duh. "I mean, did he want you to get an abortion?"

"Of course he did." Her smile seemed bitter. "How were we supposed to raise a baby with both of us being in college, playing volleyball—with his mother running for *president?*"

What a nightmare. What would I have done in that situation? I wouldn't have elected to kill my baby—*right?* I swallowed. "What happened to you and Dane...after?"

She shook her head and sniffed. "He didn't want to be with me anymore." A tear rolled down her cheek. "I was damaged goods."

I gasped. *¡Cabrón!* How could he have done that? Didn't he have *any* morals? "I'm so sorry. I, I can't believe he did that. I'll try not to talk about him around you anymore."

"Thanks."

"Does...does the whole team know about this?"

"Amy—she was a senior last year—she was the one who took me to Planned Parenthood. And Maddie made up some story to Coach about why I missed practice for a while." She picked at the shards of torn tissue in her lap. "I don't know who Dane told, but I bet Josh knows. And his coach, Phil, looks at me different since this happened." Her head shot up. "Neither of us is supposed to talk about it, and I'm sure it was stupid of me to tell you. Please don't say anything."

I paused. How on earth would I handle this bombshell without talking to someone about it? With a jolt, I also realized how this tidbit about Dane impregnating a girl then dumping her could help my Dad's campaign. But Nina's pleading eyes implored me to keep her secret, and I finally nodded. "I won't. I promise."

When she gave me a weak smile, I suddenly became aware of my exhaustion again. And hunger. I sighed and gathered my sore-ass body off the floor, feeling lightheaded as I stood. "C'mon." I reached out and helped pull Nina to her feet. "Let's hit the showers. I bet Secret Service is wondering where I am."

As predicted, Frank's bushy eyebrows lifted to the ceiling when I finally emerged from the locker room. "I was about to send a squad in there to see if you'd collapsed."

"Sorry," I said. "I'm surprised I didn't collapse after *that* practice."

"No joke." He fell into step beside me. "It was hard to watch Coach yell at you like that. I had to sit on my hands so I wouldn't grab my gun and shoot the man, just to get him to shut up."

I grinned. Maybe having Secret Service in my life wasn't so bad.

"But I could kind of see his point," Frank said. "You and Nina weren't clicking at all. Is everything okay between you two?"

"It is now."

He gave me a questioning look.

I sighed. "She told me something that happened between her and Dane last year. She needed to get it off her chest." *Something that rocked my world.* When he'd hooked up with Nina, not only had Dane proved he would never be attracted to someone like me—someone who looked nothing like supermodel Nina—he'd also taken zero responsibility for his actions. And, he seemed to be a creepy womanizer to boot.

"Ah" was all Frank said, but it seemed like he wanted to say more.

I studied him as he slid on his sunglasses. He patted my arm in a fatherly way.

We exited the gym, and I let out a long breath, thankful for the lack of media swarming our SUV. I never wanted to see another photographer again. Frank scanned the parking lot and held open the rear door, then climbed in after me.

Allison drove away. "How 'bout some lunch?"

"So they can take more fat photos of me?"

In the rearview mirror, I watched her forehead crease. "I thought Dane helped you feel better about that stupid photo."

I glanced out the window. It was starting to rain, which made me want to cry. "He only makes things worse."

12

Dane

Our afternoon flight was sunny and smooth until we neared the Highbanks Regional Airport. That's where things got interesting. Rain pelted the plane's small windows, and winds buffeted my mother's private jet.

"I thought they said the weather would clear by the time we arrived." China frowned.

Brad blew out a breath. "One thing I learned on military ops: Mother Nature's a finicky bitch."

I tried to maintain my tough act, but all I could picture was the CNN headline: *Presidential Candidate's Son Dies in Small-Plane Crash.* I felt the tightening of a Lucia-sized panic attack in my chest. My consternation must have leaked onto my face because Brad said, "Relax, girlie. Your mother has good pilots—they'll divert to another airport if they need to."

"I'm cool." *Liar.*

China peered over the top of her bodybuilding magazine and smirked.

We bumped and dipped along. At one point it felt like a rollercoaster—but not one I ever wanted to ride again—and finally we skidded along the runway and rolled to a stop. I hustled to unclick my seatbelt before rising to open the side door.

"Uh-uh, Mr. Monroe." China held out her arm. "You know an agent has to deplane first."

I sat back down with a huff. Terra firma beckoned outside. The high-pitched whirring of the jet engines gradually declined as Brad unlatched the door and let the hydraulics push it outward, unfolding narrow steps down to the tarmac. He scanned the area before descending. Once China nodded at me, I got up to follow, and she exited the plane right after me.

The rain had lightened to a drizzle by this point, and an airport tech wheeled a cart of luggage around the wing. Despite my protests that I could carry my own damn bag, Brad grabbed my duffle and led me inside the small building. I made a beeline for the popcorn machine, dumped a fluffy scoop into a white paper bag, then chilled on the leather sofa while I waited for China to bring the car around. Free popcorn was the best part of these small airports.

The only person in the building was a ponytailed woman behind the counter. "How was your flight, Mr. Monroe?"

"Peachy." I crunched on more popcorn, then turned to Brad. "What's taking China so long?"

He frowned. "Why are you in such a rush? Classes don't start till Monday."

I slowed my chewing. Why *was* I eager to get home?

When I didn't answer, Brad crossed over to the popcorn machine and helped himself to an overflowing bag. He plopped down next to me, and all we needed was a big screen to complete the movie-theater ambience. "Settle in—China's gonna be a while. She has to scan the SUV for explosives."

Half-chewed kernels froze limply in my mouth. "Why's that?"

"Your mom got some more threats this morning." He shrugged. "We're beefing up security for now."

"*More* threats?"

"You know those pantywaist jihadists. They're not too impressed with a woman who wants to be president."

My heart thudded, and I wasn't sure which was stronger: my fear for Mom's safety or my anger toward the sexist pigs trying to thwart her rightful place as president. "What kind of threats?"

"Eh, same old crap. 'We'll cut your head off and mount it on a stick, infidel.' You know, terrorist bullshit."

My face felt hot. "You think you could've told me about this earlier?"

"We typically don't share threats with protectees. And now I see why."

"Great policy, Marine." Not feeling hungry anymore, I set aside my popcorn and took out my phone. I wasn't in the mood for games, so I opened my browser. On the university's website, I pulled up the syllabus for my social science statistics class, and I checked out the required readings. "You guys have to take me to the bookstore later—gotta buy textbooks by tomorrow."

Brad grinned. "Already taken care of, Danester."

"Yeah?"

"We got an agent to buy your books yesterday. And we've already mapped out the route to your classes. You just need to show up."

"Will you do my homework for me too?"

He laughed.

"No, I'm serious. My stats and research methods classes are supposed to be *tough*. They're weed-outs for psych majors."

"Then you'll have no problem, Mr. Four-Point-Oh."

My stomach tensed as I felt that old pressure to maintain my straight-A average. I wished I could allow myself a B and get it over with. But Grandpa Monroe and Mom had both excelled at Yale, and they expected a strong effort from me no matter how many classes I missed travelling for volleyball—or campaign events.

I had to admit that a pass on the suffocating crowd at the bookstore *did* make the start of the semester slightly more palatable. And I also didn't mind the agents driving me to class. I could direct my energy toward practice instead of wasting it by walking around the sprawling campus.

"Dude, where were you guys last year when I was a clueless freshman? I totally got lost trying to find my classes the first day."

"At least Lucia won't have to go through that," he answered.

A smile threatened to show itself when he mentioned her name, and I found myself agreeing with him, feeling compassion for her once again. *What is my deal?*

An hour later, we pulled up to the greenhouse. *Ugh, must be a slow news day.* Eight or so reporters and cameramen lingered by the gate, and China slowed the vehicle. "I'll let them ask a few questions out here," she said.

Next to me in the back seat, Brad shook his head. "Boss doesn't want any interaction out in the open today."

"That's why I'll take a question or two here and won't let them follow us in."

Brad's attention was already focused on the throng of media outside the tinted SUV windows, and his hand rested on his weapon inside his jacket. "Make it quick."

China rolled down her window a smidge. "Mr. Monroe will take a question or two out here, but nobody inside the compound."

I waited a beat until a reporter asked, "Dane, do you support the student loan forgiveness program Senator Monroe unveiled last night?"

That was a no-brainer. I darted to unroll the back window, but Brad reached over to block me, shaking his head.

"But they won't see me!"

"That's the idea, kid," he whispered back.

I frowned. This was the tightest security I'd experienced, and the hairs on the back of my neck prickled. "Of course I support my mother's program," I shouted to the interior of the car, feeling like a dork. "Education should be our highest priority, and we need to make it easier for people to complete college degrees."

China smiled at me in the rearview mirror.

"But what do you think about Governor Ramirez's rebuttal?" another reporter asked.

Shit. I hadn't heard how Adolf had replied. I'd been too worried about Lucia's response to that horrid photo to read the news this morning.

"I didn't hear the governor's take on the program," China said, rescuing me. "Would you enlighten me?"

The reporter looked down at her phone and tapped it a few times, probably accessing her notes. "Governor Ramirez said the US government is already twenty trillion in debt, and therefore can't afford to bail out student loans."

Naturally Adolf had said that—he was from the party of *no.* I cleared my throat. "I think it's important to make fiscally sound decisions, and supporting education is one of them."

"Dane, how do you feel about living with the governor's daughter?"

I smiled as I looked through the gate to the house. *Not as bad as you'd think.*

"That's all for today, guys," China said as she rolled up the window and inched the car forward. She must have intimidated the reporters as much as me because they did as she asked and stayed outside the gates.

"Why didn't you let me answer that question?"

Her eyes met mine in the rearview mirror. "I thought I'd save your ass from saying something mean about Lucia. It might hurt your mom's campaign."

I nodded. "Right...of course." *Everything for Mom's precious campaign. And thanks for assuming I'd say something mean.*

After I tossed my duffle bag on my bed, I noticed Lucia wasn't in her room. Had her afternoon practice run late? I strolled into the TV room and stopped short. Fucking Fox News was on, and the headline's ticker tape ticked me off:

Twenty Trillion in Debt and the Liberals Keep On Spending

The Republicans *had a lot to do with building that debt,* I wanted to shout at the blond bimbo anchorwoman. *Gulf wars, anyone?*

Then I looked at Lucia curled up, sleeping on the sofa, and my anger dissipated. Her head rested on the oversized pillow by the armrest. She'd loosened her thick hair from its omnipresent braid, and shiny black strands fanned over her shoulder, partially obscuring her face. Her long legs, covered in black yoga pants, were tucked up to her body, leaving much of the long sofa free. For me.

But how could she sleep with the screechy Barbie in her ear? I reached over and scooped the remote off the ottoman to decrease the volume. *Much better.*

"Don't change the channel," Frank said in a low voice as he entered the room. "I'm watching that."

I frowned as he placed his beer on the end table and settled onto the very sofa cushion I'd coveted. I pointed at Lucia. "I was just lowering the volume."

"Heh." He took a long pull from the bottle. "She's been crashed for a while now." He looked me up and down. "A stampede of donkeys couldn't wake her."

I ignored that jab. "Why is she so tired?"

"That coach of hers kept her hitting for an extra hour today. Poor thing could hardly walk after."

"What an ass."

His eyebrows drew together as he stared at me, surprised.

"Well, he *is* an ass."

Frank nodded. "You got no argument from me. Why she came here to play for that man, I'll never understand— "

A long, luscious moan drifted from Lucia's mouth, interrupting him. I noticed her arm twitch and a slight smile play on her lips. Just watching her made me smile, too. What the hell was she dreaming about?

I glanced up to find Frank glaring at me.

"What?"

He looked down at his beer bottle, then mumbled, "Thought you hated Fox News."

Lucia shifted, and the leather crunched as she rolled onto her back. I could see her peaceful face in entirety now, her dark eyelashes casting shadows on her olive skin. A feeling of tenderness warmed my chest. "I do hate Fox News." *But I don't hate* this *fox*, I silently added, then almost snorted at my brain's cheese factor.

She exhaled a long breath, and with it the hint of a soft moan. My tender feelings vanished, replaced by a jolt of excitement in my groin. *Let me jump into your dream, Luz.*

"Then why are you still here?" Frank demanded.

"You want to keep your voice down?" I gestured to Lucia and jumped when I noticed she looked right back at me. "You see? You woke her up."

As a blush bloomed on her cheeks, she smiled at me. "You're back from Milwaukee." She lifted her arms over her head and stretched, and I tried not to gawk at the soft curve of her breasts as her shirt tightened across her chest. *Tried* being the operative word. When her long-ass legs extended down the sofa and the tips of her pointed toes brushed Frank's thigh, she sat up a little, appearing surprised. "Hey, Frank."

"Hi, Lucia. How ya feelin' after those practices?"

Then she scrambled to sitting, and her entire demeanor changed. Her lips parted and her eyes narrowed as she looked up at me, and she scooted away toward Frank's end of the sofa. Her chest seemed to heave with quick breaths.

I tensed. Was she *scared* of me? Why the hell would she be scared of me? "What's wrong?"

"Nothing." Her voice sounded strangled. She crossed her arms and wouldn't look at me. She simply stared at the TV.

What the hell just happened? "F-Frank told me Holter kept you long today." My heart galloped as I searched for some way to connect with her. "Did he make you practice the same play over and over?"

She acted like she hadn't heard me.

"So…classes start tomorrow. You're so lucky the agents will drive you to your classes—you won't get lost like I did."

Nothing. Her coldness felt awful. Mute Girl had been sort of endearing, in her shy, girlish way, but Ice Girl froze me to the spot, cutting into my heart. She glanced at Frank, then back at the TV.

"Do you want to watch another channel?" he asked her.

She shook her head.

"Then would you like me to leave?"

"No." Lucia bolted to her feet. "*I'll* leave. I need to go study my playbook."

She gave me wide berth when she circled around to go to her bedroom.

"Hey." My stomach clenched. "I could help you—quiz you on different plays?"

She stopped with her back to me. Finally she'd acknowledged that I'd spoken, and I breathed out. But when she looked over her shoulder, her eyes dark and cold, my chest seized again. "I don't want any of your *help*."

I watched her walk away, and my mouth still hung open when I turned back to Frank.

He shrugged, then grabbed his beer and got up to leave.

"What's going *on* with her? Why is she mad at me?"

The muscle lining his jaw twitched. "What goes around, comes around, I guess."

"What does *that* mean?"

But he'd already left the room, leaving me alone in my dumbfounded state.

"*Dane, how do you feel about living with the governor's daughter?*" the reporter had asked me. I now knew how to answer: *Ass loads of confusion.*

Confounding Variables flashed on the screen as the header for my psychology professor's PowerPoint slide.

Sounds about right, I thought as I settled into the back row of the two-hundred-seat classroom for my research methods class. It had been two weeks since Lucia had spoken multi-syllable words to me, and at first I'd definitely been confounded. But I'd since determined that Nina must have told her about the abortion, which had likely disgusted Ms. Catholic Right-Winger. Hence the silent treatment, which didn't seem fair. She hadn't even talked to me about it, and it's not like that was a simple situation. And anyway hadn't Lucia been the one to insist it was okay to disagree when Alejandro and I almost came to blows? I sighed. My past with Bitchy Nina still haunted me.

Now that it was September, less than two months remained until the election. At least I wouldn't have to live with Lucia "Ice" Ramirez after that. The polls showed our parents tied. The volleyball standings showed the girls' team undefeated. And the update on my dick showed flaccid futility.

Brad nudged my elbow, and I glanced at him. His bulky upper body spilled over the small college desk. "*Pay attention*," he mouthed.

I scowled and snatched my phone out of my pocket to text him.

What are you, my father?

His wary eyes scanned the class as he typed a response without even looking at his phone. I had to admit his technique impressed me.

UR the one who said this class was tuff.

Shit. He was right. I had to start listening to the lecture.

"One confounding variable is the Hawthorne Effect," the professor said as she clicked to the next slide, "which refers to the tendency for participants to alter their behavior when they're part of an experiment."

I pulled up her presentation online and clicked to the current slide to type in some notes on my laptop.

"The Hawthorne Effect refers to a lighting experiment done at the Hawthorne electric company in the nineteen-hundreds. Researchers found that increasing the factory lighting improved productivity during the experiment. But after the experiment ended, productivity decreased, *despite* the lighting changes. How could this be?"

She looked expectantly at the class. Did she honestly think someone would speak up in this huge lecture hall? I knew the answer because my mom had told me about the study years ago, but no way I'd raise my hand. People already stared at me like I was a freak, given my armed companions. Last autumn my gargantuan height and student-athlete status had seemed to prevent students from approaching me in class, and this year the protective bubble around me had solidified.

When nobody answered, she went on to the next slide. "The factory workers likely improved their productivity not because of the lighting, but because the researchers were watching them. It feels good to be noticed, to be cared for."

Yeah, it does. And it feels craptastic to be ignored.

"Later research shows this effect was likely overstated—other variables may have been at play. Still, this study warns us not to make spurious conclusions about cause and effect…"

As she droned on, I opened my browser and perused Facebook posts, ignoring Brad's disappointed scoff. My concentration was toast.

When class ended, Brad's thick arm shot out across my chest, blocking me from getting up. "Today we wait until everyone else has left."

I rolled my eyes. The agents constantly changed my routine as a security precaution, even making me skip class some days. The election couldn't come soon enough.

Finally, Brad and I stood. "This way." He pointed the opposite direction from where we typically exited.

"Where's China?"

"She's meeting us by the car."

Right outside the building's side exit sat not only my vehicle but another black SUV as well. "You're in that one," Brad said as he pointed to the unknown vehicle.

I paused mid-stride. "Why?"

"Dane, do as you're told for once, dammit."

I flashed back to China's lecture about following orders in public: *"You defy us, you die."* I sighed. "Fine."

As I climbed into the backseat of Vehicle #2, the changeup all made sense.

"Hey, buddy."

I gritted my teeth as I stared into blue eyes just like mine, only aged thirty years. "Hi, Dad."

Patrick DuPont extended his arms like he wanted to hug me, and I noticed the two agents in front watching, despite their efforts to pretend otherwise. I swallowed and accepted his hug. It seemed he'd shrunk since I'd last seen him, though he still topped six-four.

"We're rolling," said the agent in the driver seat.

I scooted an inch away from Dad as we stopped to let a teeming river of students pass by on the crosswalk. "Why are you here?"

"Good to see you too, son."

"I have practice soon." Mom always told me guilt-trips take a sender and a receiver, and I refused to let him play off his absence in my life as *my* fault.

"I know. They're just taking us somewhere private to talk."

"So you're not staying?"

"Do you want me to?" When I didn't answer, he ran his hand through his silver hair. His tanned face sported a few more wrinkles, but he looked every bit the debonair artist he'd been when he met my mother years ago: tall, lean, and charming. She'd first fallen in love with his abstract paintings, and it hadn't been long before she'd fallen for *him*. At least that's what the documentaries said, propping up their marriage as a story of devoted love between two passionate, creative souls. *What a farce.*

We arrived at a metro park with wooded paths. Although it was a beautiful day, the parking lot wasn't very full in the early afternoon.

"How 'bout a walk?" When Dad smiled, his white teeth dazzled.

Do I have a choice? "Sure."

Phil had taken the team to this park last spring, the day after we'd played like shit in a conference game. He'd gathered us by the entrance to the main path—a hilly, three-mile loop. "Take a long, easy, run, guys," he'd told us. "Work that despicable play out of your system. Commune with nature." After two loops, he'd sat us down in the grass and had us meditate for thirty minutes. It had become one of my favorite places in town after that.

I hoped my dad taking me here wouldn't screw that up.

Brad and China walked about a hundred yards in front of us, and Dad's protection detail walked about the same distance behind. Sunlight filtered through the leaves, dappling the packed-dirt path, and birds chirped as they flitted overhead. The light breeze and tree cover kept the temperature comfortable. I inhaled the smell of leaves and felt a blessed letup of the irritability that had plagued me the past two weeks.

We'd walked a few minutes before I realized Dad hadn't spoken. "I see you're planning to take Mom's advice," I offered.

"What's that?" He shook his head, seeming to shake off distraction.

"Talking while walking. It's better for guys to do something active while discussing something important. They're less likely to get emotionally flooded."

He stopped and stared at me. "When did you get so smart?"

When I grew up without you. "I'm just citing John Gottman's research. Mom used to take me for a walk when she had to drop some bad news on me."

He grimaced, then resumed walking. "You're right. I do have something important to tell you...some bad news." The light feeling I'd experienced vanished. "And this does have to do with your mother. She told me you've been asking about me."

Some more minutes elapsed in silence, and I braced myself for him to get it over with already.

"How much do you know about my painting career?" he asked.

Random. "Um...you won some award when you were twenty-two."

He chuckled bitterly. "Yes, the famous award." He looked at his Italian leather shoes. "Then it all went downhill."

"I thought you were a well-known artist when Mom met you."

"Well-known for my earlier work. I'd hit a dry spell when I met her." He kicked a rock, which seemed uncharacteristic for a suave, mature man like himself. "I remember when I met her at that gallery the night of my show—she was so smart, so classy..." His soft smile faded. "I was embarrassed that the place was just about empty. I'd become a has-been painter. Then she told me she'd convince her father to be my benefactor. 'Talent like this needs to be nurtured,' she said."

Whoa. I'd never heard about Grandfather bankrolling Dad's painting.

"But I lost my touch. The more money Mr. Monroe gave me, the uglier my paintings became. God, I created some monstrosities back then. I was frozen." He grunted. "Just like that old man."

I felt my eyebrows arch. I'd never heard anyone brave enough to disparage my grandfather. Had Dad always disliked the far-reaching influence of the Monroe family? He'd claimed he was fine with Mom keeping her surname after they married, then passing it along to Jessica and me, but for the first time I wondered if that was true.

"Finally, after seeing how frustrated I was, Lois asked me if I wanted to quit painting and work for her father. There was an opening in one of his property management companies." He blew out a breath. "I never should've done it, Dane."

I tried to figure out how this meandering story related to the bad news he promised to deliver. "Why?"

"Because it fucking *emasculated* me!"

His shout carried over the treetops, and I looked ahead to see Brad and China turned toward us, appearing ready to draw their weapons.

Dad must have noticed their alarm because he held his arm out and yelled, "We're okay!" He turned to wave to the agents behind us, then swiveled around and smothered his face with his hands. "Christ, I'm a mess."

I'd never seen him like this. "Uh, let's keep walking, okay?" I moved forward and exhaled when he joined me.

"I can't live without my art." His voice was tight and controlled. "I can't live someone else's life, under someone else's rules. I can't play hired hand, living off *Daddy's* coattails, pretending I give two shits about corporate domination."

"So then quit." I shrugged.

He shook his head. "If only it were that simple." He walked a couple of steps, then grabbed my shoulders, turning me to face him. "Don't ever give up on your passion, Dane. You're such a gifted athlete. Keep pursuing your dreams, okay?"

After failing to attend *any* of my matches during the past three years, he had no right to spout this Hallmark greeting card bullshit at me. "What about supporting Jessica's dreams? Have you been to any of her swim meets since she started high school?"

His eyes flared. "I know I haven't been there for you two…I've been too disgusted by the whole charade." He shook his head. "Dane, don't be like me. Don't let your mother's ambition prevent you from pursuing your passion."

"This isn't about Mom! We're talking about *your* shitty parenting." I looked ahead and noticed Brad and China had stopped walking as well, waiting for us to finish our bitch-fest. *They must think my family's fucked-up beyond repair.*

"This *is* about Lois," Dad said. "She's making me tell you what's going on."

I scoffed, "You're a grown-ass man, Dad. She can't *make* you do anything."

"You're so naïve."

Swear to God, I want to punch him.

"Your mother's convinced that me telling you is the only way to prevent you from turning out like me."

"Not a *chance* that will happen."

"Yeah? She told me you got a girl pregnant."

I inhaled all the air in the park as my vision narrowed until all I could see was scarlet. How could Mom have done that to me? Apparently all the secrets she kept were only secret from *me*. I fought for air and squeezed the sides of my head, trying to keep my brain from bursting through my skull.

"Dane, you okay?" China shouted from somewhere in the distance.

I pried my eyes open and lowered my shaking hands as I nodded at her. Then I spun around to Dad, and the rage he must have seen in my eyes made him take a step back. "Don't you *dare* talk about that," I hissed. "I didn't even know—"

"I don't love your mother anymore." He delivered the news in monotone, like he was ordering room service.

"What?" I demanded.

"It's why I haven't been around. I didn't want to hurt you kids. But I'm in love with another woman—a woman who *truly* gets me, *truly* supports my art. I'm painting again, Dane. It's just flowing from me now!"

I froze speechless, my heart on overdrive.

"I haven't told Jessie yet, because your mother and I don't think she can keep it secret. Maybe when she's older. *You'll* keep it secret, of course. An affair getting out would destroy your mother's campaign."

He cupped my shoulder. "Whew." He looked up to the sky. "I'm sorry to drop that on you, but what a relief to get it off my chest."

The rush of blood in my ears whooshed to a deafening roar, then suddenly, there was silence. I swallowed and watched a squirrel scurry across the path.

When I saw Dad's hand resting on my shoulder, I knocked it away. I stepped up and got in his face. "*Fuck. YOU.* I will *never* become like you." I shoved his chest, and he sprawled to the ground on his butt. Then I pivoted and sprinted toward Brad and China.

"Get me out of here," I panted.

Without hesitation, my agents came up on each side of me, and we ran wordlessly back to the car.

13

Lucia

"Let's see that ankle," Tina said as she unwrapped the compression gauze from my right foot. The makeshift training room was dark like my mood. A little less than one month into my college volleyball career—and only one week into my college classes—I'd already sustained an injury. I'd rolled my ankle after coming down on a blocker's foot a few days ago and hadn't been cleared to practice since. Fortunately I had Secret Service to drive me to class, but I *had* to get back out there if I wanted a starting role on the team again in this lifetime.

I braced myself as the athletic trainer rotated and pressed on my ankle. But the shooting pains were gone—it was just a little sore.

"Looks better," Tina said, then blew out a breath. "From what I can see in this janitor's-closet lighting, anyway. They need to pick up the pace on building the new arena." She opened a cabinet drawer and took out a tube of gel.

"So I can play today?"

Tina frowned as she hooked up the ultrasound machine. "How did your ankle tolerate morning lift?"

Our six a.m. weightlifting session seemed like eons ago. "It was fine. I didn't do jumps or anything with impact." And that was because our bald strength coach had watched me like a bald eagle, claiming he didn't want Tina to yell at him for letting me do too much.

"Good."

I neglected to mention that I could barely lift one-fifteen on the bench press. For some reason my strength had been crap recently.

Tina squirted some cool gel and rubbed it over my skin. She took the metal ultrasound device—it looked like a showerhead to me—and smoothed it over my ankle in slow circles. "Tell me if this starts to feel too warm."

I leaned back, rested my elbows on the cushioned training table, and closed my eyes. *Don't fall asleep.* I'd already dozed off in one of my classes earlier. Allison typically woke me up when I drifted off in class, but this morning she'd let me sleep until the end of the lecture. When I'd snapped at her for not waking me up, she'd flinched. Then she'd told me I needed to take better care of myself.

I winced, remembering the hurt look on her face. She probably hated me now. Just like Mateo had stopped texting me after I'd yelled at him for not taking his blood sugar readings. Just like Coach had scowled when I'd stunk up the gym with my horrible hits the practice before I'd sustained my injury. Just like Dane had started going out of his way to avoid me. He hadn't even come home between class and practice today. Not that I could entirely blame him. It had been two weeks since I'd found out about Nina's abortion, and I knew I'd hurt him with my silence. But I had no idea what to say. How could he have done such a thing?

"So how's your nutrition going, Lucia?"

I opened my eyes to see Tina looking straight at me. My heartbeat kicked up a notch. Why was she asking me that? "Really good."

"It looks like you've lost some weight."

Score! I'd been worried about gaining fat without being able to practice. I certainly hadn't wanted to negate all my hard work due to a stupid injury. "Yeah, well, I'm following the nutritionist's advice."

"Really?" Tina cocked an eyebrow. Her dark blond ponytail swung as she shook her head. "Whitney said you no-showed your second appointment."

My throat tightened as I sat up. "Oh, no! I-I forgot about it, I swear. I'll call her to apologize. Am…am I in trouble with Coach?"

She kept rubbing circles on my ankle. "Your coach doesn't know you missed the appointment. Whitney only called me because she knew I was worried about you."

"You're worried about me?" I gulped.

"I'm concerned, Lucia. You need to reschedule your appointment." The gel began to feel as hot as my face did. "What have you eaten so far today?"

"I had a banana after our lift."

Her brown eyes blinked at me, like she was expecting more.

"…And, um…" *Think!* "…a sandwich for lunch."

"What kind of sandwich?" She clicked off the machine and reached for a towel.

My face now blazed. "Why the hell does that matter?"

Her head shot up from toweling the gel off my ankle, and I realized I'd just snapped at yet one more person who hadn't deserved it. I squeezed my hands together to hide their trembling, then swallowed. "Turkey. Turkey and cheese, on wheat bread. And, and I'm drinking lots of water."

"That's not enough." Worry lines creased the corners of her eyes. "It's nearing dinnertime, and you need more fuel in your tank than that. I want you to eat more, okay?"

I nodded. *Not a chance.* I grabbed my sock and rolled it on. "So can I play?"

She sighed. "You can warm up, then let me know how it's feeling." She pointed two fingers at her eyes, then rotated her wrist to point them at my eyes. "I'm watching you, Lucia. Watching to make sure you'll be all right."

Despite her threat, my shoulders drooped with relief. I could practice! When I hopped down from the training table, a woozy lightheadedness overtook me, and I swayed for a moment. Luckily, Tina had turned away. "Thanks, Tina." I took deliberate steps out to the gym, away from her scrutiny.

A few teammates had gathered on the bleachers to watch the end of the men's team practice, and I joined them. But a quick scan revealed the absence of my roommate. "Where's Dane?" I asked Kaitlyn.

She shrugged. "Dunno."

Nina leaned around Kaitlyn to look at me. *Whoops.* I hadn't seen her there—I hoped she wasn't mad at me for saying his name.

"Dane got kicked out of practice," Nina said with a wide grin.

I guess if she brought him up, she must have been okay with it. But Dane got kicked *out?* "What happened?"

"Pete told me on a water break that Dane mouthed off to Phil. When Jason—he's the assistant coach—when Jason got in Dane's face to shut him down, Dane *pushed* him. He's in truuhhh-*bull*."

I covered my mouth with one hand. What had made Dane lose it? It was unthinkable to disrespect a coach like that. "What'll happen to him?"

"Suspension, probably." Nina snorted. "Maybe loss of scholarship. Not like his family would have trouble affording a state school, anyway."

My parents could definitely afford Highbanks without an athletic scholarship, but that wasn't the point. It would be so shameful to lose my scholarship, and I knew Dane must have felt embarrassed, probably even devastated. I couldn't believe it, but despite everything, my heart ached for him. Nina was sitting right here, suffering from what he'd done to her, and still I worried about him. Still I had dreams about my beautiful blond *gigante*. Really sexy dreams. I wished those dreams would stop. *Well, maybe not.*

"Whatever happens to him," Nina said, her voice lowering now that the men's team had finished and our coaches approached, "he deserves it."

"Ladies." Coach's sharp tone set me on edge. "We have three days to prepare for the number-five team in the nation. If *that* doesn't focus your energy for this practice, nothing will. This is the time for volleyball. I want you to leave behind all worries about classes..."

I could do that. I knew I should be worried about classes, but I could barely stay awake for them. Concern for my grades took energy I didn't seem to have.

"...your families..."

That would be tougher, with my dad running for leader of the free world.

"...and all boyfriends, boys, boys who are friends, and anything of that nature."

Yeah. *That* was impossible. Especially when my boy crush played the very sport that was supposed to elicit my unwavering focus.

"Madison, get us started on warm-up."

I looked behind me and noticed Maddie and the rest of my teammates had arrived without my seeing them. Of course they were there. None of us was ever late to practice.

When I popped up, the gym spun, and I started to go down. I scrabbled for Kaitlyn's arm and clung onto it until my dizziness subsided.

"You okay?" she asked.

"*Sí, estoy bien.*" My heart raced, and I glanced up to see Tina eyeing me from across the gym. It didn't help that she stood right next to Allison, who stared at me with her own brand of perceptiveness, honed from years of law enforcement.

As my teammates and I hustled onto the court, Coach's voice stopped me short. "Lucia."

"Yes?" I forced myself to look at his face, which still felt unnatural.

"Tina said you're cleared to rejoin us today."

"Yes, Coach."

"Our offense has missed your big arm. Make us proud." He gestured for me to get going.

I nodded as I jogged to the net. In other words, *No matter how much your ankle hurts, keep going. Suck it up.* When I jumped for the blocking drill, my ankle didn't hurt at all, happily. Unhappily, my legs felt like refried beans. Limp, wobbly beans. I barely cleared the top of the net—wait, they'd set the net at women's height, right? My stomach tightened as I realized the problem wasn't the net…it was me. Besides feeling too heavy to get off the ground, I was breathing so hard it felt like I'd just run ten suicides. This would be a long practice if I couldn't force my body to get with the program.

Maddie started us on the footwork combination, and all I could hear was my rapid panting for air. My vision seemed to narrow, with blackness creeping in at the edges, and my lips felt numb. I crouched down to shuffle to one side of the court, then pivoted…

"Oh my God!"

I heard a voice from far away but couldn't see anything.

"Lucia! Lucia, open your eyes."

Who's talking to me?

"Call nine-one-one!"

That's Allison.

"I'm on it."

And that was Tina.

My eyes flipped open, and I realized I was on my back. About twenty faces crowded my vision. I had a sudden urge to vomit.

"Get back!" Tina hollered, then her face hovered over me. Allison's curly blond hair made an appearance, too.

"Are you okay, Lucy?" Frank's widened eyes popped up over Allison's head. I'd never seen him look scared before.

It took an inordinate amount of energy to speak. "I'm fine." I lifted my head an inch, but Tina grasped my shoulders.

"Stay down, Lucia. It looked like you hit your head."

Now that she mentioned it, the crown of my skull *did* throb with each heartbeat. "Oh." I lifted my hand to massage it. "What happened?"

"You collapsed during warm-up. Did you faint?"

I tried to keep my eyes in focus.

"Did your ankle give out?" Allison asked.

I was pretty sure my collapse had nothing to do with my ankle. "Yeah." I closed my eyes and willed myself to keep speaking. "There was this shooting pain, and then I woke up with everyone hovering over me."

Allison nodded, and she and Frank straightened.

"I'll go meet the ambulance," Frank said.

"*Ambulance?*" My heart thundered, and I tried to get up again, but Tina held me down. She frowned as she looked into my eyes.

"It's protocol when an athlete loses consciousness. Does your head hurt?"

"Just a little where I hit it."

"Headache? Dizziness?"

I answered no to both.

"What day is it?"

"Uh, Monday?"

"What's the date?"

"September seventh. Why are you asking me this?"

"Standard questions. I'm going to tell you five words, and I want you to repeat them to me." She leaned forward. "Book, monkey, geology, foot, cat."

With her expectant look, I had no choice but to comply by parroting the words. She made me repeat the list back to her two more times before a couple of guys in navy blue uniforms entered my field of vision.

The process of lifting me on a gurney—those EMTs were stronger than they looked—seemed to take forever and was completely unnecessary. I knew I could've walked out of there. *Claro*, I could've rejoined practice if they'd let me. But by telling them my ankle still hurt, I'd shot myself in the foot.

Coach appeared beside my gurney as they wheeled me toward the exit. I expected him to be angry with me for missing yet another practice, but he didn't sport his usual frown. "Go get taken care of, and we'll check in with you later," he said.

I nodded, and for some reason his light pat on my shoulder made me want to cry. As sucky as it was to have zero control over my destiny, I felt safe for the first time since I'd arrived at Highbanks. The sheet draped over me was warm, and a gurney felt like the right place to be, given my intense fatigue. Then I noticed Allison talking to her wrist.

"How 'bout we pull the sheet over her head?"

I realized she was conferring with Frank over the comm-link. When she exhaled a loud sigh as we neared the door, I asked, "What's going on?"

"He didn't like that idea. He said it would make them *more* predatory, if they thought you were dead."

"Who are *they?*"

Allison paused. "I'm sorry, Lucia—we tried to avoid this. But the ambulance chasers are living up to their name."

The EMTs pushed open the double doors, and my senses flooded. Blinding sunlight and flashbulbs, jostles and bumps into my gurney, shouted questions in my face:

"Lucia, why'd you collapse during practice?"

"Are you sick?"

"How long will you be out?"

"What do your parents think about this?"

I groaned as I imagined my family watching Fox News video of paramedics rolling me out to an ambulance.

My mother was going to *freak*.

Three hours later, when I heard her rapid-fire Spanish from all the way down the hall, I stopped fiddling with the IV taped inside my right elbow. I sat up and looked over at Allison next to the hospital bed. "Uh-oh." Hurricane Silvia was about to hit land.

A Secret Service agent I didn't know stuck his head into my curtained area of the ER a second before my mother rushed in. "*¡Dios!*" She scuttled forward and cradled my head between her warm hands. "Are you okay, *hija?*"

"I'm fine, Mom."

"*¡Ay!* You're so skinny!"

I rolled my eyes. *Hardly.*

"Are they feeding you?" She frowned at Allison. "I *knew* you shouldn't come up here, so far from home."

Mateo waltzed around the corner and flashed his shy grin, rescuing me from my mother's scolding. "*Oye*, Matty." I lifted my left fist to give his a bump. "I swear you got taller in just a month."

"Not as tall as you." His shaggy black hair fell in his eyes.

"*Yet,*" I added. "Just wait."

Allison approached my mother's agents who stood awkwardly by the foot of the bed. "I'll give you some privacy with your daughter, Mrs. Ramirez." Then she ushered them out. My mother assessed me while resting her trembling hand on her heart, and I fought the urge to call for Allison to stay, *please*. I knew the Mexican Inquisition was about to begin.

"Why did you faint?"

I pointed to my right foot. "I guess my ankle gave out. Maybe it wasn't ready to go yet."

"They why on earth did they let you practice? Where's your trainer? I want to talk to him." She lifted the sheet and studied my ankle.

"Tina went to find the attending physician."

"But your ankle looks fine. You said on the phone it wasn't hurting you anymore."

I swallowed and shifted away from my mother's intense gaze. As I looked around the room, I noticed Mateo playing with the heart monitor, which they'd disconnected from my finger a while ago. He certainly knew his way around a hospital. "How're things going, Matty?"

He shrugged.

"Your numbers are okay?"

"We had a scare last week," Mom answered for him as she stepped around the bed and cuffed him lightly on the ear.

He held up his lanky arms to protect his head. "Child abuse!"

I laughed. But when my mother spun and glared at me, my laugh caught mid-throat.

"We're talking about *you*, not him. And I don't think this is about your ankle. There's something you're not telling me."

I splayed my hands out to the side. "I don't know what to say."

"You've never fainted before. You're a strong girl. I want to know why this happened."

"The blood test results will explain everything," Tina said as she stepped into the curtained-off area. She looked at my mother. "Mrs. Ramirez? I'm Tina Young, the athletic trainer for women's volleyball."

"Silvia." They shook hands, and my mother pointed to my gangly teenaged brother. "This is Lucia's younger brother, Mateo."

Tina smiled at him. "How old are you?"

"Sixteen."

"Do you play volleyball too?"

"I don't play sports." When he stared at the floor, I felt a pang of sadness in my heart. Diabetes had stolen that from him.

"But he's killer on the guitar," I said. I thought I caught a hint of a smile from him.

Mom butted in. "I want to hear those test results."

"And I want to share them with you," Tina said, "assuming I have Lucia's permission." Both women turned to me.

"Y-Y-You need my permission?"

"Yes. You're eighteen, right?"

I nodded. I would turn nineteen in a few weeks. I ran my tongue over my front teeth. "If I don't give permission, my mom can't hear the results?"

Mom's hands flew to her hips. "Lucia Ramirez, I will *not* leave this hospital until I know what's wrong with you." When I didn't respond, she added, "And we will pull your father off the campaign trail to talk some sense into you, if we have to."

He wasn't the one I was concerned about. He would be reasonable. My mother—not so much. But I believed her when she said she wouldn't leave without hearing what Tina had to say. *Tenaz*, my father had called her. Tenacious. *Terca como una mula*, Alejandro had said behind her back. Stubborn as a mule.

"Fine, tell her." I laced my arms together in front of my chest. "Tell the whole world. I just want to get out of here."

Tina glanced down at the paper in her hand. "There's a problem with your glucose levels."

"¡Oh, *Dios!*" Mom's hand shot to her ample bosom. "She doesn't have diabetes too?"

"There's a family history of diabetes?" asked Tina.

Mom and I glanced at Mateo, who scowled.

"Oh." Tina nodded. "No, it doesn't appear to be diabetes."

Mom closed her eyes as she blew out a breath. "But there has to be a reason for her weight loss."

"There is," Tina told her, then turned to me. "Your glucose is low, Lucia. So is your iron, and your potassium. Your resting heart rate is only forty-two beats a minute."

"But that's because I'm an athlete."

"No, it's because your body's trying to conserve energy."

My mother shook her head. "Why?"

Tina stared at me. "How about you tell her."

"What?" My heart started thumping, surely faster than forty-two beats a minute. "Tell her *what?*"

My athletic trainer gave me a sad smile as she approached the bed. She rubbed my shoulder. "Your ankle's much better, and I'm glad you'll be back on the court. It's tough to adjust to this program—to this school—but you're doing a great job. I know you've been trying really hard."

My nose burned as I blinked. I wished she wasn't so nice to me, because that made it harder to fight her. I was just so tired.

"I'm on your team, Lucia. I want you to reach your goals." She rubbed my shoulder some more. "I think you felt like you had to lie to me before practice. There *was* no sandwich. Right? You haven't been eating. It's okay, you can tell me."

No! She knew. I couldn't stop tears from leaking out of my eyes.

"*¡Hija!*" My mother came up to the other side of the bed and stroked my braid. "What's she talking about? What sandwich? You need me to make you a sandwich?"

As I wiped the traitorous tears away, I noticed Mateo staring at me. Fear filled his deep brown eyes, and his grip on the bed's railing couldn't have been tighter. I felt like a total poseur when I realized *I* was the source of his worry. Here he was, stuck in another hospital he hated, because of me. He had to deal with a real sickness every day of his life, yet I was choosing to do this. My face burned with shame.

I finally found my voice. "I guess I haven't been eating enough."

Mom gasped as her hand stilled on my head. "The photo in *USA Today*!" She threw her hands up. "You don't look like that at *all*, Lucia. You're a beautiful girl! *Eres bonita. Hermosa*." She pressed the heel of her hand into her forehead. "Oh, this is my fault. You heard me yell at the TV when they made fun of my size. You watched me try to lose weight all my life. But, *hija*, you have to eat! You can't starve yourself."

"So it's okay for *you* to diet, but not me?"

"You are muscular, Lucia. I am *gorda*."

"*Nobody* should starve themselves," Tina said. "It causes low energy, depression, and irritability."

"Yeah, Lucy *has* been pretty bitchy," Mateo piped in.

I glared at him.

"Is that why you stopped eating?" Tina asked me. "Because of that unflattering photo?" She tapped her finger on her chin. "But you seemed lethargic before that."

I winced. I hadn't known anyone had noticed.

"Wait a minute. Did Wyatt Holter talk to you?" she asked.

I swallowed. When I nodded, Tina's face changed.

"What'd he say to you?"

"He said…I needed to get fitter if I wanted to be a starter."

"I'm going to kill him." Her eyes flared.

My mother tossed her hair. "Not if I get to him first. Telling my baby she needs to get fitter?" She gestured to me. "I've never seen a girl more in shape than Lucia."

If by "in shape" she meant fat, then I agreed with her. "Guys!" My voice came out louder than I'd planned. "He's my coach—he's just trying to make me better. Please don't say anything to him. He'll never play me again."

Tina frowned. "I don't know...I'll think about it." She nodded. "And you'll talk it through with Whitney and Dr. Valentine."

"What?"

"You have appointments with the sport dietitian and sport psychologist tomorrow."

"You can't make me do that!"

Tina nodded. "Yes, I can, if you want to play volleyball for Highbanks."

"I..." I clamped my mouth shut. *¡Chin!*

"And you're eating something before you leave this ER. Stay put—I'll get you some food." She darted behind the curtain.

"I *like* her," Mom said.

My throat felt tight. "Of course you do."

Mom let out a long breath, seeming relieved that the problem had been identified. "You kids are going to kill me one day." She sat on the side of the mattress and took my hand in hers. "Lucia, you're usually so level-headed. I get rattled, go *loca*, but you...you have your father's coolness under pressure. This is unlike you to let some coach—and some stupid media hound—get to you like this. Is there anything else going on?"

I felt tears well up again, and all I could see was Dane's tanned face, the spark in his sunny eyes when he smirked. I'd only wanted him to be attracted to me, too, and I'd thought losing some inches from my thick body might have made that happen. But I could lose fifty pounds and never be as pretty as Nina. Now that I thought about it, Dane was probably a big reason I was in this stupid hospital—not that I'd ever share that with my mother. I shook my head. "It's just been hard, Mom."

"It *is* hard, and I'm not even in college," Mateo offered. "It sucks having agents follow you twenty-four-seven."

"Yeah." I sniffed and smiled at him through my tears. "But you're handling this better than I am, *hermanito*."

He shrugged. "*You're* the one who finally got Mom out of the house."

I took that in. *Huh.*

"That's right!" Mom chuckled. "You got me to leave my fortress. And I didn't even care when those vultures snapped photos of me as I came into the hospital. I was just so worried about you." She kissed my hand.

I took a deep breath. *Get it together.* My family was dealing with enough without me passing out like a weakling on the volleyball court.

"Dad will shut 'em up when he wins this thing," Mateo said. "Don't let those asshat reporters get to you, guys."

Mom reached out and lightly smacked the back of his head. "Watch your mouth."

"Child abuse!"

She shook her head as she dug into her massive purse. "Just like I thought." She scowled at her phone, then shoved it into my hands. "Your father and brother have blown up *el teléfono*, worrying about you. Call them right now and tell them everything. I mean *everything*, Lucia."

I pouted. *Now* that's *child abuse.*

14

Dane

"*Get out of my gym.*"

I rolled over to my side and faced the wall of my bedroom. But instead of seeing sage green wallpaper, all I could picture were Phil's darkened eyes and the taut lines of his mouth after I'd pushed Jason.

"*Get out of my gym.*"

I'd never seen my zen-master coach look so mad. And no wonder, with me swearing at him, then manhandling his assistant. *Way* out of bounds. I was surprised Jason hadn't taken a swing at me—he'd looked like he wanted to. But he obviously had more self-control than I. And Phil ejecting me from practice…that was much worse than a physical blow.

He wouldn't kick me off the team, would he? This was *my* team, damn it! Phil had told me so. But he'd looked so furious, so…*disappointed.* My stomach tightened just remembering his face. I wondered how getting booted from the team would affect my mom's political chances. I flashed back to her campaign speech at Highbanks in the spring, when she'd announced, *"I love our state so much I sent my son Dane to play for the Cougars!"* The crowd had roared with chants of *"Go, Monroe! Go, Monroe!"*

Of course my dad hadn't been there that day. He'd probably been off with his floozy mistress, soaking up her adoring praise of his precious paintings. How could he have betrayed Mom like that? And how could she possess the strength to run for president when her marriage had crumbled like a stale piece of coffee cake?

I fought off an image that invaded my consciousness, but it wouldn't go away: a woodsy path, the canopy of trees, my dad looking to the sky. *"What a relief to get that off my chest."*

Thanks, Dad. I'm so glad you're *relieved now.* My hands tingled with the urge to shake him.

I pushed off my bed and stalked out of the room. Brad lounged at the kitchen table reading some papers, but I ignored him as I walked by and headed to the fridge. I shoved aside some protein shakes and cans of soda and hunted around for several moments, but I couldn't find what I wanted. "Where's the beer?" I yelled.

"Uh, *that.*" Brad grimaced. "Frank said our boss stopped by for an inspection last night. He went apeshit when he found alcohol in the presence of minors."

I gasped as I clutched the fridge door. "*No.*" In a few strides I made it to the cabinet next to the sink, and my stomach sank when I found it empty. "No, not the liquor, too! *Christ.*"

"You're nineteen," he said.

As if that matters. I straightened and glared at him.

"And Lucia's only eighteen."

"I don't give a damn about Lucia. And I'm almost twenty, by the way."

Brad shook his head. "Still not legal. We're lucky we weren't fired over this."

"Too bad you weren't." My eyes narrowed, and he returned my glare. I tried to unclench my fists. "You have to take me to a bar, then."

"Dude, did you hear what I said? I'm not taking you to get booze. And besides, just how would you order a drink, Mr. Underage?"

Shit. The fake ID Josh had gotten for me our freshman year would hardly work now that the media had plastered my face all over television. Dumbass presidential race.

"Have you talked to your mom?" he asked.

I felt heat rise to my face. "Why would I do that?"

"She's worried about you. Steve called me—he said you weren't answering your cell phone."

Mom's pussy campaign manager could go screw himself. She'd been the one to sic my dad on me, therefore she was the last person I wanted to talk to. "C'mon, go buy me some beer, Brad. It's no big deal."

"No can do, Danester. Why don't you join China in the weight room downstairs? The punching bag's a great stress release."

"She's a bitch. I don't want to be anywhere *near* her."

China's voice came from behind me. "I thought I told you to go to your room."

Whoops—her pissed-off tone made it clear she'd overheard me. I wheeled around. "And I told *you* that you weren't my fucking mother."

"When you act like a child, I'll treat you like one." Sweat beaded on her forehead. "Really, Dane. Telling your head coach to fuck off? Then *shoving* your assistant coach? You're out of control."

I scoffed. She thought *this* was out of control? *Ya ain't seen nothin' yet.*

"What'd your father say to you to make you this unhinged?"

"None of your goddamn business." My dad's words competed with the pounding of my heartbeat in my ears: *"You'll keep it secret, of course. An affair getting out would destroy your mother's campaign."* I clenched my teeth. "Just stay out of my life, both of you. I don't need babysitters!"

China's face reddened as she blew out air. "That's our job, to protect you. But we don't get paid near enough to tolerate crap like this. Just go back to your room, Dane."

"You can't order me around!"

"The hell I can't." When she darted toward me, I let out a surprised laugh. Then she was on me, and before I knew it, she'd locked my elbows behind me with one arm. Her other arm tightened across my chest, pressing down on my lungs. I could smell the disgusting man-sweat pouring off her bulging muscles.

"Get your sweaty paws *off* me!" I strained to wiggle out of her lockdown hold to no avail. My right shoulder screamed with pain. *Crap*—I couldn't afford an injury. But I was so ticked off I kept thrashing in her arms.

"Stop struggling!" At least she was breathing hard too. She pushed into me, and I took a stutter step toward my bedroom. "Go to your room!"

There was no way in hell I'd let a woman take control of me. I dug in my heels and strained my quad muscles, managing to stand my ground despite her forceful shoves. Our grunts filled the kitchen.

"Brad!" she panted.

He stood by the table watching the showdown, arms folded across his massive chest, a big grin on his face. Once I got free of China, I was going to kill him.

I wasn't wearing shoes, but I stomped my socked foot down on China's sneaker hard enough to elicit a yelp. "Son of a bitch!" she hollered, then tightened her grip.

"My shoulder," I groaned.

"China." Brad wasn't smiling anymore. "Let him go. We don't want to hurt him."

"I'm not…hurting him." The force of her push intensified. "I'm teaching…this…little…shit a lesson."

"China." His voice sharpened.

From her throat came a sound like a grizzly bear in heat. "Damn!"

In an instant, I was free. My shoulder throbbed, and I spun around to face the aggressor. "Don't you fucking touch me again!"

"Go to your *room*." Her chest heaved.

Brad stepped between us. "China, hit the weights." He looked at me. "Go somewhere and chill."

"Are you going to let her get *away* with that?" I pointed at the she-beast. "She attacked me!"

"Dane, *go*." When I didn't move, he added, "And I'm not buying you alcohol."

"You're *both* assholes!" I stomped out of the kitchen and into my bedroom, throwing the door closed behind me. The damn ergonomic hinges didn't provide nearly the satisfying slam I wanted, though. Mother-effing greenhouse!

I searched my room for something to crush. My hands itched with the desire to destroy.

"What a relief to get that off my chest." He'd thrown his head back and looked at the sky with a peaceful smile.

"Fuck!" My body buzzed with rage as I paced. God, did I need a drink. Then my feet froze. I hopped over to the window to peek out the thick wooden blinds, and I liked what I saw. "Bingo."

I inched up to my door and listened to my agents' hushed voices, undoubtedly discussing what a nightmare I was to protect. *Shitheads.* When the voices died off, I shoved gym shoes on my feet and waited a few minutes. Then I strolled out to the kitchen.

Brad looked up from his papers.

I swallowed, then let out a breath. "Sorry. Didn't mean to take it out on you."

When he cocked his head, suspicion still evident, I knew I had to be more convincing.

"Dude, you realize how humiliating it was for a *woman* to dominate me like that? I lost my shit. Sorry."

"China's not any woman. She's trained to take people down."

"I see that." I rubbed my shoulder. "And, I'm taking your advice. I'll work out with her, try to get strong like her."

He smiled. "Good idea."

"Would you…?" I chewed my lip. "Would you go down there, ask if she'd let me join her?"

Brad hesitated.

"She doesn't like me very much, but you have a good way with her. Please, Brad? Grease the wheels a little for me?"

He got up. "Sure. Give me a couple minutes. I'll get her to come around."

"Thanks, man."

He headed to the basement, and I patted the back pocket of my khaki shorts to double-check that my wallet was there. Butterflies dive-bombed my stomach as my heartbeat kicked up a notch—just like the excitement I felt before a big match. When I was sure he was safely downstairs, I crept to the foyer, hoping they couldn't hear my footsteps in the basement. I scanned the camera feed of the area beyond the gates and my eyes landed on a curvy blonde. *Okay, that one.*

I lunged for the front door and heard the alarm sound behind me as I flew through it. I sprinted for the gate, and the flock of media fluttered and scrambled for their cameras.

"*Dane!*" Brad hollered from the bowels of the house, and I knew I only had seconds to make my getaway. I scaled the seven-foot gate with ease and heard snapping cameras as I climbed over the metal spikes. With grace, I hopped to the concrete.

"You!" I panted as I pointed at the blond reporter. Flashbulbs blinded me. "You want an exclusive?"

Her eyes lit up. "You bet!"

"Then get me outta here, and you got it."

Her head bobbed, and she scuttled to a TV news van with her cameraman in tow. The other reporters shouted questions at me.

"Not him." I jerked my thumb at the idiot with the bulky video camera. "Just you."

She halted.

"Dane Monroe!" China burst through the front door with Brad on her heels. "Stay right there!"

I swiveled back to face Blondie. "Now or never—how bad do you want this story? But your cameraman's not coming with."

She exchanged a look with him then nodded. "Okay, get in."

As I hustled around the van to the passenger side, I had to weave in and out of reporters hurling questions my way. I heard the house gates slide open over their shouts and the rush of blood in my head. *Please get me outta here.* Hoping for the best, I ducked into the van, and we screeched out onto the neighborhood street.

I peered over my shoulder and felt a colossal grin spread on my face. The media had parked their vans and cars up against the gate, and they now stood in the way of my pursuers' SUV. In a gorgeous twist of events, the reporters chasing after me with questions meant they wouldn't be around to move their cars anytime soon. As we sped away, the last sounds I heard were China's frustrated honks.

"Where to?" Blondie asked.

I eyed her long, styled hair and luscious rack as my heartbeat slowed. "Kroger. I need you to buy me some groceries."

She gave me a sideways glance.

"I'll pay, of course."

"That's not what worries me. Why'd you hightail it out of there just to buy groceries? The agents could get those for you."

I angled my body toward her and wiped sweat off my forehead with the back of my hand. Maybe that getaway sprint had made up for lost conditioning from leaving practice early. "What's your name?"

"Beverly Jackson." She extended her right arm from the driver's seat, took her eyes off the road, and shook my hand.

"I guess you know my name already."

"Sure do, Mr. Monroe."

"Call me Dane."

We stopped at a light, and I tried to figure out what felt familiar about her.

"So, Dane, why the dramatic escape? I hope Bob captured that on film—you gave us some great footage."

I cringed—Fox News would have a field day with my hijinks. At least they hadn't been allowed inside the gym to witness my ejection. "I've had a really shitty day, Beverly. Have you ever had a day like that?"

The light had turned green, and she inched the van forward as she waited to turn left. "Yes." As her manicured hands tightened on the steering wheel, it struck me why she looked familiar. She was shorter and bustier than Nina, but when her mouth tensed into a frown, she totally reminded me of my ex. And she didn't seem attractive anymore once I realized the resemblance. She didn't have Lucia's shiny black hair, soft smile, or that little dimple on her right cheek. She didn't possess her power or athleticism.

Had Lucia ruined me for blondes like Nina? I frowned. It was more like Nina had ruined my chances with spicy girls like Lucia. And I could no longer deny (at least to myself) that I kind of wanted one, crazy as that might be. I'd never have a chance with Lucia if she knew about the abortion. I'd never touch her silky brown skin or discover what sexy tigress hid beneath that blushing naiveté. I just knew a *caliente* spark sizzled inside Lucia, but now it would never come to light, at least with me. *Awesome*. Thinking about what I'd miss just made my day shittier.

"So you said you've had a bad day?" Beverly prompted.

"Yeah." The air conditioning had cooled me off. "What do *you* do after a bad day?"

"Bob and I usually hit *The Library* for drinks."

I smirked. *The Library* was one of the most popular campus bars—undergrads loved to tell their clueless parents they'd stayed at 'the library' late into the evening. "I can relate. I just need you to get me some beers, okay?"

Her mouth tightened as she pulled into Kroger.

My phone buzzed in my pocket. *Not my mom again.* But this was a text from China.

If you return now, we won't be mad.

I blew air out my nose. As if I cared about the emotional status of my agents. I'd never wanted them in the first place! Then I realized they could track me through my phone, so I quickly powered it down.

Beverly parked the van far from the entrance to the grocery store. "I'm not sure about this. Buying alcohol for a minor could get me arrested."

"Who's gonna know?" I flashed my most charming smile. "*I* certainly won't tell anyone."

She studied me. "Damn, you're cute." I followed her gaze as it dropped to her hands, and I noticed the absence of a wedding ring. "But I shouldn't."

"I thought you wanted an exclusive interview."

Her head shot up. "I do. Very much."

"Blue Moon loosens my lips." I grinned and held out a twenty.

She shook her head, but the beginnings of a smile emerged. "Anything for the story, right?" She snatched the money and stepped out of the van, saying, "Don't go anywhere," before shutting the door.

Where exactly would I go? She'd taken the keys. Boredom set in quickly, and I took out my phone only to remember I'd turned it off. I swiveled in my seat and marveled at the technical equipment lining the van walls. So *this* was where the media made our lives miserable.

I had to stoop as I stepped to the rear of the van to look more closely. *Aaagh!* I flinched at the network logo emblazoned on one of the TV monitors: Channel 8 Fox News. *Damn it*! Why did I have to choose a Fox reporter?

Duh. She was the hottest one out there.

They'd taped a few pieces of paper above the video editing equipment, and my mouth dropped open as I leaned in and read "Highbanks Fall Semester: Lucia Ramirez." Her practice schedule hung next to her class schedule, and my schedules were there too. How had they tapped into our private calendars? They were *hunting* us! I ripped down the information and jammed the folded sheets into my pockets. "You don't need this, d-bag stalkers."

I heard the door open and scrambled back to the front passenger seat.

"What were you doing back there?" Beverly asked as she set a plastic bag between the seats.

I ripped into it with greedy fingers and extracted a cold beer. After I twisted the cap off and downed a long guzzle, I turned to her. "Just figuring out how you invade my privacy."

"But you're a public figure." She sounded defensive, and her voice rose as she watched me down the beer. "Jeez! Take a breath."

I placed the empty bottle back in the carton and reached for another. "I wouldn't have chosen you if I'd known you were with Fox."

"We're the local affiliate."

Whatever. I closed my eyes as the golden liquid slid down my throat. "God, I love beer." I wondered how many beers it would take to obliterate the image of my dad gazing at the blue sky. *"What a relief to get that off my chest."*

She watched me drink the second bottle. "Well, I held up my end of the bargain. What do you have for me?"

Crap. I'd forgotten my promise to give her the scoop. Possible responses flooded my mind: *Did you know my parents' marriage is a sham? How about the fact that my narcissistic father is diddling his mistress?*

I peered at her over the mouth of my beer bottle, considering how awesome it would be to unleash that shocking story to the world. Mom's campaign manager would kill me! And, I thought with a scowl, Mom would be devastated. I didn't want to hurt her. It wasn't her fault she'd married a selfish asshole.

Beverly kept waiting. What else could I tell her? *Oh, by the way, I have the hots for Governor Ramirez's daughter*. Yeah, that would go over real well. Her reporter's stare was so intent that I had to come up with something to stall her. "When I tell you something, aren't you going to take notes?"

She looked startled, then shifted her cell phone in her lap. "I have a good memory." She tapped her temple.

The screech of tires exploded to our right. *Oh, no*. I turned to find China's fierce glare piercing into me from the SUV. How had they found me? She stepped out of the vehicle as I lunged for the door lock.

China came right up to the van. "Open the door, Dane."

I tried to peer around her. Where was Brad?

"Open the door right now."

I followed a sound to my left and, to my horror, saw Brad open the driver's side door.

"Why didn't you lock your door?" I cried as I glared at Beverly.

"Step out of the car, ma'am," Brad ordered. He glanced at my beer bottle. "Party's over."

"Hey!" Beverly turned to me. "You haven't given me my exclusive interview."

I heard my car door lock click open a second before I lunged for it, but China had beaten me. *Damn!* Brad must have unlocked it from the driver side. China yanked the door open as I seized the bag of beer bottles. We stared at each other for a few long seconds.

China's eyebrows rose. "Will I need to handcuff you, Mr. Monroe?"

"You wouldn't do that." *She won't* handcuff *me, right?*

"I *will* do that, unless you get your ass into the SUV." She still wore the sweaty Spandex workout top and tight shorts she'd had on earlier, showcasing her muscles, but she'd also strapped on a belt with a gun holster and dangling handcuffs.

I swallowed as I tried to come up with a way to evade them both. Now that Brad had taken Beverly's seat, my odds for escape were dismal.

"We can do this the easy way or the hard way, hot shot," Brad said. His bulk crowded the space between us.

To help me think, I took the last swig of my third bottle. I still had no brilliant ideas. "How'd you guys find me?"

Brad tapped the dashboard. "We tracked the van's coordinates via satellite."

"If you try to pull that stunt again, blocking us in..." China put her hand on her weapon.

"I'm sure you have backup," I said.

"Well," Brad said, "we tried to reach the other team, but they couldn't leave Lucia."

I frowned. "Why not?"

Beverly gave a sudden shout, and we turned to see her jumping up and down. "I need my van back to pick up Bob!" She pointed at her cell phone. "Lucia Ramirez is in the hospital!"

"*What?*" I looked at Brad.

He nodded grimly. "She passed out at practice."

"Is she *okay?*" My heart raced.

He cocked his head and studied me. "Yeah, she'll be all right."

"She was just discharged," China said. "They'll bring her back to the greenhouse."

As I scooted out of the van, China backed up to let me out. "Then we're headed to the greenhouse," I said decisively.

She massaged her temples. "I need a raise."

15
Lucia

"Frank." I wiggled against his hand cradling my elbow as he ushered me through the front entrance of the greenhouse. "I'm okay. You don't have to do that."

He jumped back. "Sorry, Lucia. You gave us all a scare when you fainted, you know."

"That won't happen again," Mom said as she came in behind me, flanked by her agents. I turned to see her take in the modern architecture of the foyer. "What a lovely house! I don't know why Adolfo was so concerned."

I doubted Dad had worried about the quality of the home—more like the quality of its residents.

"Are you okay, Lucia?"

And there was the primary resident, his voice sounding oddly shaky. Dane angled against the wall with his hands jammed in the pockets of his shorts. His eyes washed over me, and I wondered why his cheeks were so pink.

I held my breath, hoping he'd never find out the reason for my hospital visit. "I'm fine."

"Is your ankle still hurting you?"

I was unaware he'd known or cared about my ankle injury. Not knowing how to answer, I searched his deep blue eyes.

When Frank chuckled as he chatted with my mom's agents, I looked away to glance at my mother, and I realized she had been staring at Dane, too. I cleared my throat. "*Mamá*, this is Dane Monroe."

He flashed his signature charismatic grin as he approached her. "*Señora* Ramirez." He took her hand, and I gaped when he lowered to kiss it. What the hell was he doing?

But Mom didn't seem charmed. Her nose scrunched up. "You smell like a brewery, young man."

Dane dropped her hand like a hot tamale and backed away. "No, I don't."

He'd been *drinking?* That would explain his flushed face and bold greeting of my mother. My mind instantly flashed to his last alcohol bender, when he'd kissed my cheek. Would he kiss me again? My heart shook with anticipation.

From behind my mother came a laugh, and I realized Mateo had entered, followed by Allison. She carried his medical bag.

"Good luck trying to tell *Mamá* she's wrong," Mateo said as he slung his arm across Mom's shoulders. "She doesn't like that." As expected, my mother's expression soured as she continued to look at Dane.

I attempted to diffuse the tension by pointing out the newcomer on the scene. "Dane, this is Mateo — my *other* brother."

Dane nodded at Mateo, whose eyes widened upon meeting my *gigante*. "Dude, you're tall!"

"He's already met Alejandro?" Mom interjected. Her scowl told me she was still unimpressed by my roommate.

"*Sí, Señora.*" Dane smirked. "And what a polite, *tranquilo* first-born son you have."

Her eyes narrowed as she caught his sarcasm. *¡Hijole!* Insulting one of her offspring was about as unwise as it got.

But like an idiot, Dane kept going. "And now the rest of *la familia* Ramirez is crashing my home, I see. Will the patriarch, Adolfo, join us, too?"

¡Cállate! I wanted to shout. *Shut up!*

My mother stepped forward. "That's *Governor* Ramirez to you, *hijo*. And you should be so lucky for him to show up. Clearly, your father hasn't taught you how to behave."

Dane blanched, and he straightened to his full, intimidating height. "You know *nothing* about my father."

I'd never seen him so angry. *What is his deal?*

"Lucia?" China's voice filtered into the foyer from the TV room.

I watched Dane to make sure he stayed put. "Um, yeah?"

"CNN says you're..." China stepped into the foyer. "Oh, hello, Mrs. Ramirez. I'm Agent China Halloway, on Mr. Monroe's detail." My mother nodded at her, and China's gaze shifted right. "And you're Matty? I've heard great things about you."

My brother shot me a dirty look. "It's Mateo."

"Of course, sir."

His face relaxed.

China rested her hand on Dane's shoulder as she looked up at him. She leaned in to whisper something in his ear, and he closed his eyes. Amazingly, his fists unfurled and he blew out a breath. China's brute force typically riled him up, but he appeared much calmer when he spoke this time.

"*Señora* Ramirez, Mateo, please come in." He extended his arm toward the TV room. "Apparently Lucia will need your support when CNN comes back from commercial."

"*What?*" I barely felt my mom and brother brush past me as China led them inside.

His eyes held the hint of an apology. "China said they're about to show footage of you being rolled to the ambulance again. Only this time they're promising to explain why you collapsed."

My hand darted to cover my mouth. They didn't know, did they?

Dane inched toward me. "You don't have to watch if you don't want to. I'll, I'll ask Brad to drive us somewhere. Take us away from here."

That *did* sound appealing, after the day I'd had. But, wait, this was Dane. Could I trust him? I wanted to. Refusing to engage took a lot of energy. I blinked up at him, wondering why was he being so nice to me.

I guess I hesitated too long, because he frowned.

"You probably don't want to do that—just take off with somebody like me—especially when your family's here." His head hung low and his hands found his pockets again.

Somebody like me? What had happened to the cocky Great Dane? Whatever his mistakes, somebody like *him* would be great to take off with, throw my cares to the wind. But carefree wasn't my life, and it wasn't his life either. Once our parents had chosen to run for president, carefree had flown out the window.

Remembering Matty's look of fear in the ER, I retracted my shoulders. "I better go in there. I have to start facing my problems instead of avoiding them."

Dane looked up, his blue eyes smoldering, and I wondered if the problems I'd referred to were about my eating or my complicated feelings for him. Too tired to figure it out now, I walked into the TV room just in time to see a coiffed brunette reporter's talking head next to video of me on a gurney.

"This afternoon at Highbanks University, Lucia Ramirez, daughter of Republican presidential nominee Adolfo Ramirez, collapsed at volleyball practice."

As my mother caught my eye from her seat on the sofa, I felt Dane come up behind me. His presence sent tingles up my spine.

"Emergency workers took her to University Hospital, where she was discharged this evening. But what caused her to collapse? According to an unidentified source…"

I held my breath.

"Lucia Ramirez is suffering from an eating disorder."

I stopped breathing.

"Obviously Ms. Ramirez isn't handling the pressure of her father's nomination well. We have with us psychiatrist Walter Downing from Emory University Medical Center. Doctor, please educate us on how an eating disorder could lead to collapse…"

I felt wetness on my face and realized I'd started crying. *Lead to collapse, lead to collapse…*how could my mortifying weakness lead to the collapse of my father's campaign? I alone would be responsible for my dad losing the election—for my dad losing his dream. When I swayed to my left, Dane grabbed me.

"Just how did they get that information?" my mother screeched as she bolted off the sofa.

Allison and China stood as well. "We'll find out," Allison said.

I had to admit Dane's solid hands cradling my elbows felt good. He guided me to the sofa and helped me sit, then crouched down to search my eyes. "So it's true?"

More tears leaked out, and I looked away. "This is so humiliating."

"Is *that* why you've avoided me?" I looked at him to find a weird smile on his face. "You've been withdrawing from everyone."

Before I could try to make sense of Dane's babble, Mateo scooted over and patted my shoulder. "It's okay, Lucy. Nobody will believe them."

"*Everyone* will believe them." To my horror, I started crying harder. Now Dane got a good look at my snotty, blotchy ugliness. "I'll ruin Dad's chances."

"That's not true." Dane frowned. "The media doesn't expect us to be perfect."

"Yeah, if you're a Democrat." I sniffed.

Dane stood and headed to the kitchen. Apparently he couldn't stand the sight of my blubbering mess. But then he was back, kneeling down and handing me some tissues.

"Thanks." As I plucked one from the box, I looked up to see my mother staring at us. My chest seized with panic. Could she read my attraction?

"Well, folks, we have even more news today from Highbanks University."

The reporter's amused tone cut through the chatter in the room, and it grew quiet as all eyes focused on the TV.

"Lucia Ramirez isn't the only student-athlete who had a bad day. Earlier we showed footage of Dane Monroe, son of Democratic nominee for president Senator Lois Monroe, making a break for it outside his living quarters."

A video of Dane scaling the greenhouse gates filled the screen, and I gasped. "When did *that* happen?"

He'd swiveled on one knee to face the TV, and I could see a blush creep up his neck. "When you were in the hospital." His voice was tight and low.

"But why?"

"Now we know why Mr. Monroe was so eager to get away from Secret Service. Beverly Jackson of WBNT News provided this footage."

"Fuck."

His utterance was so soft that I was the only one who heard it. I watched with fascinated horror as the grainy video of Dane guzzling a bottle of beer flashed on the screen. He was in some sort of vehicle—*oh, no*—he started in on another bottle and the liquid disappeared with dam-breaking speed.

Then he lowered the bottle and closed his eyes. "*God, I love beer.*"

"Her cell phone camera," he murmured as he sank to the floor in front of me. "I'm so screwed."

"That was quite a show today: an eating disorder and underage binge drinking." The reporter turned to the stupid psychiatrist, who was still on set. *"Dr. Downing, what's causing this acting out? Is it tied to the stress of being the child of a presidential candidate?"*

"Ya think?" Dane hissed. He massaged his forehead with his palms as my mother gestured wildly above us, yammering about security leaks with Allison and security breakdowns with China.

Shaking his head at Dane, Mateo snorted. "I can't believe you did that. You're sooo busted."

"No doubt. I royally screwed the pooch." Dane flexed his hands then turned them over and stared at his palms. "That asshole stunt just ended my volleyball career."

I inhaled sharply. He looked so defeated! What would he do if Phil kicked him off the team? I touched his shoulder. "Don't say that. You love volleyball. You've got to fight to keep playing."

When he glanced sideways at my hand on his shoulder, I snatched it back. Why was I voluntarily touching him like that?

"I hope you don't get kicked off the team," Mateo offered. "Lucia told me you're an awesome setter."

Dane's eyes moved to my face, which flamed with heat. "She did?"

I looked away, only to notice my mother staring at us again. I swallowed.

Mateo said, "Actually, we should thank Dane for being such an idiot, Luce. He took the heat off you."

Dane nodded slowly. "You know, he's right." He managed a smile—quite a different look from his earlier self-flagellation. "The story became about the pressure we both face. At least *something* good came out of my insanity."

"I would hardly call you a hero," my mother snapped. "Mateo, *ven acá*. Help me in the kitchen."

I could tell she was worried Mateo might think Dane's beer binge was cool. But it wasn't like my brother had the chance to hang out with kids from the bad crowd, or hang out with kids at all—not with the Secret Service shadowing his every move. Mateo rolled his eyes but followed her.

"*I* think you're a hero," I whispered once they'd left. "You busted out of our prison."

"It *was* pretty sweet." His smile broadened.

An hour later, I sat at the table with a huge plate of food glaring at me, and Brad's moans of pleasure filling the kitchen. "Mrs. Ramirez..." He spoke between bites, standing by the fridge. "This is the *best* enchilada I've ever had!"

"It's not spicy enough," my mother scoffed as she leaned on the counter. Where had she gotten her apron? "What respectable kitchen doesn't have jalapeños?"

She was fishing for compliments.

Dane's fork scraped against his plate. "Could I have another, *Señora?*"

That was the best compliment he could've given. My mother *tsked*, but took Dane's plate and handed it back to him loaded up with two more enchiladas. Then she filled a glass with ice and water from the fridge and set it down by his plate. "No Corona for you." She smacked his head.

"Ow." Dane rubbed his ear.

Mateo laughed. "Better you than me, bro." He shoveled a bite into his mouth.

"*Hija*." Mom glanced at my uneaten food.

"But I ate at the hospital."

"Small, frequent meals, sweetheart." She leaned close so the four agents snarfing her cooking around us couldn't hear. "You can do it."

This was *small?* My heart pounded. I felt Dane's gaze and managed to look up at him. His eyes seemed sad, but he gave a slight nod, like he urged me to take a bite.

"Did I tell you about the hotel fire alarm last year?" he asked.

I shook my head.

"We were at an away match, at Penn State, and some idiot pulled the fire alarm at three a.m. We all had to go to the hotel parking lot. It was February, and *freezing*, and Josh..." Dane glanced at Mateo. "He's my best friend on the team. Anyway, Josh waltzes out of the hotel wearing only his underwear and flip-flops."

As Mateo snickered, I managed a bite of tortilla and chicken.

"Tell me you snapped a photo of that," Mateo said.

"Are you kidding? No way I'd miss that Kodak moment." He whipped his phone out of his pocket and scrolled through his photos.

My fork suspended in midair as Mateo and I looked at Mom.

"What?" Dane asked, noticing we'd frozen.

"*Mamá* doesn't let us have phones at the dinner table," Mateo explained.

"Why?" Dane shook his head.

Mom approached the table and placed her hand on Dane's shoulder. "This is Dane's house, so we'll let him use his phone just this once." She cupped my shoulder with her other hand. "Besides, I want to see this Josh character for myself."

16

Dane

★★★

The next day, all I heard were my steady breaths and the thumping drumbeat of my favorite band as its music piped through my earbuds. I tucked in my chin and added a muscle-burning kick as I zoomed up a steep incline. "Attraction Infraction" was next on the playlist, and I wanted to crest the hill before that song, which always made me think of Lucia. Sadness and longing didn't pair well with a get-it-out-of-your-system hard run.

When I neared the end of the metro park trail, I slowed to a walk, feeling alive and exhausted. My quad muscles quivered, and sweat poured down my spine. A few minutes later, my agents came up on either side of me. I yanked out my earbuds.

"Thanks for bringing me here—I needed that."

A bead of sweat dripped from China's chin as she nodded. "Thanks for asking us to drive you instead of engineering your own transportation."

We shared a smirk.

"Can we…stop a second?" Brad gasped for air, and I came to a halt on the dirt path. His drenched T-shirt stretched across his sprawling chest, and gym shorts squeezed his sizeable thighs. He'd started the run ahead of me but had fallen behind in the first mile.

"C'mon, Brad, how will you keep up with assassins if you can't keep up with me?"

He continued breathing hard. "I doubt assassins…have the stamina of…a scholarship athlete."

"That *was* a punishing pace, Dane." China's eyes flared with excitement, and I knew she thrived on tough workouts just like I did.

"Well, I had to make up for missing practice this morning." As soon as I spoke, the reality of my suspension hit me, and with it came the deflation of my positive mood. Maybe "punishing" was an apt description for this run…punishing myself for my stupidity yesterday.

"*I have to start facing my problems, instead of avoiding them,*" Lucia had said last night. I grimaced. She was right. By the time I'd awoken from my beer bender, she'd already done just that by eating breakfast and leaving for weights. I assumed her mother and brother had flown back to Texas.

On the ride back to the greenhouse, I glanced at my phone to find more missed calls from my mother. I closed my eyes and leaned back against the headrest until we made it home. Then, after a shower, I clenched my teeth and called Mom from my bedroom. To my surprise, I didn't have to go through Steve this time.

"Oh, *Dane,*" my mom said, and the concern in her voice made me want to cry. "Thank you for finally calling back, honey."

"Sorry." I took a deep breath. "How's the campaign?"

"We're not talking about me. How are *you* doing?"

I swallowed. "I might…I might get kicked off the team." I hated the hitch in my voice.

"That would be devastating. I hope your coach can appreciate the pressure you're under."

"I think he does, but that's no excuse for how I acted at practice. And that was *before* I got drunk on national TV."

She paused. "There's *more?* I'm almost afraid to ask what happened at practice."

"I, uh…" She wasn't going to be happy with me. "I kind of told Phil to fuck off."

"Dane!"

I figured I might as well tell her everything—I knew she'd use her psychology techniques to drag it out of me anyway. "And I screwed myself even harder when I shoved Jason. Phil suspended me from the team."

"Oh, Dane. So you took a crisis and made it worse."

Basically.

"This is why I kept calling you, to try to talk you down. Patrick told me you didn't take his news well—"

The understatement of the year.

"—and we both know you have trouble with your temper."

I closed my eyes as I slumped back in my desk chair. When would I learn some self-control? Mom had tried to help me over the years, but I still threw tantrums like a two-year-old. As a psychologist, she was probably embarrassed to call me her son.

"I don't know why I'm lecturing you—that's not going to help anything." Her voice softened. "I'm sorry, Dane."

"Why are *you* sorry? I'm the one who messed up."

"This is my fault. I'm the one who cajoled Patrick into speaking to you."

I sighed. "I was going to find out some time."

"If only I could've held onto him...made him love me...none of this would've happened—" Her voice broke, and I could hear her choke back a sob.

"*Mom.*" I clenched my fist. "What he did wasn't your fault, not at all. *He's* the asshole, not you."

Her voice trembled. "They say an affair's a sign of a problem in the marriage." She sniffed. "I should have seen it. I should've done something about it."

"*He* should've supported you more. You're the most powerful senator in our country, and he can't handle it."

"Well, Patrick is in a tough spot. It's not easy being married to a successful woman."

My lips parted. "You're *defending* him?"

"No! I..." She exhaled. "I'm just so sorry about how this is affecting you. Patrick promised not to make his relationship public until after the November election, and that's a long time for you to hold onto this. I know how destructive secrets can be."

I was quiet for a moment. "How could you tell him, Mom?"

"Tell him what?"

"About last year...about Nina."

"Oh!" She made a strangled noise. "I'm so sorry. Please believe me, I didn't mean to tell him. Patrick was just acting so smug, like his absence in your and Jessie's lives was no big deal, and I let it slip about the pregnancy...maybe I was trying to show him you do indeed need him in your life—"

"I *don't* need him!"

"Honey...everyone needs a father figure."

"Phil's been a better father to me than Dad ever was." And I'd gone and destroyed that relationship, too. *Good job, dickwad.*

When a rustling occurred in the background, I noticed the substantial uninterrupted length of our conversation—a first since she'd started campaigning. I was probably making her late to something. "Don't you need to give a speech, tape an interview somewhere?"

"I cancelled my appearances today. I was just about to get on a plane to come see you since you weren't answering my calls."

"Mom, you don't have to do that. I can take care of myself."

"I know you can, but you deserve some TLC. I want to be there for you." She sighed. "I'm so wrapped up in this stupid presidential race that I'm neglecting you and your sister. Maybe...maybe I should drop out."

"No! You *are* there for me. I always remember what you taught me, especially if I'm having an emotional freak-out, and I know you'd be here more if you could. But Mom, you're doing something incredible right now—you're gunning to become the first female president of the United States. That's amazing! That's historic. Of course you won't be around for the next couple of months."

"I'm not acting like a good mother."

I realized how alone she must feel. My dad had abandoned her, and Jessica was a self-absorbed teenager, which left me to support her. "Jess and I will be fine. We will."

"I wish you could have a normal college experience. I wish you could go out there and make mistakes without ending up on the national news because of me and my campaign."

I winced as the van video replayed in my head. "I brought that one on myself." *Jackhole.* "Look, Lucia's dealing with the pressure too, and I don't hear *her* dad planning to drop out of the race. I don't hear him feeling guilty for how this affects his kids."

"He's not a mother. He's not the primary caregiver, so what would he know?" As she spoke, her voice grew stronger, capturing a hint of that competitive spirit I knew so well. The competitive spirit I'd inherited from her. "I do not like that man. He'd ruin this country if he got the chance. But poor Mrs. Ramirez—she's probably so worried about her daughter. All the sexism and objectification of women in this patriarchal society…no wonder Lucia's struggling with body image."

"*Señora* Ramirez came to the house last night."

"She did?" Mom paused, and I thought I detected a twinge of guilt in her voice. She probably felt badly she hadn't visited me this year. "What did you think of her?"

"Loud—she talks nonstop." I grinned. "Lucia calls her 'Hurricane Silvia.'"

Mom chuckled. "I guess I'll see the hurricane at the last debate in October."

I'd forgotten about the last debate. Mom had told me to focus on my classes instead of attending the first two. But both our families would be there for this one, and I wondered what it would be like to meet Lucia's dad. Would I hate him as much as I predicted? Would he hate me? He probably would, particularly if he knew how much I lusted after his daughter. But it was a no-brainer that Mom would love Lucia. Her beauty lit up a room.

"Thank you for the pep talk, Dane. Thank you for being you. I'm so proud you're my son."

I gripped the phone tighter. Though I'd shooed her away, the truth was I did want my mom to visit. I missed her. And I abhorred hearing such a strong woman doubt herself because of her shithead husband.

"Your father and I disagree on many things, but we both know how much you love volleyball. You belong out there, leading the team. Is there any way to make this right with your coach?"

"Phil hasn't called me yet."

"Then you call him."

I blew out a breath. "He doesn't want to hear from me."

"Dane, don't mind-read. You don't know that—all the evidence I've heard suggests Phil likes you. You're letting your feelings for your father get in the way of your relationship with your coach."

"Don't psychoanalyze me, Mom."

"Sorry. Listen, you probably have to get to class, so I'll let you go. Please call if you want to talk more about the situation with your father, or…anything. I'm here, okay?"

"Okay."

"I love you, Danish."

My cheeks warmed. "Love you, Mom."

I checked my watch after I hung up, and she was right that I needed to leave for class soon. After staring at my phone for too long, I typed a text to Phil:

**I screwed up big time, and I want to apologize.
Can I meet you before practice?**

After class, I clenched my teeth as I knocked on Phil's door. *Here we go*. The door swung open, and I faced my assistant coach. "Uh, hey, Jason."

"We're waiting for you, GD." He gestured to the small table where Phil sat. Next to him was a woman who looked familiar. As she stood, Phil got to his feet as well.

"You remember Michelle Farris?" Phil asked.

I nodded as I shook her hand. She was an associate athletic director—my team had met her during orientation.

"I oversee the department's drug testing," she explained as we sat.

I paled. "Did I fail a drug test?"

She cocked an eyebrow. "I don't know, *did* you?" Her eyes nailed me to my chair. She'd been an All-American basketball player somewhere, and her tall frame and elegant business suit conveyed intimidation all the way. "Are you using drugs besides alcohol?"

Phil glared at me. This wasn't getting off to a good start.

"No, ma'am." I gulped.

"Good." She pushed a paper across the table toward me. "We treat alcohol violations, like your flamboyant underage drinking stint last night, the same as positive drug tests."

Waves of nausea roiled in my gut. No way I'd stay on the team now.

"Here's what we expect you to do." She pointed at the paper in front of me. "You need to schedule an assessment with our sport psychologist, Dr. Valentine, and follow her recommendations regarding further treatment."

I looked up at Phil to find a serene smile on his face. He'd urged me to see the psychologist over a month ago, and now he was getting exactly what he wanted.

"Secondly," Michelle said, recapturing my attention, "you'll be tested more frequently. When your athletic trainer calls you for a drug test, you're to report immediately, no questions asked."

I nodded. Drug tests were so embarrassing, with Tina forced to watch me take a piss. Now that mortification would multiply.

Michelle pointed at the third bullet point on the contract. "If you have another alcohol violation or positive drug test, you'll be suspended for two weeks from your competitive season."

"And if that happens," Phil said, leaning forward, "you'll find another position or leave the team. I won't have our starting setter missing two weeks in season. You'd lose all credibility with the guys."

I felt my chest fall with a long exhale. Though Phil was obviously still angry with me, he'd used the words "starting setter." I latched onto those words. Whatever they did to me, I could handle it, as long as I still got to play.

"A third positive and you're done," Michelle said.

I looked her in the eye. "That's not going to happen. I *need* volleyball."

"You sure didn't show that commitment last night, Mr. Monroe. As a scholarship athlete, you represent Highbanks. Evading your government protection detail, running off to guzzle alcohol as a nineteen-year-old—that is *not* an image we want to portray. You need to get your act together."

"I will." I swallowed. "I promise. I'm very sorry."

After all of us signed the contract, she scooped it up and pushed off her chair. The rest of us stood as well. "Are your agents outside?" she asked.

"Yes."

"Good. I'd like to speak with them, make sure things are running smoothly. Anything else we need to cover?"

Phil cleared his throat. "There's a disciplinary issue we still haven't discussed."

"*Another* one? Do you need me to stay?"

"I think we can handle this on our own," Phil said.

My heartbeat surged at his ominous tone.

Once Michelle had left and we'd retaken our seats, the coaches stared at me as I fidgeted in my chair. I wove my shaking hands together to still them. "I, I want to apologize to both of you. Phil, I should've never cussed you out—"

"I don't mind your colorful language—it's part of your passion. As long as you don't let the officials hear it." His hand skated through his grey hair. "But I *won't* tolerate your lack of respect."

"Yes, sir." I hated that he'd questioned my respect. I had to do better. I turned to Jason. "And it was absolutely wrong of me to shove you."

Jason fumed. "Damn right it was!"

"I…I know you wanted to deck me right then. And I appreciate your self-restraint, Jason. You're a better man than I am." I watched his shoulders lower a half-inch as he sat back a bit in his chair.

"You've both treated me so well," I continued. "You put up with the stupid Secret Service, and you've given me every opportunity I could ask for. I definitely respect you, and you didn't deserve that from me."

"What the hell made you act like that, then?" Phil's eyes searched mine. "You've always channeled that fire of yours into the game, where it belongs, but this time you targeted *us?* We're on your side, Dane. We want to make you exceptional."

"I know." I looked down. "I messed up. I had an argument with my dad before practice, and I was so pissed off at him. I think I took my anger…and misdirected it onto *you*. Unfairly. I'm really sorry."

Phil nodded and was quiet for a moment. "I've never met your dad. What's he like?"

"He's a pompous prick."

"Whoa," Jason said as he cracked the first smile I'd seen from him all day.

"So I guess you'll have much to discuss with Dr. Valentine." Phil's eyes twinkled.

I sighed. "Played right into your hands, huh?"

His slight smile faded. "I meant what I said. You're under inordinate pressure, Dane. Anyone in your situation would need some support."

I nodded.

"And that's why I'm letting you return to practice. Today."

"Really?" I grinned.

"But don't think you're in the clear." Phil folded his arms across his chest. "You need to build back trust with us, and with the team. I think you're mature enough to suggest just how you'll do that."

When they kept staring at me, I rubbed my hands over my face. "I'm supposed to decide my own punishment?"

Jason nodded.

Ugh. This sucked. I couldn't float something too easy, or it would look like I was making light of my horrid behavior. But I didn't want to commit myself to consequences too hellish. "I guess you could make me run extra?" When they didn't respond, I added, "After practice, I could run sprints, or long distance…"

"What did you do this morning?" Phil asked.

"Ran at the park."

"How many miles?"

I shrugged. "About six."

Phil unclasped his arms. "Physical fitness has never been your weakness. Your work ethic is unparalleled on the team—it makes the guys want to follow you."

I never expected my coach to compliment me after how I'd treated him.

"Extra running won't do much for you. Give us some other way for you to rebuild our trust."

Crap. I tried to drum up ideas. He'd said fitness was my strength, but what were my weaknesses? I knew in an instant: pride and anger management. My cockiness had gotten me into quite a few scrapes throughout my life, which had then escalated due to my hot temper. I chewed on my lip. "Um, I could apologize to the team? Take responsibility for my blow-up?"

"Now we're talking," Phil said. "That would show leadership."

And cause humiliation.

"What else?"

He wanted more? My gaze drifted to his bookshelf. "And..." I couldn't believe I was about to suggest this. "I could learn about meditation, and teach it to the team?"

When Phil beamed, I knew I'd hit pay dirt. "Excellent idea. You can start by reading this one..." He reached behind him to pull a worn book off the shelf. "It's a primer on meditation by Jon Kabat-Zinn."

As I accepted the book, I noticed just how many mindfulness titles lined his bookshelf—this was clearly his wheelhouse.

"We'll see you in the locker room in fifteen for your apology."

"Uh, sure." My stomach twisted as we stood. I hadn't expected things to proceed so quickly. "Thank you, Phil. Thank you, Jason." I squared my shoulders. "This will never happen again."

After I hustled to dress for practice, the team gathered in the locker room. I stood next to my coaches with a suddenly dry throat. I shifted from one foot to another.

Jason raised his hand, and the guys got quiet. "Dane's got something he wants to say."

Shit...it's show time. "I...I want to apologize for my behavior yesterday." That sounded way too stiff. "I let my personal life interfere with my commitment to the team, and I behaved disrespectfully—in practice...and later." Still too formal, and not very heartfelt. A couple teammates looked uncomfortable, and the rest looked bored. I sighed. "In other words, I was a total dick."

A few laughs drifted toward me. When Josh stood, everyone stared at him. I wondered what he was up to as he lifted his hand to his mouth then tilted his head back—oh, no, he was miming drinking beer. Then he lowered his hand and gave his best stoner smile as he closed his eyes. In his cheesiest voice, he drawled, "God, I *looohhve* beer."

Laughs erupted in the locker room, and even the coaches cracked up. Everyone was laughing but me. When Josh opened his eyes and grinned, I couldn't help it—the bastard made me start laughing too.

In that moment, I knew the team had accepted me again. I was back.

17

Lucia

"You had quite a day yesterday, hmm?"

"Yes." I felt my cheeks warm and glanced away from Dr. Valentine to her bookcase. A framed photo of a grey, fuzzy cat perched atop shelves jammed with books.

"That's my cat, Annabelle," she explained.

I nodded. The cat was *huge*.

"She's, uh, plus-sized." I looked at the sport psychologist to find her grinning at me. "I think she might have binge-eating disorder." She waited a beat. "Do you have pets at home in Texas?"

"We have a cat, too." I imagined his soft, black fur spilling over my lap, making me sweat as I completed biology worksheets on a hot day. Then, if Alejandro entered the room, I'd feel the sharp prick of claws on my bare legs. "His name's Squinky."

"Squinky?" Her head tilted.

"Short for *Escuincle*, or Brat. My brother Alex named him that because he hisses at him all the time." I chuckled as I pictured Alejandro's scowl. "The Squinkster doesn't like my dad either, but he cuddles with me and my mom."

"How sweet—not many cats like to cuddle. So, Tina told me your mom came to the hospital to visit you?"

I nodded.

"She must have been worried about you passing out at practice."

I looked down. "She was."

"Is she still in town?"

"She had to get my brother Mateo back to school, so they left this morning."

"How old is Mateo?"

"Sixteen."

"Squinky doesn't like him either?"

I bit back a smile at hearing a classy professional like her repeat his ridiculous nickname. "Actually, Matty told me Señor Squink has resorted to sleeping with him, now that I'm not there."

"He must miss you."

"Squinky or Matty?"

"Both, I bet." She smiled. "You light up when you talk about Matty. You're closer to him than Alex?"

I paused and shifted in my chair. It was one thing telling her about my cat, but I knew my dad wouldn't want me to discuss the inner workings of my family with a liberal, which this psychologist *had* to be. "You said this is private, right?"

"Yes. You signed releases of information to the athletic trainer, team physician, and dietitian, to let me speak to them, but otherwise this stays between us."

"You can't talk to the media?"

Her eyes widened. "Hell, no! And if I did, you could sue me for breach of confidentiality."

That sounded okay.

"Lucia, I know you're under tremendous pressure and scrutiny. I realize you just met me, and you're forced to be here, to boot. Trust takes time to build, but I'm hoping this might become a safe space for you. A place you can be yourself, let it all unwind. Even if…" She gestured to the door. "Even if Secret Service is right outside in the hallway."

I rolled my eyes.

"How do you *do* it, by the way? I'd go nuts if I had agents shadowing me all the time."

"I…I did go nuts, I guess." I gestured around me at the therapy office.

She laughed. "You seem pretty clear-headed to me—not nuts at all. The way I see it, from the little I know, you're a hard-working athlete who simply wanted to get better at her sport. You wanted to please your coaches and everyone around you. And you thought losing some weight would help you reach that goal."

My heart fluttered as I stared at her. It was like she'd read my mind.

"Unfortunately, you took it too far. Athletes are extreme people… they really *go* for it when they set a goal. I mean, who else would *want* to practice five hours a day?"

She seemed to get my particular brand of insanity, that's for sure.

"How could *you* know what starving yourself would do to you? It's not like you wanted to collapse at practice. It's not like you wanted all this attention on you, with people thinking you're crazy for getting an eating disorder."

"Exactly!" I sat up in my chair, and my head bobbed with the satisfied beat of somebody finally understanding.

"The thing is, Lucia, you didn't need to lose weight in the first place."

I leaned back in my chair.

"I can tell you don't believe me. But Whitney shared your testing results with me—do you know your body composition?"

I shook my head and braced myself to hear the fat news.

"You have seventeen-percent body fat."

"Ugh." I cringed. *Ballena.*

"Why are you making that face? That number means you're quite lean. A normal range is twenty to thirty-two percent for women. With body fat that low, you shouldn't lose weight."

I stared at her, trying to discern why she would lie to me. "But I weigh the most on the team."

"Of course you do—you're one of the tallest and most muscular."

"But Coach said I was too fat to get to the double block fast enough."

Her eyes flared. "He will never say something like that to you again. And if he does, tell Tina or me. His job's riding on this."

I groaned. "He's going to hate me."

"No, he won't. Michelle from administration will make sure he treats you fairly. This goes way back before you, Lucia. Highbanks coaches aren't allowed to tell athletes to lose weight, but he's violated that rule countless times over the years. This is the last time."

Huh. I wasn't the only volleyball player he'd told to lose weight?

She studied me. "Let's look at the facts. The past few practices, before you hurt your ankle—an injury that might relate to malnutrition, by the way—how were you performing? You had lost some weight. Did you block better? Spike better?"

"Um..." I frowned. "Not really." My vertical leap had turned pathetic, actually.

"How was it going in the weight room?"

"My bench press sure sucked."

"Well, there you go—you saw it for yourself. If you lose weight, you can't selectively lose fat. You lose muscle, too. And with muscle loss comes a loss of power."

I absorbed that information.

"You want all the power you can get when you play Bridgetown, right?"

I chewed on my fingernail. "But we play them in a month. I'm not strong like I used to be."

"One month. Is that how long you've been restricting your food intake?"

"About."

"Listen, eating disorders aren't easy to recover from—I'm not going to bullshit you. But catching them early is key. Huh." She tapped her pen on her chair. "Now that I think about it, maybe the early identification is one good thing coming from this being leaked to the press."

I narrowed my eyes.

"Or maybe not." She smirked. "If you've only been restricting for one month, I'm pretty confident we can get you back to full strength relatively soon, hopefully by the time you play Bridgetown. It's going to take a lot of work on your part, though. Are you committed?"

"I *should* be committed."

"Ha, ha. That sense of humor will definitely help you through this. Now, tell me what you've eaten today."

Why did she want to know that? "Uh, well, for breakfast, Mom made me eat an egg burrito." I cringed.

"What's that face for?"

I pointed to my stomach, which seemed to be protruding. "It's still there, like, sitting there, ballooning my stomach."

"Delayed gastric emptying," she said. "Your digestive tract slows down when you're not eating regularly. The food sits there like an uncomfortable lump."

I nodded.

"Do you know the best way to get your metabolism clicking again?" When I shook my head, she said, "Small, frequent meals."

I groaned.

"So now that it's afternoon, what else have you eaten?"

"I had soup and salad that Allison, one of my agents, got for me."

"Did you finish both?"

I considered lying, but I thought she might know if I did. "No."

"Okay. Time for a snack, then." To my horror, she reached into a desk drawer and placed assorted three protein bars on the coffee table between us. "Pick one, and I'll eat one with you."

"I'm really not hungry."

She nodded. "I bet you're not. Your hunger signals are messed up right now, so you can't rely on them to tell you when to eat. Instead, you need to follow the meal plan Whitney gave you. We're not trying to make you fat—we just want to help you reach your goals. So, which flavor will it be?"

"Please, don't make me eat." My mind filled with chaotic noise as my vision swam with fattening bars. Peanut butter, oatmeal raisin, or blueberry? All of them looked disgusting. *You're fat. You're disgusting. You shouldn't eat. You have no self-control.*

"You can do this, Lucia. I'm here to support you."

Ay Dios mío, I was about to start crying. My throat tightened, and I tried to blink back tears. My chest trembled. *You're a fat slob.* This was so mortifying.

Her voice gentled. "It's okay if you cry. This is really tough stuff."

"It's just a stupid protein bar!" I felt tears on my cheeks. "I shouldn't freak out like this."

"I'd freak out, too, if I had mean thoughts shouting at me in my head. But this will get better with each day that you follow your meal plan." She held out the three bars. "You want to beat Bridgetown?"

That did it. I snatched a protein bar from her hands and grumbled as I peeled open the wrapper. *Cállate*, I told the fat voice. *Shut up*. Dr. Valentine took a bite of her bar and wrote something on her pad of paper. I nibbled on the sickeningly sweet oatmeal raisin bar. *¡Guácala!* It tasted like shit.

"Okay, guess a letter." She held out the notepad to me, and it took me a second to recognize the quick sketch of gallows and blank spaces for letters on the page.

"Hangman?"

"Yep, we're playing a game to distract you from the eating disorder thoughts. Go ahead and take another bite, then pick a letter."

She's crazier than I am.

After a series of turns, I guessed her phrase: *Bite it Bridgetown*. Then I wrote spaces for an eight-letter word. She supplied quite a few wrong guesses, and she only had one guess left before she would hang herself. I laughed at her scowl.

"No E, R, S, I, or L? You're killing me over here." Dr. Valentine tapped her forehead. "How about N?"

I nodded. Now the word was _ _ _ _ N _ _ _ .

Her forehead creased. "A?"

"Yep." *Drat*. Alejandro had beaten me with this word once, and I didn't want her to figure it out. Now it was A _ _ _ N _ _ _.

"D?"

I smirked as I hung her man.

"Damn it!" She tossed her brown hair over her shoulder. "I can't believe a freshman beat me. What the hell is this word?"

"It's autonomy."

Her mouth dropped open. "That was cruel, Lucia." She grinned as she reached for a small box and held it out to me. "But you get a sticker for finishing your protein bar. Excellent job!"

My heart rate spiked as I crumpled the empty wrapper in my hand. I'd eaten the whole thing? I hoped she didn't see my hand tremble as I accepted the box from her and flipped through the stickers.

"Autonomy's an interesting word. Why autonomy?"

"Um..." I selected a shiny star, and stuck it on my phone case. "It's what my family believes in...autonomy, self-reliance." I chewed the inside of my mouth as I looked at her. "We think people deserve to live their lives without government interference."

"Ah, that makes sense. Republicans believe in a smaller government."

I rubbed my finger over the sticker. "You're a Democrat, right?"

"What makes you think that?" She tilted her head.

"Because you're a psychologist. All psychologists are liberal."

She shrugged. "Not necessarily. What makes my political beliefs important to you?"

A realization dawned on me. "You're not going to tell me, are you?"

"Lucia, I'm not trying to be evasive, but my beliefs aren't really important here. What *is* important is that this is a nonjudgmental space—you can talk about anything, explore any idea, and I won't judge it. I support you. I want to help you find your own answers, which have nothing to do with my opinions or advice. What's right for me might not be right for you."

Though I was uncomfortable with the idea that she probably was on Dane's side, her words made me think that she valued autonomy too. *My* autonomy.

"So, how's your social life? Do you have some close friends?"

I didn't want to admit how lonely I'd been—it seemed pretty pathetic. "I've texted a couple of club teammates."

"Your volleyball club in Texas?"

"Yeah."

"Anyone you're growing close to here?"

"Um...It's kind of tough with Secret Service following me around."

"I can imagine that would be difficult."

"But Maddie Brooks—she's our captain—do you know her?"

Dr. Valentine paused. "I've certainly heard what an excellent athlete she is. Has she befriended you?"

"Well, she's a senior, and I'm just a freshman, so we don't hang out much, but she's been really cool." I thought back to a practice in August when Coach had screamed at me. "Early on I had a meltdown in the locker room after practice, and Maddie told me about *her* freshman year. She'd stayed up late studying the night before practice, and she couldn't stop herself from crying when Coach yelled at her. You'd think he would yell more when the tears came out, but instead he got all nervous, like he didn't know what to do—totally uncomfortable. He had Kara talk to her, and he kind of avoided Maddie after that. She said she's cried a couple more times since then and every time he freaks out and avoids her, but he's nicer afterward."

She shook her head. "He is an enigma of a man, isn't he?"

"Maddie told me if I'm at the end of my rope, about to lose it, just cry and he'll back off. But I haven't played my crying card yet."

"You seem proud of that."

I thought about it. Maybe I was a little proud. *You haven't broken me yet, Coach!*

"Maddie sounds like a keeper. Sometimes friends can offer more support when they know about the eating disorder. Does Maddie know?"

"*Everyone* knows now."

"Right." She grimaced. "Has she said anything to you about it?"

I chewed on my lip. "This morning at weights she said 'Rez, you're a total badass. You'll kick this thing, no problem.' Then she told me I was all muscle, and as the team captain, she forbids me to lose any more weight."

"Wow. She *is* a good friend. Do you think she could eat with you at team meals? Not to monitor what you're eating or anything, but to help keep the mood light. Maybe play Hangman or another game with you?"

"Maybe."

"Would you ask her?"

I considered that. "Okay."

"Again, this might be another unexpected advantage of your private life splayed over the national news. Typically it's nerve-wracking to 'come out' about your eating disorder to your friends and family. But you've already got it covered."

"Awesome."

She caught my sarcastic tone and laughed. "So, any friends outside the team?"

"There's one girl, Ellen, in my poli sci class—we've talked a few times."

"That sounds promising. Do you have much in common?"

"She said she's going to vote for my dad." When Dr. Valentine nodded, I added, "She told me she's glad I'm in the class, because that will make the professor less blatant about his liberal views."

"Really?"

"She told me to be careful what I say, or my grades might suffer."

"Whoa. I hope that's not true."

I tapped my foot on the floor, wondering what to say next.

"Are you feeling nervous?"

I willed my foot to stop tapping. "Yeah, I guess."

"Individuals who develop eating problems often suffer from high anxiety. Do you worry a lot?"

"All the time." *No te preocupes*, my dad would always say to me. *Don't worry, Lucy*. Too bad I couldn't stop stressing about everything, no matter how hard I tried.

"Do you experience times when your heart races, your chest tightens, and your body trembles?"

I nodded.

"When that happens, do you feel nauseated? Like you're out of your body?"

"Check and check. And I get all sweaty and gross."

"So you're experiencing panic attacks. When did you most recently experience one?"

I winced. "Did you happen to see that photo of me spiking the ball in *USA Today*?"

She paused. "No, but this morning Tina told me how the photo contributed to you starving yourself." Her mouth tightened. "I want to kick that photographer's ass for his indiscretion." She shook her head. "The good news is that panic attacks are quite treatable. Let's talk about how to handle them."

"Take deep breaths? Tell myself to float through it, and it will get better?"

Her eyes opened wider. "Exactly! Who taught you that?"

"Well..." I sighed as I imagined his deep voice over the phone... the sexy baritone of his laugh. Then I realized I hadn't had a panic attack since that day. "Dane did."

"Oh, Dane Monroe, your roommate." A hint of a smile played at one corner of her mouth. "The enemy."

"That's him." The gorgeous enemy. Who made a girl get an abortion. And who's been pretty kind to me. *Stop thinking about him.*

"How did Dane know about panic attacks?"

"He said he'd overheard his mom on the phone, talking to her patients who were freaking out. He called me right after I saw the photo, and he got me to calm down." Remembering that morning filled me with warm fuzzies. "I'm not sure how he knew to call me right then, but he really helped. I owe him one."

Dr. Valentine studied me. "That sounds quite sweet of him."

"He's not that sweet, really. Not most of the time."

"No?"

"He's cocky and righteous and inflexible and demanding and—"

She started laughing. "Tell me how you really feel, Lucia."

I blushed. I was being rude. "Sorry."

"No need to apologize for having strong feelings. I like it when you're being honest. Sounds like we have a lot to discuss in our next session, like your rooming situation and what it's like to be a Latina at Highbanks. It must be pretty different from Texas."

"*Sí.*"

She smiled, told me to find the Dove evolution video online for homework, and we scheduled for the following week. The only time we both had free was during my study tables, so I hoped that would be okay with my coaches. *Ugh.* I didn't look forward to seeing Coach Holter later. He hadn't been in his office when I'd passed by this morning after being unable to get Dane out of my head.

As I slung my backpack over my shoulder, I wondered about his fate.

18

Dane

As she came down the sports medicine hallway, I caught the shine of Lucia's glossy black hair a second before I noticed Allison's presence at her side. Lucia's long legs were taking her away from me—she looked hell-bent on getting out of here. I popped off my chair. "Lucia!"

She spun around and her eyes widened. "What're *you* doing here?" Her gaze darted to the other patients in the waiting room.

"Same thing as you, I guess." As I stepped closer, I felt Brad follow me. Lucia wore a shirt with the logo *Pretty in Pink... Wicked in Spandex.* I lowered my voice. "Mandatory counseling with Dr. Valentine."

"Oh." Her hand flew to her mouth, and her eyes crinkled as a little snorting sound escaped. "For your alcohol bender?"

"Don't laugh." I narrowed my eyes, though I was grateful to see her open up to me a little. "There are about one million places I'd rather be right now." Her bright smile made my day.

"I hear you. But she's not too bad. Just get her talking about her fat cat and the hour will fly by."

"Gotcha." My reward for winking at her was a soft bloom of pink on her face.

"Uh, um, so you get to stay on the team?"

I exhaled. "Yeah. Phil took pity on me."

"That's awesome news." She looked as relieved as I felt. Then she leaned into Allison as the agent whispered something in her ear. "Well, I gotta go." She squirmed. "I have to meet with the dietitian." A fake smile plastered her face. "*Fantástico*."

I knew how hard it was to swallow pride and deal with jacked-up emotions—we were both trying to figure that out. And only we knew the discomfort of salvaging our personal lives in front of three hundred million people. "You're doing great, you know."

She looked up at me with big, brown eyes, and I realized I'd surprised her by saying something nice. That wasn't right. Lucia hadn't deserved my initial goading simply because I disagreed with her father's politics—okay, and hers too. Apparently my problems with building trust weren't limited to my coaches—I had quite a few relationships to improve.

"Are you ready, Dane?" a female voice asked behind me.

I turned to find a solidly built woman with hazel eyes looking up at me, her hand extended. "Carly Valentine."

I swallowed as I reached to shake her hand. "Let's do this." I swiveled to face Lucia. "See you at home, sweetheart?" *Whoops, that just slipped out.*

She froze in place, and I'd never seen her face so flushed. Her cheeks almost matched the color of her hot pink shirt. Lucia's panicked eyes darted to Dr. Valentine, whose expression remained neutral, before she looked back at me. "Uh, yeah. I…better go. Bye!"

I watched her zoom off, and Allison almost had to jog to keep up with her.

"Shall we?" Dr. Valentine gestured to the entrance of the sports medicine office. I let her go first, and Brad introduced himself as we walked down the hall.

Once he'd checked out her office and planted himself outside the door, she turned to me and said, "You're probably familiar with how this works, since your mom's a psychologist, but I need to review informed consent anyway."

I nodded and signed a couple forms as she explained them. I wondered what Lucia had thought of all of this psychobabble.

"So, Dane…" She settled back in her chair with her pen poised over a notepad. "Why here, why now?"

"You know what happened yesterday, right?"

"Your beer video's had a lot of hits online, yes. You're quite the celebrity."

I closed my eyes and stifled a groan.

"But I want to hear from you about what's bringing you in."

"You mean, why I went on a rampage?"

"If that's what you call it." She shrugged.

"What the hell would *you* call it?"

She clicked her pen. "How about we back up a bit? How old were you when you started playing volleyball?"

This seemed like more comfortable territory. "Ten."

"You're a setter, right?"

I nodded.

"What do you love about volleyball?"

"Winning." She smiled but kept looking at me like she wanted more. I scratched my neck. "And, diving for a save. Setting the perfect ball." I pictured the old arena in my mind. "Acing a serve. Dumping the ball over the net when they least expect it." I was on a roll. "But the best part is when we're deep in the fifth game, and both teams are toast, our jerseys stick to us with sweat, and the coach calls a time-out—we're staring at each other in the huddle and it's like a total connection, total brotherhood...nobody knows who's gonna win, but we know we're gonna fight like rabid pit bulls, and the crowd's going nuts, my muscles tingle...then the ref's whistle blows, and it's time to unleash holy hell..." I noticed her smile widen. "What?"

"You got my heart pumping!" She placed a hand over her chest. "Sounds like you feel truly alive in that moment."

"Yeah. It's amazing." I looked away, silently cursing myself. "And I almost flushed moments like that right down the toilet."

"You thought you'd be dismissed from the team?"

"I was worried. Phil had already suspended me, then I pull that shit with the beer? I mean, how many chances will he give me? He's the best coach I've ever had, and I went and jeopardized the whole thing." I rubbed the lifeline of my palm as I sighed. "He kept telling me to come see you, and, like a jackass, I ignored him."

A line creased her forehead. "I'm trying to keep up, here. Michelle told me about the underage drinking, but you were suspended before that?"

"I thought Phil talked to you."

"Only the administrator calls me in these situations. What were you suspended for?"

"Anger management problems," I explained, accenting with air quotes. "I stepped over the line with my coaches."

"What happened?" When I didn't answer, she said, "You know, many athletes struggle with anger. We ask you to be ultra-aggressive in your sport, then expect you to just shut it down when you walk off the court. It's not that easy."

"I should know better."

"Why's that?"

"Because I'm not just a dumb jock."

"Clearly. What's your GPA?"

I shrugged. "It's an A average. But psychology research methods might bring me down this year."

"Every psych major's nightmare." She smiled knowingly. "What made you so angry that you acted out on your coach? You seem to respect him."

"What a relief to get that off my chest." My dad's smug face filled my mind, and I felt my right hand clench into a fist. "I can't say."

"You can't?"

"No." But I wanted to. *I* wanted to '*get that off my chest*' too. "Not when you're telling the AD and my coaches what I say in here."

"I have to report your attendance and overall progress to them, but not specifics." She studied me. "I realize you have unique security considerations with your mother's position, and I'll be extra careful with privileged information. Secret Service already briefed me this morning."

"They did?"

"I could get into a lot of trouble with the government if I leaked any information. But Dane, I would keep your secrets even without Secret Service calling me. That's what confidentiality is about."

I sighed. "I guess it helps that you're voting for my mother, too."

She blinked at me.

"*Aren't* you?" I sat forward on the sofa.

"How I vote is important to you?"

"Uh, *yeah*. I won't feel safe disclosing secrets to a crazy conservative."

"You seemed to feel pretty comfortable talking to Lucia out there."

"She's different."

"How so?"

"She's... *Wait* a minute! Are you telling me you're a fucking Republican?"

"I'm not telling you jack shit, Dane." She leaned forward. "My political beliefs aren't important right now. *Your* beliefs are. Your feelings, thoughts, behaviors—that's the focus here."

I crossed my arms over my midsection as I slumped back.

"Whether I share your political philosophy doesn't influence my ability to be a good psychologist for you. We may be different in many ways. For example, I'm not a guy, I'm not your age, and I don't play volleyball. I don't hear you questioning those things."

"Did anyone tell you you're a pain in the ass?"

"All the time." She relaxed in her chair. "Did anyone tell you you're blunt and feisty when somebody challenges you?"

I unfolded my arms. "All the time." We shared a small smile.

"I'm guessing this anger management issue that got you suspended is also related to your alcohol use. Is that right?"

"Yesterday was one giant clusterfuck, yes."

"So what started the clusterfuck?"

I liked how she swore—it felt like I was talking to a teammate. Though teammates were a hell of a lot more trustworthy since they wouldn't evaluate every word out of my mouth with laser-beam psychological insight. I jiggled my thigh as I studied her bookcase.

"You're a high-energy guy, aren't you?"

My thigh stilled. "I guess."

"Feel free to stand up, walk around as we talk."

"Really?" I'd itched to get off that sofa from the second I'd sat down. I hopped up and stepped over to check out her book collection. I noticed several titles my mother owned. As I thumbed through one of them, I asked, "What do you know about my dad?"

"Um, he's an artist, right?"

"A painter."

"I'm afraid I don't know much about him. He hasn't been in the news lately—I haven't seen him at your mother's campaign stops."

I blew air out my nose.

"That bothers you?"

I replaced the book and walked over to examine the posters of fall sports teams on her wall. The Highbanks volleyball poster featured the seniors on the team, including Maddie in an action shot blocking the ball. I noticed Bridgetown looming on the girls' schedule in October, and wondered if Lucia's parents would attend the match. I knew there'd be no way good ole Patrick would travel to watch me play Bridgetown next March. "My dad has basically ignored us the past year."

"You have a younger sister, right?"

"Jessica."

"You're angry and hurt your dad hasn't come to watch your games."

I turned to look at her, and she stared back at me. Feeling unnerved by her intuition, I returned to the sofa. "Is it okay if I lie down?"

"Fine with me, though your legs won't fit."

I stretched my body lengthwise, with my head on an overstuffed pillow resting up against one armrest, and my feet dangling over the opposite armrest. "It's okay, I'm used to it. I never fit." I watched her scribble something on the notepad. "What did you just write down?"

She paused. "I wrote, *He feels like he doesn't fit in.*"

"That's not what I said."

"You're right. I was just thinking how hard it is for you to be in the spotlight all the time—not only on the national stage, with your mother running for president, but also as one of the best athletes at a big sports school. And then there's your height. You must stick out like the Jolly Green Giant, only not so jolly, maybe."

I thought about her words. "It's *not* hard, most of the time. I like it, and I'm proud of my mom. I don't want to be average. I want to be exceptional."

"So you thrive on the attention most of the time. When is it not so great?"

"When I lose control in front of everyone." I smacked my forehead. "I've got to get my shit together."

"You get mad at yourself when you're not exceptional."

"Pretty much. That was so cliché of me to take out my anger on the wrong person. I should know better."

"Who deserved your anger?"

I sat up and rested my elbows on my knees. "You tell me, Dr. Valentine."

"You're challenging me." She grinned. "I like that. Based on what you've told me so far, I'd guess you were angry with your father for not being around, and you took that out on your coaches."

"Bingo. My head has now been shrunk. Can I go now?"

"You hate being here, huh?"

"I don't…" I exhaled. "I don't hate it, and I'm not mad at you." I punched the pillow. "I hate talking about my dad, though."

"What do you notice inside of you right now?"

"What do you mean?"

"Where in your body do you notice your anger? Is your heart beating fast? Your stomach clenched?"

I held still for a moment. "Yeah. My face feels hot, and my mind, it's going really fast."

"What color is your anger?"

I thought for a moment. "Scarlet."

"What is its shape?"

"It's, um, like lava. But not oozing—it's racing through my body. And when I think about my dad, the lava explodes." I flicked my hands up, fanning them out over my head. "I want to destroy shit."

"Nice job. That's a vivid image. The more you know about your anger, the more you can manage it."

"My anger makes me out of control. I don't *want* to know more about it."

"You want to get rid of your anger. Obliterate it."

"Yeah."

"And that's where alcohol comes in."

I froze. How did she know I was craving a drink right then? "You're trying to get me to admit I'm an alcoholic. I don't drink to numb my emotions. I drink for fun—to celebrate good times."

"First of all, I don't believe you're an alcoholic, and labels like that aren't helpful anyway. Secondly, you didn't seem to have a good time when you drank with that reporter."

I scowled. "I can't believe she secretly filmed that." *Fox News Bitch.*

"Well, she did get her comeuppance."

"She did?"

Dr. Valentine tilted her head. "You didn't hear? She got fired, and she's facing criminal charges for buying alcohol for a minor."

Whoa. Despite my fury, I felt guilt squeeze my chest. I'd been the one goading her to buy me beer.

"Shit just got real, huh?" She smirked at me.

I glared at her. "Are you saying it's *my* fault she got fired?"

"Not at all. That reporter's an adult who made an adult choice to break the law in order to get a story. But there *are* negative consequences from your drinking. You wouldn't be here otherwise."

I said nothing.

"Repeating a behavior despite negative consequences—do you know what that's called?"

Addiction. "I'm not an addict."

"Good to hear. Prove it to me and your coaches, then."

Frustration simmered in my gut. *I hate this shit.* Therapy wasn't so bad, though I should be the one asking the questions, not the one answering them. But I was tired of my jackhole behavior. *I just want to play volleyball, go to class, and be done with it. Why do I get myself into these situations?*

"You look angry."

I clenched my teeth. "Shocker."

"I'd be angry too if I had to face feelings I'd rather keep buried."

A few seconds went by as I fidgeted on the sofa. "So why face them, then?"

"Because suppressing feelings gives them more power. You can't just get rid of feelings, no matter how hard you try. Alcohol, other drugs, eating disorders, gambling...they're all an effort to squelch negative emotion. They provide temporary relief, but then the emotion comes roaring back."

I thought of Lucia and me. Were we both suppressing emotions we didn't want to face?

"But they're just feelings. They can't hurt you. Trying to suppress them—*that's* what can hurt you. If you acknowledge feelings and deal with them effectively, they can help you."

"No way anger can help. It always screws things up for me."

"I think you're confusing anger and aggression." She studied me. "Anger is a healthy feeling we all experience, whether we're aware of it or not. Anger can help by communicating our needs. For example, if I feel angry, that might be a sign my rights are being stepped on, and I need to assert myself. Think about it for a second...how does your anger help you?"

I felt my eyebrows draw together. "I got pissed off when Bridgetown beat us last year...and I guess it motivated me to work out extra hard this summer."

"Yes, feelings can motivate behavior. Anger the feeling is normal and healthy. Aggression the behavior is not okay. Yelling, name-calling, and violence can hurt others."

Lucia's wounded eyes filled my mind—one of many times she'd reacted to my insults about her father.

"Looks like you're doing some thinking over there."

I realized I'd been quiet for a few moments. "I'm an aggressive asshole."

She laughed. "Now *that* doesn't sound fair. Just because you've behaved aggressively doesn't make you an aggressive person. And you need to be aggressive on the court."

I frowned.

"Let's talk about effective ways to deal with your anger off the court, besides drinking alcohol or lashing out. You already know about diaphragmatic breathing, right?"

"Yes." I remembered teaching it to Lucia when she freaked out.

"Have you heard of paced breathing?"

I shook my head.

"It's when your exhale is longer than your inhale. Paced breathing actually slows your heart rate. Let's take some breaths where you inhale to a count of two and exhale to a count of four." She nodded at me.

I humored her by practicing. *One, two...* I held my breath a moment, then breathed out *One, two, three, four*. I was surprised I still had breath left at the end of the long exhale. *One, two...one, two, three, four.*

"What do you notice when you practice paced breathing?"

"Uh...my mind slows down, I guess."

"Yes, and a clear mind helps you avoid acting like an 'aggressive asshole.'" She smiled. "Your self-talk—how you coach yourself in your mind—is also important in managing anger. Have you studied Albert Ellis in your psych classes yet?"

"A little bit...he's a cognitive therapist."

"Right. He found that 'should' statements increase anger. Shoulds are unwritten rules or expectations that we might want to be true, but aren't necessarily true. Earlier you said 'I should know better.' How'd you feel when you thought that?"

"Ticked off at my stupidity."

"So the 'should' statement increased your anger. But where's it written that you *should* know better? You wish you could have avoided repeating the same mistake, but we humans often do just that. It's not true that you should know better. It is true that you'd *prefer* you made another choice. You wish you'd acted differently. When you say 'should,' you're shoulding all over yourself."

I groaned. *Total cheeseball.*

"When you hear the word 'should,' challenge it with 'want' or 'prefer' and your anger will decrease."

I wondered if I could do that.

"What are some other should statements you believe? How about 'The government should take care of people'?"

"That's not a belief. That's truth."

"That's a philosophy, Dane." She shook her head. "It's no different from the other side believing 'People should take care of themselves.' They're both valid beliefs."

I huffed, "But I agree with that too, to a point. People should take care of themselves, but sometimes they're oppressed and need the government's help. They shouldn't have all these roadblocks to getting the help they need."

"I'm not questioning your philosophy. What I'm saying is that 'shoulds' increase anger so much that people have trouble discussing different points of view." She sat back in her chair. "You're living with somebody who has polar-opposite political beliefs. How's that going?"

I hesitated. "Did Lucia talk about me? What'd she say?"

Dr. Valentine's expression remained placid. "I'm not at liberty to discuss other athletes I may or may not be seeing."

What a joke for her to pretend Lucia wasn't her client—she'd run into us together in the waiting room!

"Hopefully my silence will reinforce my promise that I won't disclose any of *our* conversation to others."

Oh. That made sense. I didn't want Lucia to know about any weaknesses I revealed in here, especially if I decided to tell Dr. Valentine about my father's affair.

"With all the should statements in your head, how have you been able to manage your anger? How well do you let mistakes go?"

A lump lodged in my throat as I considered my long line of mistakes—my harsh words, stretches of provoking Lucia, and most of all, the abortion. "Not great. And I think Lucia hates me."

"You sound so sad when you say that."

I swallowed as I looked away from her sympathetic eyes. Maybe I *was* just like my father—hurting those I cared for, thinking only of myself.

"You know, Dane...*hate* implies strong emotion. I'll take hate over indifference any day."

"Are you saying I still have a chance with her?"

One eyebrow arched. "Do you want one?"

Hell, yes. And I hadn't realized how much until she asked me that. Was it too late to salvage things between us?

19

Lucia

My stomach dropped as Coach Holter called us into a huddle. I'd been seeing Dr. Valentine for a while now—it was already October!—and though she'd encouraged me to take deep breaths during our little team "chats," I still stressed out about them. Maddie had just hit the ball into the net right after I'd hit the last two sets out of bounds, and the rest of my teammates weren't exactly killing it this practice either. I braced myself for an epic tongue-lashing.

Instead, Coach said, "I can tell by your tired play that midterms are this week."

I'd had two today. My biology test had gone okay, but I wasn't sure about the political science exam.

Coach folded his arms across his chest. "Get out of here, go study, and get some rest tonight."

We stood there for a long moment, stupefied, before he jabbed his finger toward the locker room. "Out of here!"

I shared a surprised grin with Kaitlyn as we jogged to grab our water bottles.

"Lucia."

As I swiveled back to Coach, I gulped. I knew his kindness had been too good to be true.

He approached me with his typical hard-set jaw and piercing gaze. "I want to talk to you about your nutrition meetings."

I'd been seeing Whitney and Dr. Valentine for a month, but this was Coach's first mention of those sessions. My shoulders tensed.

"I hear you're making good progress. Excellent job."

"Um, thanks." My voice shook.

"You're looking stronger out there. Keep it up." He turned and walked toward his assistant coach. "Kara! Cue up Bridgetown's latest game video. I want to figure out their service patterns."

I stood alone in the middle of the gym floor. My breath quickened as I looked down at my thighs. Everyone knew "stronger" was code for "fatter," and I tugged my Spandex down an inch to hide the rolls of fat.

"Hey." Allison's voice startled me. She stepped closer. "Are you having a rough body image day?"

With a forced exhale, I nodded.

"Remember, you're not seeing reality. You look great. Now let's get out of here like Coach said, okay?"

I forced a smile. "Okay."

Twenty minutes later, we zoomed away from the gym. "Coach needs to let you guys out early more often," Frank said from the driver's seat. "It's easier to make a getaway without those media dogs hounding us."

"For sure." Chilled from the cool October rain now pelting the vehicle, I tugged my warm-up jacket tighter across my chest. Any night without my media stalkers was a good night. Still feeling unsettled from my chat with Coach, I took out my mp3 player. Neil Diamond's "Sweet Caroline" always brightened my mood.

When we pulled up to the greenhouse, I took out my earbuds.

"Go on in, Lucy," Allison said as she looked down at her phone. "Frank and I need to coordinate travel plans for this weekend."

I jogged through the rain as I groaned about more out-of-town matches in my near future. All the volleyball travel had blended together in a blur the past month. On the plus side, our match at Penn State had interfered with the first debate, so I didn't have to squeeze that travel into my busy schedule. On the down side, we'd played matches in Oregon on my birthday, making that a non-event. But my dad had promised we would celebrate my nineteenth year after the election.

I was also starting to miss Dane when I went out of town. His gentle smiles and sweetness the past month had confused me, especially after he'd been such a *pendejo* my first days at Highbanks. But once I began opening up to him again, I'd discovered he was cool to hang out with—not to mention still hot, of course. Maybe we were learning how to move past our differences?

Brad met me at the door. "You're home early." He glanced over his shoulder and, when his eyes returned to me, seemed anxious.

"Damn, she's *hawt*," China said. It sounded like her voice came from the TV room. "Especially when she's pissed off."

Dane's deep laugh rippled into me. "You do like the blond ones."

What were they watching? I studied Brad, who wouldn't meet my eyes.

"I like Maria better," Dane said. "She's *caliente*."

My breath caught at the back of my throat. Just who was this Maria? I pushed past Brad to the TV room. Sprawled on the sofa with a half-empty tub of popcorn between them were my roommate and his agent, both too absorbed in the onscreen action to notice my arrival.

I watched as a raven-haired actress dabbed her tears with a tissue.

"*Stay away from my husband, bitch*," the blond actress hissed at her.

Dane gasped. "No, she did-ent."

"Oh, Maria completely deserved that!" China retorted. "She's a total ho."

I couldn't believe what I was witnessing. I marched closer to the TV. "You're watching a *soap opera?*"

"Shit!" Dane scrambled off the sofa, his eyes flashing surprise. "You're home early."

China paused the recorded show and stood as well. "Don't knock it till you try it. This show is addicting."

"Hey, my mom watches *telenovelas* all the time," I said. "I just never expected *you*—" I smirked at Dane. "Or *you*—" I pointed at China. "To watch this stuff."

Dane looked away. Was this the first time I'd seen him blush? It was definitely the first time he'd been speechless in my presence.

"Why aren't you still at practice?" China asked.

"Coach let us out early."

Dane whirled to look at me. "Did you collapse again?"

"No." I leaned back, feeling offended. "Why would you say that?"

"You're obviously lying. Coach Holter *never* ends practice early."

"Well, hell froze over, 'cause he did let us go. When monkeys fly, or whatever."

Dane's concern seemed to morph into amusement. "I think you mean 'when *donkeys* fly,' not monkeys."

I smiled. "In my family, we don't use the word *donkey*."

"Ugh." He rolled his eyes. "*Republicans.* Like elephants are any better?"

"Elephants are majestic animals!"

"The correct expression is when *pigs* fly," China said. "It's not about donkeys or elephants. You two argue about everything. I feel like I'm living with an old married couple." She walked past us out of the room.

Dane and I looked at each other for a second, then quickly looked away. *I can't believe she just said that!*

"So, um..." Dane stretched his back and cracked his neck from side to side. "If I make you dinner, will you promise not to tell anyone about the show you caught me watching?"

He wanted to make me dinner? My heart twittered with joy, then thudded with fear. *Dinner.* "You know how I feel about eating. Is food supposed to *entice* me to keep your secret?"

"Oh." He winced. "I wanted to do something nice for you, but obviously I wasn't thinking. You, um, you seem to be getting better..."

"Why'd you want to do something nice for me?"

He shrugged. "Late birthday dinner, I guess." One corner of his mouth slowly lifted. "A bipartisan celebration, a week before the final debate."

"Well, if you put it that way, I guess it'd be okay if you cooked dinner for me."

"Really?"

"I don't want to be from the 'party of no.'"

He smiled as he reached for my hand and led me to the kitchen. "I'd planned to finish cooking by the time you got home, but now you can be my sous chef."

He'd planned to cook me dinner? That was so adorable. His hand cradling mine felt amazing, and I hoped he couldn't detect my trembles of excitement.

Dane set a cutting board on the counter and parked me in front of it. "Here you go." He slowly handed me a huge knife. "I know conservatives have a love affair with guns…how do you feel about knives?"

How does that charming smirk work every time? He made it nearly impossible to keep my guard up. I pointed the Ginsu at him. "Keep up the snark, and you're about to find out."

"Whoa!" His hands shot up, and his eyes danced. "Cut the food, not the defenseless Democrat." A few bell peppers and an onion plopped on my board. "I want thin strips."

"*Oui*, Chef." I curtsied and began slicing sections off the red pepper, avoiding its seedy core. "Is the sous chef allowed to know what we're preparing?"

His head popped out of the fridge, and I noticed he held tortillas and a bowl of chicken marinating in some sort of sauce. "Your favorite."

My knife paused mid-slice. "How'd you know fajitas were my favorite?"

"I, uh…" His second blush of the night! "I sort of texted Mateo."

"You texted my *brother?* How'd you even know his number?"

"We exchanged numbers when he was here with your mom. He liked the music I was playing, and he seems like a cool kid. Well, nicer than Alejandro, anyway."

My face felt hot, and I returned to chopping to conceal my inevitable blush. Not only had he asked about my favorite meal, he'd planned to make it for me? Was it possible he liked me as much as I liked him? Glancing at my fat, sausage fingers clasping the knife, I knew that wasn't likely. And the abortion thing still never really left my mind. How could he have killed that baby? Our values were too different for a romance. We'd barely found our way to being friends.

His hip bumped mine. "Earth to Lucia."

Over the pungent tang of red onion I smelled his clean, soapy scent, and my heart thumped wildly. I knew Alejandro wouldn't approve of my physical reaction to Dane—or anyone with beliefs so different from mine, actually. "Matty *is* much nicer than Alex, you're right."

I dared to look up at him, and a line creased his brow, as if my response had disappointed him.

"Thank you for making my favorite meal," I added. "It means a lot to me."

He stared at me for a few more seconds, then nodded. As he left my side and squatted to retrieve a frying pan, I stared at his taut butt encased in charcoal grey workout pants. My eyes zipped back to the cutting board when he rose, and I tried to think of something to say. "I get to meet your sister next week, right?"

The muscles in his forearm rippled as he added some oil to the pan. "Yep, Jess will be there."

"What's she like?"

He shrugged. "Sixteen, smart, pain in the ass." He added the chicken breasts to the sizzling oil. "She's always at swim practice, so she's tired and grumpy all the time." His nose scrunched. "She *reeks* of chlorine."

Belying his critical words was his fond smile, which stretched into a grin when he said, "I think she has a crush on one of Mom's agents."

"Really?" I laughed.

He snorted. "Poor guy. Jess is the determined type."

"Like her brother, huh?"

The depth of blue in his eyes made my breath catch in my throat. "I'd say we're both pretty determined." He held my gaze as the chicken crackled in the pan.

I was certainly determined to stay next to him for as long as possible, and I swallowed but didn't look away. The moment lengthened between us, timed by the pulsing metronome of my heartbeat. Was it getting warm in here? I unzipped my hoodie and hung it on a kitchen chair.

When Dane stared at my boobs, my heart raced.

"We like to spike," he said with a smile, and I realized he'd just read my T-shirt. "Where'd you get all those shirts?"

Oh, he wasn't staring at my boobs. Wait…*why* wasn't he staring at my boobs? "My dad buys them for me."

He nodded, and for once he didn't make a mean comment about my dad. "Are you *finally* done chopping?" He gestured to my cutting board.

"Jeez!" I returned my attention to the last pepper. "Just a second, Chef."

"You can work on the lettuce and tomatoes next, slave."

"So bossy." I smiled to myself.

A few minutes later he piled the cooked chicken breasts on top of each other on a plate and molded aluminum foil over them to keep them warm. The kitchen smelled so good. I paused my tomato chopping to hand him the strips of peppers. "Do you know where the word *fajita* comes from?"

He finished sliding the vegetables into the pan. "Little *fajas*, right? Only…I hate admitting this, but I don't know what *faja* means."

"It's a belt, or strip." I pointed to the peppers in the pan.

"Yummy." He stirred the peppers, then bellowed, "Fried belts for dinner tonight!"

A second later Brad meandered into the kitchen, rubbing his belly. "Did you say something about dinner, GD? It smells awesome in here!"

"This is for Lucia and me," he said.

I looked down at the bowls of fixings I'd prepared. "This *is* a lot of food."

Dane frowned. "Fine. Dinner will be ready in fifteen."

"Hey." Brad thumped him on the shoulder. "Sorry, man…we won't crash your party." He strolled out of the kitchen.

I chewed my lip as I dolloped sour cream into a bowl. I would *not* be eating any of that lardaceous goo. "So, why do you like Maria?"

"Huh?" He turned to me.

"The soap opera actress. What makes her attractive?"

His gaze slid down the side of my head. "Her hair. It's long and…shiny."

Self-consciously, I twirled a strand of my hair. Dane's eyes followed my fingers.

"And, um…" He rubbed the back of his neck. "She's kind of shy and sweet." His eyes traveled to my face, then he grabbed the package of tortillas and turned back to the stove. "I think the actress is from Puerto Rico. She's just pretty, I guess."

Once the tortillas were warming in the oven, Dane pulled out some ranch dressing. He winced as he set it on the counter. "I'm not a fajita purist—I use ranch instead of sour cream."

"So does Matty!" I grinned. "It drives Alejandro nuts."

"Good to know I'm not a freak."

"Oh, you're still a freak."

His eyebrow arched, but he didn't seem mad. He surveyed the spread and sighed. "Margaritas would go really well with this." His shoulders slumped.

"Is it hard?" He looked at me. "Not drinking, I mean."

"Nope." He'd rushed his response, and he paused, like he realized he hadn't been honest. "If I say yes…that means I have a problem, right?"

It was rare to see him vulnerable like this. "It just means you're strong. It means you're fighting."

He seemed to stand an inch taller. "What do you think of Dr. Valentine?"

"She's pretty cool." I thought about her for a moment, then scowled. "Except for the times she makes me eat."

"Yeah. I was pissed when she made me do an alcohol swab test."

I recoiled. "What's *that?*"

"She had me swab the inside of my mouth to test for alcohol in my saliva. I told her I hadn't partied, but she said she still had to test me." His eyebrows pulled together. "I wish she'd trust me."

"Trust—" I started, and he joined me to finish Dr. Valentine's platitude, "—takes time to build."

When we both laughed, I noticed his face relax, and his eyes shone like ocean waves. Were *we* building trust? Could I trust him?

He took a step closer, smiling down at me, and I froze. Maybe I forgot to breathe. Was he about to kiss me again? That's what I wanted, right? Then why did I feel so scared? Why didn't I feel ready? "Um…" I looked at the counter. "How 'bout I tell the agents dinner is ready?"

The crease returned to his forehead. "Yeah. Yeah…sure." He turned his back and grabbed an oven mitt to take out the tortillas.

As I skittered toward the agents' bedrooms, my heart felt heavy. I knew I'd let him down. Why couldn't I just say what I wanted to him? *What do I want?* Why was it always so complicated?

Three of four bedrooms were empty, but I heard a rustling behind China's slightly open door. I pushed it open. "Hey, Dane cooked fajitas if you want—"

China's head appeared from under the covers, and I blanched when I noticed she was topless.

"Sorry!"

Then a movement beneath the duvet rolled toward the headboard. I saw a flash of blond curls a second before Allison's face emerged next to China's.

"Oh!" I stepped back. Allison's eyes might have been even wider than mine. "I..." *Mierda.* I closed my mouth, and swallowed. "I just..." I spun on my heel, determined to get the hell out of there.

"Wait!" Allison's voice was higher than normal. "Will you tell your father about this?"

"What?" I inched back another step and felt my heart squeeze in my chest. Why would she care about that?

"Of course she won't," China said as she tossed the covers down and pushed off the bed to stand nude in front of me, in all of her muscular glory. Her breasts were round and perky, surrounded by pectoral muscle. She didn't seem embarrassed at all, but I was literally dying. "We aren't on duty."

Allison shook her head as she pulled the duvet up under her chin. "That's not what I'm worried about."

I pursed my lips, trying to figure out that comment.

"Ohhh." China grinned, then kneeled on the mattress and climbed up the bed. "Governor Ramirez might not approve of same-sex sex."

I looked away from her butt dancing in the air but the sound of a wet kiss was unmistakable. And *that* was my cue to leave. I rushed out of the room and raced down the hall—I couldn't get to my bedroom fast enough.

¡Dios mio! I plunged back on my bed and pressed my hands against my skull. I'd never walked in on a man and woman having sex before, much less two women. Why hadn't I just knocked? I thumped my fist to my forehead several times. *Estúpida.*

"Lucia?" Dane knocked on my door.

I sat up. "What?"

"Where'd you go? The food's getting cold."

I didn't know what to say. I couldn't let him find out I'd walked in on China and Allison. *Way* too embarrassing.

After a few moments passed, he asked, "Can I come in?"

I tossed my hair over my shoulder and stood. *Crap.* "Uh, sure." I grabbed the knob and found him filling the doorway.

"Are you okay?"

"Yeah, I'm fine."

"Do Allison and China want to join us?"

"Um..." I looked away as my cheeks lit on fire.

"Listen, if you don't want to eat dinner with me—"

"No, I do! I really do. I just, ah, I just need a moment..."

I watched a fully dressed Allison come up behind Dane. "Lucia?"

Dane swiveled. "Oh, hey. Are you guys going to eat with us? Did Lucia come find you?"

I sure did find them. Mortifying!

"Are we cool?" Allison asked me.

What should I say to that? I tilted my head.

Dane looked back and forth between us. "What's going on?"

"Lucia, I need to know if I should start looking for another job."

My chest tightened, and my mind went blank. Why did she keep hounding me? How could she think my dad would be so cruel? I just needed everyone to leave me alone!

"What the fuck happened?" Dane asked, his hands perched on his hips.

"Lucia walked in on us," China explained. She came up behind Allison, thankfully dressed in a robe. "And evidently it was a surprise for her."

I cringed. Now he knew.

As an understanding dawned on Dane, a smile stretched his mouth, followed by a few chuckles. "You walked in on them having sex?"

I squeezed my eyes shut, which only elicited more laughter from the *cabrón*. Deep belly laughs filled the hallway. "I wish I could've seen the look on your face!" He slapped the wall. "Hell, I wish *I* would've been the one to walk in on them."

"You're an ass, Monroe," China said.

"You've never seen lesbians get it on?" he asked me.

I hadn't seen *anyone* 'get it on,' but I wasn't about to admit *that.*

"Lucia." Allison blinked at me. "Are you going to tell your father?"

"No, okay?" My voice came out louder than I'd intended. "I don't know why you keep asking me that—I won't tell him. It wouldn't matter anyway."

China exhaled loudly. "I guess I have to spell it out for you. Allison needs to know if your dad will get her fired once he finds out she's a lesbian."

My lips parted. "He wouldn't do that! He knows I like Allison."

"He's hardly the champion of gay rights," China replied.

I hesitated. Our church had taught us that being gay was sinful, but I knew Dad would never get Allison fired just for that.

"What do you think, Lucia?" Allison's worried eyes bored into me. "Do *you* support gay marriage?"

"I..." My heart hammered. I'd always agreed with my family that marriage should be between a man and a woman, but it felt wrong to say that in front of them. Allison had been good to me, and I didn't want to hurt her feelings.

"Are you homophobic like your father?" China demanded.

I glanced at Dane, who'd been surprisingly quiet through this interrogation. I didn't know why he hadn't jumped on the bandwagon to accuse me of prejudice as well.

He reached out and patted my shoulder with his warm hand. "You look kind of freaked out."

I nodded.

He turned to the agents. "Guys, give her a second. She's overwhelmed. Let me talk to her."

The next thing I knew, Dane had pushed me into my bedroom and closed the door behind him.

20
Dane

I guided Lucia to her bed and waited for her to sit before plopping down on the desk chair across from her. "Do you want to take a few deep breaths?"

She nodded, and I gave her some time to collect herself as she perched on her light yellow comforter. She'd made her bed—something I rarely did. In fact, her entire room was neater than mine. A faint scent of lavender, with maybe a twinge of lemon, floated in the air.

"So *that's* not something you see every day, huh?"

She looked up at me, and her eyes crinkled as she gave me a grateful smile. "Definitely not."

Allison was probably pacing her room, worried about unemployment, and my jaw clenched thinking about the unfairness of it all. But I'd seen enough of Lucia to know she wouldn't intentionally hurt another person, and yelling at her wouldn't solve anything anyway. I tried to figure out a way to talk about gay rights without initiating a shouting match.

"Before Allison, have you ever known anyone who's gay?"

She twisted her hands together. "I don't think so."

I shook my head. "How is that *possible?* Ten percent of the population is gay!"

She scooted back on the bed, away from me, and I blew out a breath. *Chill, amigo.* "No gay or bisexual teammates? High school classmates?"

"I…I think there were a few students at my school who were maybe gay—I was too busy with my club team to get to know them."

"But they weren't out?" I couldn't imagine that. It had seemed *de rigueur* to be gay or bi at my private school.

She swallowed.

Then it hit me. "Your school was Catholic."

"Yes."

"So it probably wasn't cool to be out." *Judgmental jerks.* I sat on my hands. "And how does, um, your religion…how does that influence your beliefs?"

Her lips pressed into a taut line. "Why do you want to know? So you can tell me how stupid I am?"

"No! I'm really trying here, Lucia. I'm trying to discuss this calmly."

"Why?" Her eyes seemed weary, weighed down by suspicion and hurt.

Okay, I deserved that. I deserved her mistrust after how I'd treated her at first. And she deserved an explanation for my attempted suppression of the jerk who got off on riling her up—for me trying not to act like Mr. Arrogant Asshat the Third. "Liberalism is about being open-minded—"

"Right," she scoffed.

"—but I know I haven't been open-minded when it comes to your beliefs."

She looked away as she folded her arms across her chest.

"I want to do better. I want to understand why you think the way you do, because…" When her gaze returned to me, my throat tightened. *Don't fuck this up.* "Because I felt like shit when I was mean to you. I swear I don't intend to be such an asshole, but I got so mad about your dad's positions that I ended up making assumptions and spewing all over you, and you don't deserve that. Not at all."

She stared at me for a few moments. "I guess I haven't been very nice to you, either."

That comment puzzled me—she was one of the sweetest people I'd met—but it also encouraged me to keep going. "You've hardly been as aggressive as me, just a little quiet from time to time." I looked at her pointedly, trying to raise a smile.

She rubbed her hands over her arms.

"Are you cold? Want me to get your sweatshirt from the kitchen?"

"That's okay." She grimaced, then blew out a breath, seeming to brace herself. "To answer your question, my church says marriage should be between a man and a woman. It's from the Bible."

I gritted my teeth. "Okay, but not everyone believes in the Bible."

"I get that. But being a Catholic means I don't get to pick and choose what to follow. I have to follow the scripture."

"But that's exactly my point!" I realized my voice had risen, and I struggled to tamp down my intensity. "The Bible also says women should cover their heads, right?" I gestured to her lush hair. "Yet here you are without your hoodie, woman." I smirked. "A hoodie-less heathen."

I'd meant to lighten the mood, but the look in her eyes was far from jovial. "So my faith is some joke to you?"

"Nooo." I groaned in frustration as my palms scoured my cheeks.

"Do you believe in God, Dane?"

I paused. "Maybe." When her eyes widened, I rushed to add, "I definitely believe in a higher power. I just don't know what form that power takes. I'm still figuring it out."

"But your mother said your family goes to church every Sunday."

My mother said a lot of things, just like Lucia's father surely did, to garner votes. "We did, as kids. I guess it never took. Anyway, my psych professor said it's healthy to question at our age."

"But how do you sleep at night, if you don't believe in God?"

"How do *you* sleep at night, thinking your religion is right and everyone else is wrong?"

"That's not what I'm saying." She sighed. "That came out too judgey, *lo siento*. What I'm really asking is how you feel any peace if you don't have faith. My faith is everything to me, and I don't know how to survive without it."

She seemed so sure of herself and her so-called faith that for a moment I wished I could have that surety as well. I jiggled my foot. "How are you so certain God exists?"

She drew back. "I…I've never thought about it before…I just always *knew*…"

She'd never questioned what Daddy Adolf had told her?

"Love," she finally said, her eyes flaring. She pressed a hand against her chest. "I get this feeling of love in my heart when I think of God. He's there to guide us, take care of us, but mostly to love us." She blinked at me earnestly. "Do you feel it?"

Yes. Her eyes gleamed with such conviction that I wanted to sweep her in my arms, our differences be damned. But how would she respond if I kissed her like I wanted to? Would she push me away, like she'd done in the kitchen?

After moments ticked by, I knew she was waiting for an answer, so I said, "I want to feel that love. But it's not that simple." I sighed, unsure if I was talking about our messed-up relationship or our religious differences. I opted to continue down the less treacherous path. "If Christians were all about love, maybe I could get on board. But your religion seems more about hate to me."

She drew in a sharp breath. "*Hate?* How are you getting that out of the Christian message?"

"You're telling people like Allison they're not worthy."

"I didn't say that! We're all sinners, but we're all worthy in God's eyes. And I like Allison—she's a good person. I wouldn't want something bad to happen to her."

"But what if something bad *does* happen to Allison or China? Without legal marriage, they couldn't get survivor benefits."

She paused. "I actually agree with you on that." Her nose wrinkled up adorably. "Don't tell anyone, but I've been working on my dad, trying to get him to support civil unions. I think he's starting to come around."

"But that's not what gay people want! They want the right to marry, just like heterosexuals. Though why they want to join that destroyed institution is beyond me." I grimaced, thinking of my parents. "Straight people who divorce like four times then have the balls to tell gay people *they* can't marry? Total hypocrites."

"I agree on that, too. Divorce sucks." She ran her hand down her long thigh, and tugged at her leggings. "I'm glad my parents are still married."

"You're one of the lucky ones, then."

Her eyes searched mine. "What do you mean by that? Your parents are happily married, too."

I hoped she couldn't hear my pounding heartbeat. She, more than anyone, couldn't know my parents' marriage was a sham. When I didn't answer, she kept speaking.

"My dad said divorce and single parenting have caused a lot of problems for America."

Stop talking about divorce!

"Single parenting in minority homes leads to crime, school dropout, unemployment..." She ticked off each issue on her fingers. "The downfall of the family has hurt our country, and we need to get back to family values."

"What, like the wife barefoot and pregnant, two-point-five kids, with abortion illegal and white people stealing back all the power?" My fists clenched.

"*Increíble*. What Alex said about your liberal guilt is spot on." She gestured to her cheeks, a pretty rose blush blooming on her caramel skin. "And how dare you lecture me about multiculturalism?"

"How dare *you* lecture *me* on liberal guilt!" My heartbeat drummed in my ears, and I knew I should walk away to rein in my aggression. But her belief system was so fucked up—I couldn't let her say these things unchallenged. "We all need more guilt, to right wrongs. Liberals feel guilty because they care about people. We care about equality."

"Equality is impossible, Dane!" Her spine snapped straight. "It's a fantasy. All we can strive for is equal opportunity—we can *never* be truly equal. Some people simply work harder than others."

"What a convenient excuse to subjugate people. That's exactly why Daddy Adolf won't support gay marriage—he thinks gay people aren't equal to him."

"I told you not to say another word about my father! This conversation is over. It's not even really a conversation!" She bolted off the bed, flying past me with a storm raging in those dark eyes. I scrambled off the chair to stop her. I clasped her wrists, and she wriggled in my arms.

"Let me go!"

"Jesus, you're strong," I marveled as I tried to contain her roving limbs.

Just like that she stopped fighting and went almost limp in my arms. The abrupt shift alarmed me.

She looked down. "I'm not strong." I thought I heard her sniff. "I'm fat."

Did I hear her right? What a horrible thing to say about herself. I let her wrists go and listened to our panting as I tried to figure out how the hell to respond to her ridiculous comment. When she wouldn't look at me, I tilted up her chin. Those shiny eyes blinked at me, full of wounds.

"You're *not* fat. You're..."

She seemed to hold her breath.

"Beautiful."

She gasped, and I realized the enormity of what I'd said. At once we hopped away from each other. The energy between us had shocked us both.

We stared at each other—eyes unwavering, chests heaving—for a long minute. What was she thinking? Did she hate me even more now? Would she run away again? Refuse to speak to me?

She twisted her hands together then softly said, "But not as beautiful as Nina."

Shit. Now I knew for sure. "You heard about the abortion."

"Nina told me." Her mouth quivered, and I could feel her judgment pouring over me like the steady rain pinging her bedroom window.

"I know I fucked up. I was just a stupid freshman, okay?"

She looked up at me from where she'd been studying her comforter.

"I'm not trying to insult you. You're, like, way more mature than I ever was as a freshman." I swallowed. "But the abortion...I know you don't understand, but the abortion needed to happen. It was a *good* thing." It sounded like I was trying to convince myself more than explain things, and maybe I was. I continued in a flat voice, "It put that nightmare behind us. It made everything better."

"The abortion didn't make it better for the *baby!* That innocent, defenseless baby!"

As I watched her face fill with horror, a lump lodged in my throat. Though I tried to fight it, the image of a little blond baby girl, swaddled in a maroon Highbanks Cougars blanket, filled my head.

"Okay, okay, you're right," I finally said. That killed me to admit. "I still regret it. I think about that...tiny baby. What she might have looked like...maybe she'd become a volleyball player, maybe a setter. I would've given a lot of love to her. I would've tried to be a good dad to her."

She cocked her head to one side, for some reason looking angry. Why was she mad at me? I'd just conceded a point to her side. "So..." She blinked at me. "You're regretting the abortion?"

"Well, yeah, of course I am."

"You've had a change of heart, then."

"Change of heart?"

"A complete one-eighty from how you treated Nina when all this went down."

"Oh. So you think I'm an asshole for judging Nina's decision to get an abortion?" I sighed. "Look, I know the guy gets off scot-free while the girl's the one who really has to deal—"

"*Nina's* decision."

I looked at her. "Yeah."

"The abortion was Nina's decision?"

My mouth dropped open. "What did she tell you?"

"She said you told her abortion was her only choice! Then after she went through with it, you dumped her—you wouldn't talk to her."

"*What?*" I paced the room, suddenly unable to take a deep breath. "Son of a bitch! No wonder you think I'm a monster."

"Why shouldn't I? What kind of guy gets a girl pregnant, forces her to get an abortion, then abandons her?"

"Not *me!*" I grabbed her hands. "Lucia, I never knew about the baby! I never knew...until it was too late." I slumped, defeated by images of that tiny girl flooding my consciousness.

She gasped. "Nina didn't tell you she was pregnant...until after the abortion?"

"Until it was too late." I pressed my lips together and fought off those wrenching images. "I think of my baby girl—I know she would have been a girl—every day. *Every day.*" I looked away from her shocked eyes, ashamed by the tears threatening to well up in mine. We stood in silence for a long time.

"Oh, Dane." She stepped into me and circled her arms around my back as she rested her cheek on my chest. "I'm so sorry. I'm so sorry you lost your baby."

Stunned she was in my arms, just like I'd always imagined and hoped, I didn't know what to do at first. Her sympathy for me, despite me being such a *cabrón*, overwhelmed me.

Then the crisp, uplifting scent of lavender wafted from Lucia's hair, loosening the tension from my shoulders and nudging me to gather her more tightly. I closed my eyes and inhaled her scent, my fingers smoothing across her strong back and her soft breasts pillowing into my chest. My hands slid up to bury themselves in the thick hair piling over her shoulders.

She tilted her chin up, letting her head rest in my hands, and my fingers weaved into spun silk. A sound of pleasure echoed from the back of her throat. When I opened my eyes, her face was right there, gazing up at me. Gone was the tightness of mistrust in her expression—her brown eyes were big, round, inviting...her red lips parted and trembling. With her chest pressed into mine, I wasn't sure whose heart raced faster. She was a tantalizing temptress, a soft seductress...hardly the uptight, buttoned-up conservative I'd expected. At that moment, I didn't give a damn that she was a Republican. I wanted her. *Now.*

"I'm waiting for a kiss, GD." Her fingertips traced the lines of my shoulder blades, and her coy smile delivered a shot of heat to my groin.

Evidently she wanted me, too. "*Paciencia.*" I leaned in to taste her sweetness but she interrupted me.

"And it better not be a lame peck on the cheek, either."

So Shy Girl was the teaser this time, and I was determined to kiss the ever-living-hell out of that smirk. I touched my lips to hers, hovering for a moment, sharing her breath—if either of us was indeed breathing at the moment—before capturing her supple lips with a rush of urgency that had swelled inside of me for two months. Her soft mouth yielded at first, pliant and warm, then thrust into me, molding around my lips, hot and charged. The unexpected aggressiveness of her kiss jolted into me and fire raced from my core up my spine. *Sweet Jesus*, this girl. How had I let her live under my roof this long without tasting the delicious merlot of her lips?

Her breathy moan sparked a surge of heat that zinged upward and escaped my mouth in a feral growl. I fell deeper into her as our kiss intensified. One hand tangled in her hair as the other caressed her cheek, and her hands inched down my back as we kept our lips locked together. When her hands cupped my ass, I almost came right there. *Paciencia*, I told my Cock-a-saurus Rex. *Tranquilo*. But there was nothing calm about this moment, and my feet moved forward of their own accord, urging her to backpedal in step with me, until we'd shuffled the short distance to her bed.

Without missing a beat she fell back on the mattress and pulled my buns down with her, dragging my body on top of hers. I was impressed we kept kissing throughout the change in position—quite an athletic feat. We stretched lengthwise on her bed, our legs entwined, and I tried to rest some of my weight on my elbows but her palms dug into my butt so firmly it was like she wanted me to impale her right then and there. *Wait a minute*—why was she touching my butt when I'd been dreaming about fondling *hers* from day one?

"I'm too...heavy," I murmured between kisses.

She shifted below me with a groan of protest as her mouth detached from mine, and I leaned my weight to one side to allow her to climb on top. But then she pushed her hand into my shoulder and in one swift move flipped me on my back. *Damn!* Her manhandling was a huge turn-on. Now that she'd gained the top position, she stared down at me, smiling as she panted. I smiled back.

This was nothing like the rushed, cold, mechanical coupling I'd experienced with Nina. Her skinny doll body had seemed almost breakable, but Lucia pressed into me with captivating strength, and I didn't have to hold back. My hands darted for her curvy ass, and she gasped when I kneaded the shapely muscles. A look of alarm flashed across her face.

"What's wrong?" Maybe it was too soon to become intimate with the two halves of her heinie?

She shook her head—I'd seen that anxious look before. Apparently the eating disorder had joined us in the bed, and I wanted to kick him the hell out. "You know, you have the most gorgeous butt."

The worried indent between her eyebrows smoothed slightly, but it was still there. "It's too big."

"Nonsense." Taking a risk, I slid my curved palms under the crease between her butt and thighs. "See?" I jostled those muscular peaches. "Your patooty fits perfectly in my hands."

Despite herself, she giggled.

"I've wanted to get my paws on this curvylicious booty from the second I met you."

One corner of her mouth slowly curled up. "You did?"

"*Sí, cariña.*"

Her smile vanished. Did she still doubt my feelings for her? To reassure her, I said, "You had me at *hola*, Luz."

Her eyes locked onto me, and I wondered if she could feel the electric connection between us. When she ran the tip of her tongue along her bottom lip, I got even harder. I lifted my head to kiss the wet spot on that luscious lip but she pulled back from me. "Then why didn't you tell me?"

The back of my head hit the mattress with a thump.

Her hair tickled my cheek as she leaned in with inquisitive eyes. "Why did you act like you hated me?"

I reached to tuck her hair behind one ear. "I was stupid, I guess."

"Uh-uh, Dane." As she shook her head, the hair loosened to fall in my face again. "I need more of an explanation than that."

Crap, how would I answer her? Why did all of us do dumb shit every day? I had no fucking clue—that's why I was a psych major…I was trying to figure it all out. From the corner of my mouth, I blew a strand of her hair off my cheek.

"Well?" One of her eyebrows arched.

I shrugged.

"Do I have to give you hair torture to get it out of you?"

What is that? From the light in her eyes and the jaunty uptick of her mouth, I had a sense it would be pleasurable. "Do what you must."

In a dash, she pinned my wrists above my head. Her head dipped and her thick hair engulfed me, sweeping across my face and filling my mouth. "Nooo!" I half-heartedly pressed against her hold.

"Give it up, Dane." I could hear the laughter in her voice.

"Never!" I thrashed my head from side to side, trying to breathe through the black curtain blinding and drowning me. "You're killing me!"

"Jeez, you take this even worse than Matty."

I groaned. "With a sister like you, I feel sorry for him."

There was a sharp rap on the door. "Are you okay in there?" China asked.

Lucia glanced at me, and we both cracked up.

"I'm fine!" I called.

As we waited in silence for China to walk away, I heard a growl from Lucia's belly. She popped up and scooted off of me, and her cheeks turned red.

I sat up. "I'm starved, too. We forgot about our fajitas—not much of a first date without dinner."

"Our first date?" Her grin stretched from ear to ear. She placed her hand in mine, and I pulled us off the bed. Then she looked at the door as her hand tensed. "What do we tell them?"

"Not a damn thing. They've already invaded our privacy too much."

My answer didn't seem to quell her anxiety. Her breathing had quickened.

"Hey." I stroked the side of her face. "We'll figure this out."

"But my dad—"

"You want to know why I acted like such a jerk when I met you?"

She paused. "Probably 'cause you hate Republicans?"

I chuckled. "That's part of it. But the real reason?" I clenched my jaw. "Fear."

She looked at me quizzically.

"Fear. At least that's what Dr. Valentine told me."

"*Fear?* Fear of what?"

I sighed. "Getting close to you, I guess. I was attracted to you, but it freaked me out." I looked down. "I thought we were way too different."

"I've been worried about that too."

"But don't you see?" I scooped her hands in mine. "We have so much in common. For one, we're both freakishly tall."

She smiled just a little at that. "*Y hablamos español,*" she offered.

"*Sí.* We're both crazy enough to need a shrink."

She nodded. "We've both been humiliated on the national news."

"Ugh." I wrinkled my nose. "And what are the chances two presidential candidates' kids play college volleyball? It's like, fate."

As she took that in, she swept her tongue along her lip. I wanted to kiss her again—hell, I wanted to rip off her T-shirt and pants and throw her on the bed. But we'd come so far in such a short time, I didn't want to push her too fast. And I really had no idea how far she could be pushed. "C'mon, let's get you some food. Dr. Valentine won't be happy with me if I don't feed you."

She swayed for a second, and I clasped her shoulders. "Are you okay?"

"I...I'm just overwhelmed, I guess. I can't believe tonight just happened." She beamed. "I..." She chewed her lip as she glanced at me. "I've wanted to be with you from the first time I saw you on TV."

"Of course you did."

She slugged me in the chest. "*Esquincle.*" Her warm hand rested over my heart, and I reached to clasp her wrist. She looked up at me. "But you just *kissed* me?" Her lips parted with wonder. "This is like the best night of my life!"

Her exuberance was contagious, and fajitas be damned, I had to kiss her again. I leaned into those honey lips and sucked the sweet nectar dry. Unfortunately, our growling stomachs pulled us apart and sent us toward the door.

"They say not to discuss politics and religion on the first date," she said as I opened the door for her.

"Well, then." I gave her a huge smile. "We're *screwed.*"

21

Lucia

I followed Dane into the kitchen to find Brad: his cheeks stuffed like a chipmunk's and a smear of guacamole on his chin. "Daneschter!" He forced a swallow. "S'okay I ate some? These are awesome!"

Dane beelined to the counter and lifted the sheet of foil. "Phew. He didn't eat it all."

"Of course I didn't." Brad brushed crumbs off his hands, then pulled a chair out from the table and gestured for me to sit. "My lady."

I glanced at Dane, who gave me an amused shrug and took a seat while offering Brad a discreet chin tap.

Brad yanked a napkin off the table and swiped the green smudge clean before pulling out a chair for Dane. "Least I can do is serve you two tonight," he said.

"Your service ain't so *secret,* huh?" Dane joked.

"Exactamundo, *señor.*" Brad bowed then crooned a bit of "Be Our Guest" as he grabbed two plates from the cabinet.

Dane scooted his chair closer to mine, and my breath hitched when he clasped my hand under the table. His soft, setter hand was warm, and each stroke of his thumb sent tingles up my arm. I still felt the humming vibration of his kisses on my lips.

"What are you smiling about?" he whispered.

Was I smiling? I snuck a peek at Brad, but he was busy with the microwave. I turned back to Dane. "Being with you."

His eyes darkened, but then he looked up, and his spine straightened. Frank had entered the kitchen. Was that *anger* in his eyes?

Dane let go of my hand and kept his eyes on Frank. "Any day now, Brad. We're starving over here."

"Almost ready." Brad looked at his fellow agent. "Hey, will you get some drinks for them?"

Frank stood statue-still for a moment, then nodded. Brad now sang "La Cucaracha" as he set tortillas on the table. *Cockroaches…how appetizing.* A few moments later, Brad swooped in with a steaming plate of chicken, peppers, and onions, which he set between us, and I had to admit I wanted to eat. I wanted to *inhale* the food.

Dane apparently felt the same way because he'd already wolfed down half his first fajita before I'd finished filling my tortilla with goodies. He reached for another as I took my first bite. *Mmmmm.* There were hints of jalapeño, cilantro, and garlic in his chicken marinade, and my taste buds did a little happy dance. "This *pollo*…" I closed my eyes as I savored the flavor…maybe I even moaned?

He laughed. "It's my mom's recipe." He chewed for a while, then added, "She used to be a pretty good cook."

"Used to be?"

"We hired a chef once she became senator, of course." He tilted his head. "Didn't you have one?"

I arched an eyebrow. "You think Sylvia would let some stranger into her kitchen?"

"Silly me." He grinned. Then he frowned at Frank, who had been staring at us. "What?"

Frank jumped back, like he was surprised to be caught gawking. "Just…" He cleared his throat. "Just seeing if you'll need the Heimlich—never seen someone eat so fast."

Brad thumped Dane's shoulder. "He's a growing boy."

"I worked up an appetite," Dane said.

¡Dios mio! He looked straight at me, his lively eyes direct and challenging, sparking a prickle of arousal inside of me. I dipped my head and focused on scooping rice onto my fork.

"It smells *so* good—" China rounded the corner, followed by Allison, but they stopped when they saw me.

"Oh." Allison fidgeted and wouldn't meet my eyes. "We'll come back later."

"Nonsense." Dane gestured to the table covered with food. "Brad already stuffed himself, of course, but we have enough for everyone." He nudged an empty chair out from the table and patted its seat. "And we know *you two* definitely worked up an appetite tonight." His grin was positively wicked, and I wasn't sure whose face was redder—Allison's or mine.

China barreled toward the table and snatched the seat next to Dane, which left the chair to my right open. Allison swallowed, hesitating for a second, before she joined us as well.

"Want me to get you a plate, Frank?" Dane asked. But my agent simply turned and left. Dane and I exchanged a confused look before he shrugged. "More for us, then."

Brad followed him out of the kitchen. "Hey, Frank, wanna watch *The O'Reilly Factor*?"

Dane cursed, and I grinned.

I watched China scoop chicken, vegetables, and salsa onto her plate, and wondered how she would fit all that into a tortilla.

"Oops, sorry." China winced as she noticed me studying her plate.

"Huh?" *Why is she apologizing?*

China peeked over at Allison. "Allison told me not to do my high-protein bodybuilder diet around you." She twisted her mouth to one side. "She said it could…trigger you, or something like that."

"China!" Allison hissed. She snuck a glance at me. "I wasn't trying to talk behind your back, I swear."

I hated how scared of me she seemed to be. I wanted my old Allison back. "Thank you." When she looked at me, I slowly lifted my hand, letting it hover for a moment, wondering if it was okay to touch her. I finally patted her forearm. "Thank you for helping me with my, uh, problem. You've really been there for me."

Her smile was faint but at least not a frown. "You're welcome, Lucia. You're doing great."

I wasn't so sure of that. As we spoke, I could feel the guacamole glomming onto my ass…my…*curvylicious* ass. My face warmed as

I recalled Dane's hands cupping my butt cheeks, sending shivers up my back then and now. I looked at him and found him watching me as he bit off a piece of the chicken strip he held. The muscles in his jaw rolled and flexed as he chewed, and his full lips drew my attention. I imagined that mouth on my neck, sucking, licking, his warm breath on my skin—

"That's *it*, Monroe," China said. "You're cooking for us every night." She took another bite. "Seriously, this is some good shit. Right, Allie?"

Allison nodded as she dipped her tortilla into ranch dressing. "Yum."

"Then Lucia has to cook every night, too," Dane said. "She deserves some of the credit—she was my sous chef." He scooped my hand into his under the table again. "In fact, she was seeing if you wanted to join us for dinner earlier, when, ah..."

China's naked body flashing in my mind killed my GD buzz, and I squirmed in my chair. Why did he have to bring this up at the dinner table, of all places? I was stressed out enough as it was. When I looked at him, he gave a slight nod, like he urged me to address the Republican elephant in the room.

The eating disorder steals your voice, Dr. Valentine had told me. *You need to express your needs to steal it back*. Dane's hand gently squeezed mine.

I swallowed and faced Allison. "I'm sorry I hurt your feelings."

She placed her half-eaten fajita on her plate.

"I'm sorry you felt judged by my family...and scared about losing your job. Please, please, don't worry about that. There are many Republicans who believe in equal rights for gay people, and I'm one of them."

The hardness in Allison's eyes seemed to soften.

China looked at Dane. "What'd you say to her?"

"Nothing she didn't already believe." He shrugged, but his eyes smiled at me.

"So you affect her like she affects you," China said.

"What?" Dane's eyebrows drew together.

She looked right at me. "You have such a way with him."

I retracted my neck.

"It's true. I told my supervisor about you and Dane."

"You did?" Allison asked.

She did? I glanced at Dane, whose eyes had also opened wide.

China blew out a breath. "My boss was chewing my ass after The Great Beer Escape. Epic security failure...Beergate! I thought for sure I was fired."

Dane clenched his fists. "They could've fired you for that?"

"Yes," Allison answered, her voice sharp.

"I'm sorry." Dane looked straight at China, then down at his lap. "I was an idiot." His apology sounded truly contrite.

"I *still* don't know why you went all trench coat that day." China paused, but Dane didn't say anything, which made me wonder. What *had* caused him to get thrown out of practice and guzzle beer on national TV? "Anyway," China continued, "my supervisor told me my methods clearly weren't working. He said I needed to be less aggressive with the protectee."

Dane looked up. "I *like* this supervisor."

China shoved his shoulder. "When I had no fucking clue how to approach you differently, my supervisor asked if anyone else had more success at calming you down—at getting you to behave. And right away I thought of Lucia."

I gulped. Her spiky brown hair didn't move an inch as she nodded at me.

"You took his insults without slinging mud back at him. Unlike me, you didn't fight back and make things worse."

If only she knew my lack of response was often more about being tongue-tied than turning the other cheek. I'd *wished* I could fight back in my bedroom minutes ago, although I suppose that situation turned out okay...I sighed. "Not always."

Dane's hand found mine again, warm fingers intertwining with mine. "It's not your fault." His gaze traveled from me to China, then to his lap. "I bring out the worst in people."

His words pierced my heart. How could he believe that about himself? Even with the mistakes he'd made...I felt absolutely amazing around him—well, when I wasn't comparing my body to his gorgeousness, anyway. He was a brilliant firecracker in a sky of dark clouds. His brightness had lit the way on my journey at Highbanks so far, and I wondered if I'd still be here without him.

"Hey," China said. "You've been a good challenge for me, Monroe."

Allison nodded. "And China sure enjoys challenges."

"Makes life interesting, that's for sure." China's chair scooted across the tile as she stood. "I'm guessing you guys need to study, so Allie and I will do the dishes."

Dane looked up. "We're being sent to our rooms to study by Mom…and Mom?"

Holding two plates aloft, China cackled. "Lord, you as my *son?* I think your mother deserves to be president simply for surviving your childhood."

"But Governor Ramirez might have a chance too," Allison chimed in as she carried a bowl to the counter. I was relieved to see her smirk in my direction.

Dane came around behind my chair and rested his hands on my shoulders. "C'mon, Luz. We don't want Moms to spank us for misbehaving."

I watched China's wrist spin a dishtowel into a twisted weapon and felt Dane jump behind me when she snapped his butt with it.

"Ow! *Moooohhhhmmm.*"

I giggled as I stood and noticed him massaging his rear end. *I'll massage it for you.* What would my dad say if he heard that?

"Go to your room, young man!" China twirled the towel, her eyes blazing with faux menace.

Dane pushed me out of the kitchen, and we laughed all the way to his bedroom. My smile faded once I entered the space. The sage-green walls and musky scent lent an earthy feel to the room, and psychology textbooks lined his shelf. Dane crossed over to his bed and yanked the duvet over messy sheets—a touching effort to tidy up for me. Then he flipped on some music.

My heartbeat kicked up as he approached me. "Do you have any midterms tomorrow?"

I shook my head. "I had two today."

"Ouch. I had one, and I thought that was bad enough. The damn professor scheduled it so I had to miss half of practice."

"That sucks." I watched his shirt hike up as he scratched one hip, revealing a taut strip of muscle. I longed to see more. He spoke again but visions of rippled chest muscles, grooves and valleys of tight skin, clouded my brain. "Huh?"

He stepped closer and curved his hand around my hip. "I asked if you needed to study tonight."

Focus! "Not really." Of its own accord, my body leaned into his touch. "I mean, I could always study more, but nothing's due tomorrow, so it can probably wait, I think..." I was babbling.

"Good." He tucked strands of hair behind my ear. "No way I could concentrate on school tonight. You're *way* too distracting."

He leaned in and scorched me with a plunging kiss. I felt myself tilt backward, but his forearm supported my back and his other hand cradled my head. I was weightless, floating on the pulsing energy his lips pressed into my body.

With apparently zero control over my hands, I felt one of them snake under his shirt and rub against the hard muscle of his ribcage. My fingers slid inward, gliding over his skin, marveling at the ridges of corded abs, and paused at the downy hair above the waistband of his workout pants. His sharp intake of air stilled his lips on mine. His entire body seemed to freeze, except for the part of him pressing against my belly, which made itself known with growing awareness. My lower body bloomed with heat, turning to mush compared to his hardness.

At once, he steadied me on my feet and backed away. He exhaled. "I don't want to mess this up."

Why, oh why did you stop? "I don't either."

"We just had our first kiss—the first relatively peaceful discussion of our entire relationship—and here I am already, desperate to *take you* on my bed."

My girly bits tingled at the growl in his voice. "I want that, too."

Shock flashed across his face, matching the flip in my stomach as I said that out loud. *What the hell am I doing?*

"Jesus, we're so screwed." He closed his eyes and lifted his face to the ceiling. Then those deep blues found me again. "I was counting on *you* to be the one holding the reins. I certainly don't have any self-control."

My feet pulled me toward him—evidently I had even less control—though I knew he was smart to try to slow us down. Niggling voices from my family and my church fought to be heard, knocking on the door of my mind. I silenced the incessant noise by stepping in and pressing my lips against his neck. Dane groaned and kissed the top of my head, burying his mouth in my hair, as he gathered me into him.

I tugged his collar down to expose his collarbone, soap mingling with the faint smell of grilled onion on his shirt, and kissed him in an alcove of skin and muscle.

"Luz." His voice sounded strained, like he was barely holding it together. "What about your father?"

When I lifted my head and looked into his troubled eyes, I sighed. He was right, and I hated it. "Dad comes between us once again."

"Look, I want you—*God*, I want you...but this is too fast. When I meet your dad at the debate, he'll kill me if his only daughter just jumped into bed with me."

I drew a hand to cover my mouth, horrified by that prospect.

Dane let me go and backed up a few steps. "You know I'm right."

"Yes." I gritted my teeth. It grew quiet between us, the only sound the strum of a guitar and the lead singer from Dane's favorite band.

"I yearn to touch you; you grasp for me
Fumbling in the dark, craving ecstasy
Your forbidden allure, a drunk man's merlot
Seizes hold of my will, inside me it grows..."

He paced the room with palpable energy. Then he stopped. "Okay, I know what we should do. When I'm so hyper I can't stand it, I go to the gym. Let's go, okay? I've always wanted to set you."

I shook my head. "But the gym's closed. It's locked."

"China!" Dane opened the door and hollered her name again as he headed to the kitchen. He was back before the next song. "Frank's taking us—he has a key, so go put on your sassy Spandex. Okay?"

I smiled at his excitement. "Okay." I left his room and headed to mine, noticing he was right behind me. "Um..." I looked over my shoulder. "I don't think watching me undress will help the situation with my dad."

"Damn, you're right." He turned on his heel and left with a giant sigh.

Five minutes later, Dane and I sat in the backseat with Frank driving. Brad drove the other SUV as a decoy vehicle—not that we really needed it. One advantage of stealth nighttime volleyball: no media! Another advantage of the dark vehicle: Dane's hand stroking mine with Frank none the wiser.

The main campus teemed with nightlife, and I watched students stream in and out of The Library bar. "Whoa, is this what college is really like?"

Dane snorted. "For everyone except the athletes."

"And the *underage* students," Frank piped up.

Dane rolled his eyes. "And the hapless offspring of presidential candidates."

I squeezed his hand and smiled at him. I didn't need the bar scene to have a good time at college. *He* was my good time.

"Just one week left until the presidential debate," a reporter said over the car radio. *"And Governor Ramirez's camp claims the selection of a liberal moderator like Molly Martins tips the scale unfairly for his opponent. Pollsters still report a virtual tie in the presidential race."*

For a moment I wondered what Dane thought of the liberal-bias claim, but I tried to drown out all worries about the election. Instead, I focused on the feel of his hand in mine until we arrived.

Once the buzzing lights of the gym flickered on, we discovered the coaches had left the net at women's height. "Do you think I'll get in trouble if Coach finds me here?"

"No way." Dane grabbed the cart of balls and wheeled it to one side of the net. "Extra practice for his players is like his wet dream."

Dane laughed at the disgust on my face. "C'mon, let's warm up."

As Frank and Brad watched from the bleachers, we jogged around the court, shuffled side to side, sprinted, and stretched. I couldn't take my eyes off Dane's powerful body as we peppered. No matter how hard I spiked the ball, his sets were right on target. I wished I could say the same for my passes, but I wasn't accustomed to the force of his hits.

After Dane chased down a ball I'd shanked toward the bleachers, he looked up at our agents. "Hey, would you guys help out?"

"Sure." Brad removed his suit jacket and hustled to the gym floor, and Dane guided him to stand by the basket of balls. Frank followed at a slower pace, staring suspiciously at us, but he did walk to the other side of the net as Dane asked.

I tugged at my kneepads as Dane nodded at me. "Ready?"

Butterflies dive-bombed my stomach but I said, "Let's see what you got."

His eyes glittered, and a smirk lifted a corner of his mouth. He nodded at Brad, who tossed a ball toward him. It was a low toss, but Dane got under the ball with ease and launched his set in an elegant arc to my corner of the net. My jaw unhinged as I marveled at its perfection, then before I knew it, the ball dribbled to the floor.

"I thought you said you were ready." Dane frowned at me.

"How'd you do that?"

"How'd I do what?"

"You just set the most perfect ball I've ever seen, at a net lower than you're used to, to a lefty hitter when all of your hitters are right-handed. How'd you do that?"

His grin developed slowly, lazily spreading across his face. "You wanted to see what I got, sweetheart." His hands gestured down the length of his body. "This is what I got."

I wanted to rip that shirt off him right then and there. My mouth felt dry, and I glanced at Frank to see if we were busted, but he simply looked bored. Maybe he'd chalked that 'sweetheart' comment up to Dane cockiness.

"Let's see what *you* got," Dane taunted. As he nodded at Brad, I shook out my hands to expel their thrumming nervousness.

The next set was an exact replication, and I slammed the ball down the line. Frank went to retrieve it. "Nice," Dane said. "But I already know you're a good hitter down the line. Let's work cross-court tonight."

I took a deep breath and nodded. With magnificent sets like that, I could hit the ball anywhere he asked. Dane set me, and I watched with satisfaction as the ball careened across the court at a vicious angle.

"*That's* what I'm talking 'bout!"

My heart soared to see his fist pump.

I didn't know how long he kept setting me, but I did know it was the time of my life. He arched his back to execute beautiful back-sets, and he timed his quick sets just right, practically handing me the ball as a gift to smash over the net. I bounced with glee when he wanted to practice the slide—my favorite. I lined up on the right side of the net, with him facing me. As Brad tossed the ball, I darted around behind Dane and jumped up for his back-set, which I dispatched like a heat-seeking missile. The run-around maneuver confused defenses, and it was a total blast flying through the air, waiting to pound his exquisitely placed set. I whooped as we high-fived.

All at once, Dane paused. He turned to the wall behind Brad, and I followed his gaze to see his coach standing there, watching. "Hey, Phil." Dane brushed his hand on his thigh. "How long have you been watching us?"

"About five minutes," Frank said from behind me.

I nodded—of course Secret Service had noticed his entrance. I'd been too absorbed in Dane's balls (hee hee) to be aware of much else.

Phil turned to look at me, and I swallowed. I'd only spoken to him once, and he'd never seen me play. Had I performed like an amateur in his eyes?

"Good hitting, Lucia."

His praise made my heart skip. "Thanks, Coach."

"A word, please, Dane."

Dane jogged over, and they spoke in hushed tones.

"Hey." Brad grinned at me, and I noticed his white button-down shirt sticking to him with sweat. "Try some jump serves. I want to see if I can field them."

Frank snorted. "It's called passing, not fielding."

"You might want to remove your gun holster first," I told Brad as I rolled the ball cart under the net so I could serve toward his side of the court.

"No way!" He crouched down, looking ridiculous in his agent attire. "I need all the defense I can get."

What were Dane and Phil discussing? Whatever it was, it looked intense. I hoped I hadn't overstepped my bounds. I grabbed a ball and took a deep breath as I backpedaled from the baseline. I tossed the ball high, approached, then leaped and whacked the ball over the net. It whizzed to the floor before Brad got anywhere near it.

"Day-um, Luce!" He stood with his hands on his hips. "That packed some *heat!*"

I grinned. He was like an oversized child. But I also knew he would sacrifice his life to protect us—all of our agents would.

After a few more serves, Phil walked away, leaving Dane to stare at me with an unreadable expression. He seemed...bewildered? I rolled the cart toward him, bending and scooping wayward balls into it as I went, and stopped in front of him. I looked over my shoulder and saw the agents gathering their suit jackets, out of hearing range.

"Are you okay?"

He blinked at me. "Yeah. Phil always gives me a lot to think about."

"Was he mad we were playing?"

"No. He said he liked my 'initiative' to be here, since I missed part of practice."

I nodded and waited for him to continue.

"He's concerned about me, about my focus." Dane rubbed his jaw. "He's worried about the effects of our relationship."

I gasped. "Did you tell him?"

"No, Luz." His fingertips grazed my cheek. "He knew just by looking at us. Hell, I bet Frank knows—I bet they all know."

My skin tingled. Would my dad know, too? Alex? It was difficult to get a full breath. "So, does Phil..." I chewed on my lip. "Do you want...to end it?"

"Are you *crazy?*" His eyes bugged. "I want to give this a shot."

I could breathe again.

22
Dane

"That's the best practice I've ever seen from you."

I beamed like a giddy schoolgirl, which was saying something since it was the night before the final presidential debate, and things were feeling pretty serious. Phil wasn't one to blow smoke up my ass—I knew if he praised me like that, he meant it. "Thanks."

We stood at the side of the court, watching Brian and Kara prepare the gym for the big women's game: Highbanks vs. Bridgetown, the top two teams in the conference. Lucia was so nervous it had taken her two hours to fall asleep the previous evening. And I knew this because when she'd finally drifted off, she'd been in my arms. It had been one of the best nights of my life.

"Why'd you play so well today?" Phil asked.

Happy athletes play better, according to Dr. Valentine, so I knew Lucia deserved credit. But I wasn't about to admit that to Phil.

When I didn't respond right away, he added, "Because it's your birthday?"

I couldn't believe I was now twenty years old. Hopefully two decades of fuck-ups wouldn't carry through to my third decade. "Maybe." I thought of another answer. "Actually, I think the meditation helped me concentrate."

He nodded. In the locker room, before practice started, we'd focused on our breath for five minutes, silently repeating the mantra *Just this…one moment.*

"Sounds like meditation should be part of your pre-game routine, then."

"Okay." I trusted Phil. He could tell me to stand on my head before games while I smoked a peace pipe and painted my toenails hot pink, and I'd do it—no questions asked.

"Also sounds like my concerns about Lucia hurting your focus are unfounded."

A tendril of unease snaked up my spine as I remembered his words from a week ago, the night Lucia and I had played volleyball together. "Well, it's not that serious—it's only been a week. And the media shitheads haven't caught on yet." *Thank God.*

"But she wants it to be serious."

I looked at him. "Why do you say *that?"* A little thrill zinged inside of me. Could he see we belonged together, despite his misgivings?

He paused. "Did she tell you she talked to me?"

"No?" My forehead creased.

"After your dumbass explosion—your alcohol binge. Lucia came to my office, asked me to keep you on the team."

Holy shit. I stared at him as I took that in.

"She said you were under a lot of pressure, said you deserved another chance."

That was possibly the kindest thing anyone's ever done for me. But why hadn't she told me? "Is she the reason I'm back on the team?"

Phil shrugged. "I'd already planned to take you back, once I found out you had to go to counseling. Assuming you took responsibility for your behavior, of course. But her pleading for you like that…it told me one thing."

"What's that?"

"You're *screwed."*

He grinned, and I managed a limp chuckle. "Tell me something I don't know, Phil."

"I warned you about conflict with Lucia attracting the media like flies to honey." He smirked. "But I should've known your bluster—your insistence that you hated her—was merely foreplay. And when those reporters sniff *this* out, they'll swarm you both."

I groaned.

"Just be smarter this time, okay?"

I understood his hidden message: *Don't knock up another girl.* "It's not..." I skated my thumbs inside the sweaty waistband of my shorts. This was as embarrassing as fuck. "It's not like that with us." I hoped it *could* be like that one day, but it was probably true that neither of us was ready for sex. At least that's what Dr. Valentine had gotten me to confess in my last weekly appointment.

Phil cupped my shoulder as he pegged me with a stare. "I know you'll do the right thing."

As he walked away, a lump lodged in my throat. My dad had never expressed faith in me like that.

I headed out of the gym, with Brad on my heels, and was almost to the locker room when I noticed Lucia and Allison at the other end of the hallway. Why was her arm slung over Lucia's shoulders, like she was comforting her? What had made Lucia look so downcast?

"Hey!" I called.

She brightened when she saw me and practically skipped down the hallway. "Happy birthday!"

I would have loved to scoop her into my arms, but I was sweaty, and the agents were right there. "You already wished me happy birthday this morning."

Brad lifted his fist to his mouth and between pretend coughs he said, "In *bed*."

When Lucia's cheeks reddened, I scowled at him. "What are you, thirteen?" So much for keeping our relationship secret from our constant chaperones.

"The Bridgetown team bus has just arrived." Allison touched her earpiece. "Let's get out of the hallway." She ushered us into a dark alcove filled with gymnastics equipment, then gave me a knowing look. "We'll give you some privacy."

My sweaty shirt felt clammy in the coolness, which drew me closer to Lucia's warmth. I caressed her thick braid. "Why'd you look upset earlier?"

"I'm fine." She shook her head. "It's nothing. How's your birthday been? I haven't seen you all day."

"Luz, *dímelo*." *Tell me.*

She sighed. "My mom called. She and Matty were supposed to come to my game, but his blood sugar numbers are all over the place, so they can't make it."

"That's too bad." My hand curled the tip of her braid up to her mouth, tickling her lips. When her tongue swept across her upper lip, I felt a shiver vibrate my chest.

"At least I'll see them tomorrow night," she said.

I scowled. My mom and sister had given me the same excuse about failing to visit: *We'll see you at the debate.* "But it still sucks for your family to miss your biggest college match yet."

"And for your family to miss your birthday."

I shrugged. "Less sneaking around for us."

Her smile stretched across her face. As she leaned into me, her hands slid beneath my shirt and spanned my hips.

"I'm all gross from practice." I recoiled a bit.

"You always smell yummy to me."

Her breathy voice and sassy grin reeled me back in. As my mouth found hers, I drowned in her soft lips and intoxicating floral scent. *You smell yummy, too.* I cradled her head as our kiss deepened.

My hands drifted to her shoulders when our kiss ended, and she gazed up at me. "October twenty-fourth. You're a Scorpio, *sí?*"

"You're into *astrology?*" I felt my eyebrows lift.

"Don't be a hater. It's mostly *ridículo*, but I read up on it, and I think your sign's perfect for you."

"Yeah...I'm a scorpion, stinging you with my venomous, ah, *appendage?*"

"*Ew.* No." She wrinkled her nose as she giggled. "But you're radiant, passionate, and, um, energetic." Her head bobbed. "Yep, that's you."

"I see. You just had your birthday—what's *your* sign, baby?" My eyes traveled lecherously up her body.

She swallowed. "Virgo."

"The virgin."

Her blush bloomed like the White House rose garden. "It's not a literal translation. But Virgos are supposed to be modest."

"That *is* you." I nodded. Sweetness also had to be part of her birth sign if there was any validity whatsoever to astrology.

"And Virgos are perfectionists." Her eyes rolled.

I'd read somewhere that perfectionism was a risk factor for eating disorders, so that fit her too. I wouldn't be surprised if she was beating up on herself for falling short of perfect at that very moment. "No wonder you're attracted to me." I let go of her shoulders to gesture to myself. "Sheer perfection right here."

"Gag." She laughed.

I laughed too, feeling happy I'd coaxed her out of her funk. My hands found their way to her hips.

"What time are the guys coming over for euchre?"

"Soon—better hit the showers. You better get dressed for warm-up, too. After the game I want to talk to you about— "

I heard a scuffling patter of footsteps and spun around to find Nina screeching to an abrupt halt, with Allison and Brad zooming up behind her. I sprang back from Lucia, but the fury in Nina's eyes told me she'd seen enough. We were busted.

Nina's chest heaved. "When I saw both your agents, I *knew* you were together."

"I tried to stop her." Brad grimaced. "But I didn't want to tackle her."

"Nina," Lucia said, "this just...happened. I meant to tell you."

But Nina wasn't looking at her. She glared right at me. "You're a *bastard*, Dane."

She was right. Though I was still angry with her for lying to Lucia, I knew I'd made a mess of things when we were together.

Nina pushed past Brad and Allison and stormed off.

"Nina!" Lucia called. She started to take off, then turned to look at me. "See you tonight?"

I nodded. As I watched her chase after her teammate, I winced and looked down at my feet. No perfection here. *No perfection at all.*

"You didn't get any veggie pizza?" Josh asked as he frowned at the steaming box.

"Oops, forgot. Sorry, dude." I lifted a huge slice of pepperoni, and a mouth-watering string of cheese dangled over the edge of my plate.

Pete jostled between Josh and me to grab the next piece. "Since when do you care about veggies?"

"Since he became vegetarian," I said. "Just pick the meat off, Josh." I shoved a huge bite in my mouth. "Hot, hot, hah..." With my taste buds now singed, I spit out a half-chewed glob of cheese and crust onto my plate.

"Classy." Josh grinned. "A stunt like that'll go over *great* at the next state dinner."

My stomach clenched. Would my mother win? Or would Lucia's dad reign victorious? The race was still neck-and-neck, and tomorrow's debate made me nervous.

Pete frowned at Josh. "Dude, how're you gonna survive as a vegetarian?"

"I know. It's dumb." I blew on my pizza. "He'll never be able to get enough calories."

"Bra, I want to take care of my body." Josh picked pepperonis off his slice and flicked them to the side of his plate. "It's my machine."

"If you're so concerned about your body," I said, "maybe you should stop smoking weed."

Josh shot a glance toward Brad, who had piled three slices onto his own plate. "Ixnay on the eedway."

"Relax, Brad won't tell." The only reason Brad was part of our euchre foursome in the first place was that the agents hadn't had time to move more of my teammates through security clearance. It was hard enough to get Josh and Pete through the doors. *What a rocking birthday party*. Not only was the guest list small, I also felt guilty for hanging at the greenhouse while Lucia had nobody supporting her at her game. Maybe Nina had already blabbed our relationship status, but without knowing for sure, I didn't want to tell the guys why I had a sudden interest in watching the women's game.

Brad sat across the table from Pete. "Tell me you know how to play euchre, Marine." I didn't want this to be a repeat of clueless Kaitlyn that night at Josh's apartment.

"Chill, amigo. I had some guys from the Midwest in my platoon, so they taught me all the tricks."

"We'll see about that." When I risked another bite, I didn't fry my mouth this time. My phone buzzed in my pocket with a text from Jessica:

Happy birthday, old man! :)

I smiled as I remembered how mature twenty sounded when I'd been sixteen. Too bad I didn't actually feel so mature. It would be rude to keep texting when I had guests, so I typed a brief response.

Thanks, little girl. About to deliver the smackdown in euchre—see ya tomorrow.

As we chomped on pizza and guzzled pop—another lame feature of the Secret Service-Sponsored Birthday Bash—I dealt out four hands of five cards each.

"So, we have to let you win 'cause it's your birthday?" Pete asked.

I grinned across the table at Josh. "There'll be no need. Josh and I are unbeatable."

But a little while later we were down nine to six (thanks to Pete's frigging loner) when Brad got a call. "Gotta take this—it's China." He stepped out of the kitchen.

China was at Lucia's match too, due to the large crowd, and I felt a stirring of disquiet in my gut.

"One more point and the game is ours," Pete gloated. He cupped his hand around his ear. "What was that about you being unbeatable?"

When I didn't respond, he gave me a strange look. "You okay?"

"Sorry, guys, game's over." Brad swept back into the kitchen. "My partner said the media presence is bigger than expected, and they need extra security at the game. Which means I gotta go to campus."

"Which means you need to take me with you," I added, attempting to sound disappointed.

Brad tilted his head. His nods started slowly then picked up speed. "Yesss, it does. Ain't no way I'm leaving you alone after that stunt you pulled with the beer, jackhole."

"*God, I looohhhvvve beer.*" Josh cracked a smile, then stood. "Well, this sucks. Will you kindly drive me to my abode, Petester?"

"Anything to get rid of you for the night." As Pete pushed Josh toward the front door, he hollered over his shoulder, "I was *beating* you, Monroe!" Brad followed to let them out.

When he returned, he scowled at me. "It would be safer if we left you home, with the alarm set and agents doing drive-bys. You sure you want to go?"

"Lucia doesn't have anyone there for her."

Brad shook his head as he chuckled. "You've got pussyitis, my man."

Yeah, I do. "Keep that to yourself, jerkoff."

"Get ready for the carnage, though."

I cocked my head, confused, as he cocked his weapon.

"Bridgetown's ahead two-nothing. Let's roll."

How was that possible? Highbanks had beaten Bridgetown three games to one in an away match earlier this season.

When we arrived at the gym, I stuck by Brad's side as promised. A few media types snapped photos of me, but I was too absorbed in the play to notice. Bridgetown was beating the Cougars in game three as well, and I soon discovered why. Though the defense passed the ball right to Nina, she refused to set Lucia. Instead, set after set went to Maddie. Maddie was an all-conference hitter, but without the element of surprise for each set, Bridgetown blockers smothered each of her spikes. *Christ,* at one point they triple-blocked her!

Coach Holter's face was fire-engine red. Why hadn't he substituted in the backup setter for Nina? I scanned the Highbanks bench. *Oh.* Murphy's bandaged foot rested on crutches in front of her chair. There *was* no backup setter.

I studied Lucia after she lunged to save a wayward pass. She looked on the verge of tears, and seeing her so upset clenched my hands into fists. I couldn't imagine how frustrated she must be. I looked over at Nina's pinched face. *I did this.* This was my fault.

When the merciful end of the match came, Brad said, "Let's get you out of here." Dejected Cougar fans spilled out of the stands and herded toward the exits.

"I need to talk to Nina."

"Why? What's going on?"

"I need to talk to her!"

Brad frowned but relayed the info into his comm link. He paused as he likely listened to his earpiece. "Okay, but we should get you to a secure location. Follow me."

We headed to the weight room, where China waited by the entrance. "Coach is blasting them in the locker room," she told me. "But when he's done, I'll ask Nina to meet you here."

"Thank you. And can you…?"

She scowled at yet another request.

"Could you, uh, try not to let Luz know I'm talking to Nina?"

"You're not going to two-time Lucia, are you?"

"Absolutely not." I then realized what she'd said. "Wait, are you standing up for Lucia now?"

She shrugged. "Allie likes her, that's all."

When she walked off, Brad and I exchanged a smirk.

Sometime later, Brad held the door open for Nina, then left us. My planned diatribe vanished from my mind once I saw her mascara-streaked face and her eyes glittering with tears. Instead, I blurted, "I'm sorry."

She sniffed and looked away. Her uniform was rumpled, and she probably craved a shower. "Do *you* want to yell at me, too?"

"No, just want to talk. Thanks for being here." I stuffed my hands in my jean pockets and lowered onto a bench. She remained standing. "You seemed, um, mad, when you saw me and Lucia together."

She blew out a breath and folded her slender arms across her waist. "She asked me not to tell anyone about it."

"I see." I pressed my lips together. "*Do* you plan to tell anyone?"

"You can't tell me what to do—we're not together anymore. Why do you care, anyway?"

"You know why I care. The media are already crazy around here. And also, Adolf might castrate me if he finds out." That drew a small smile from her. "Though I realize that would probably be quite okay with you."

She rolled her eyes. After a beat, she sat on a bench across from me and fidgeted with the hem of her Spandex shorts.

"So..." I inhaled stale weight room air. "You told Lucia I *wanted* you to get an abortion." Her hand stilled. "Is that how you saw it?"

"Of course you did. You didn't want to be saddled with a baby."

"You never gave me a *choice!*"

When her eyes opened wide, I knew I'd been too forceful. I swallowed. "I mean, why'd you think I wanted the abortion, when you didn't tell me until after it was over?"

"I was scared, and alone...My family doesn't even know. And I was trying to make things easier...for you."

"For *me?*" What the hell kind of logic was that?

"I knew you didn't love me." Her tears started anew.

"Oh, Nina." I blew out a breath. Unfortunately, she was right—we didn't belong together. Most guys would call her beautiful, but I found her boring and kind of mean. And every time I looked at her now, I thought about my mistakes and her lies—hardly a turn-on. But if she'd given me the chance, would I have stepped up to the plate as her baby daddy? If I had, would the scandal have ruined my mom's chance to become president? Nauseating guilt swirled in my belly as I realized the abortion *had* made things easier for me. "You still should have let me know," I said softly.

"I want to be…with you." Her lips trembled as she swiped her face. "But you don't want me."

I looked down. "I'm sorry." I pressed my fingers into the lifting bench cushion. "There's probably been too much history between us. But a lot of guys would kill to be your boyfriend. You deserve a guy who's totally into you."

"Like you're into Lucia?"

I didn't know what to say.

"How the hell can you want *her?*"

Her superior tone churned my gut, splashing the walls of my stomach with acid.

"I mean *really*, Dane. She's against everything you fight for. Her beliefs are ridiculous. Not to mention how big she is—"

"Shut *up*." I fought the urge to spring to my feet and throttle her. *Anger's just a feeling*, Dr. Valentine's voice cooed in my head. *Breathe through it. Notice it without reacting.* "You lie to Lucia about me, then you dare insult her right to my face? Just because her beliefs differ from yours doesn't make them wrong."

"So you want Adolf to win?"

"Of course not! My mom's the smartest person I know, and she's clearly the best choice to lead the country."

"But how can you be physically attracted to someone like Lucia?" Her tiny Barbie nose scrunched up with disgust. "She's *huge*."

What a bitch. How had I once felt attracted to *Nina?* "Lucia's strong," I forced out through clenched teeth. "She's got substance." My hands twitched, remembering the feel of her curves in my caress. "She's a beautiful athlete."

She made a scoffing sound. "I don't understand you."

"And I don't understand *you*. How could you let your petty vendetta against Lucia hurt the entire team?"

Her eyes flared, spitting fire at me. "I don't know what you mean."

"Bullshit, Nina. You refused to set Lucia tonight. You alone lost the match." I gritted my teeth. "*I'm* the one you're mad at—not her. Don't let my mistakes hurt Lucia and ruin the season for your whole team."

She opened her mouth, probably to hurl more venom my way, but then pressed her lips together and looked down. She likely knew she couldn't deny what she'd done, especially to me. As a setter, I knew what was what.

"You're the leader of the team." I tried to temper my tone. "The team lives and dies with your leadership. You owe it to them. You owe it to them to give your best, and you didn't do that tonight. You let them down."

She sniffed, and I wondered if she'd resumed crying. At first I let the silence extend between us—she was much nicer to be around when she wasn't bitching at me. But then I worried Lucia might wonder where Nina had gone, so I spoke up.

"Do you ever think about our baby?"

Her head snapped up, revealing glassy eyes. A tear leaked out.

"*I* do." My heavy heart thudded.

"I don't want to think about him." She swallowed and brushed at her cheek.

"Him? I always thought we'd have a girl."

When the tiniest of smiles formed on her face, I felt my anger slip away like a puff of smoke. "I'm sorry you felt alone with this."

Her eyes turned down, and more tears escaped. "I guess I should have told you I wasn't on birth control."

No shit!

"And I probably should have let you know about the baby."

Yes, you should have.

"Do you think...?" She blinked a few times. "Do you think God will forgive me?"

I exhaled. "Don't know if we'll be forgiven. Lucia's praying for us, though."

"She is?"

Nobody had ever prayed for me before. "Yep. I don't deserve her." I grimaced.

"I'm such a bitch."

I barked out a laugh at her sudden confession.

"You've got an edge, and I thought…I thought you liked bitches."

I paused. "I thought I did, too." I stared at her. "But turns out I like sweethearts. Who knew, huh?" I rubbed the back of my neck. "I know I'm not good enough for Lucia. I can't explain her attraction to me, or my attraction to *her*. It doesn't make sense…but it's powerful. It's right. I can feel it. And I won't stand for anyone hurting her. Got it?"

Somewhere in my little speech I'd risen to my full height, and Nina looked up at me with big eyes. She looked as if she were going to say something for a moment, but then she just nodded.

"You're going to set her? Treat her like a teammate? Act like a *leader* out there?"

She pursed her lips. "Okay, okay. Geez! You're not my coach."

"Praise God for that."

"He already had a shit fit about us losing tonight. Now we're forced to play the first match of the conference tournament."

"You'll win it no problem, especially if you play like you're capable of." I reached for her hand and pulled her to her feet. I took a deep breath. "Truce?"

She studied me for a moment. "I'll try."

"Good. Now go shower, stinky."

"Asshole."

I attempted not to smile as we walked out of the weight room. Nina turned toward the locker room, and I turned to Brad.

"Let's get back to the greenhouse," Brad said. He rubbed his belly. "Time for some birthday cake when Lucia gets home?"

"Sure." I hadn't envisioned celebrating my birthday by talking down the girl who'd almost had my baby. But, spending the rest of the evening with the girl who'd stolen my heart…yeah, that would more than make up for it.

I followed Lucia into the kitchen and watched her shoulders tense the second she saw the cake. My hand came up to cradle her neck and gently swivel her to face me. "How 'bout some euchre to take your mind off that awful match?" *And distract you from the cake.*

"But I don't know how to play."

My eyes widened as I let go of her. "Blasphemy! You can't go to school in the Midwest without knowing the best game ever." I extended my palm and adopted a stern frown. "Hand in your Cougar card, right now."

The crease between her brows eased a bit, but she still remained tense.

"C'mon. I'll be your partner, and I never lose."

"You sure were losing earlier tonight," Brad said as he entered the kitchen. "Pete and I *schooled* you, son."

I scowled at him. "Josh and I would've made a comeback."

"You stopped your game early?" Lucia asked. "Why?"

"*Señor* Pussy-Whipped wanted to see your match," supplied Brad, drawing a smile from Lucia. "Wha-*cha!"* He dipped his wrist like he was cracking a whip.

I shook my head. "You can *leave* now, Jarhead."

"What, and miss this cake? I've been drooling over it all night." He swiped his finger through the thick vanilla frosting and stuck it in his mouth.

"Hey!"

Ignoring my protest, he closed his eyes. "Mmm." He grabbed a few plates from the cabinet and opened the drawer for a knife. When he noticed me glaring at him, he paused. "Okay if I dig in, GD?"

I grunted, then turned to Lucia. "Let's leave him to his cake orgasm and ask China and Allie to play." But she still hesitated, seeming appalled by the huge piece Brad cut for himself. I needed more distraction. "Are you afraid you'll suck at euchre?"

That did it—a spark of fire blazed in her eyes. "I'm sure I'll be just fine." She bustled out of the kitchen toward the agents in the TV room.

I grinned as I trailed her.

After my quick tutorial with Lucia and Allison—China had played before—we started the game. Lucia and I were up six-five when it was my turn to deal. I hid my grimace as I looked at the hand I'd dealt myself. *Total crap.* I couldn't give Brad more gloating ammunition, so we had to win this game. To my left, China passed, and I waited to see if Lucia would pass or instruct me to pick up the top card of the blind.

She frowned at her cards for a long moment from across the table. "Pass?"

"You don't want to order me up?"

"Table talk's beneath you, Dane," China said.

She thought I'd hinted that I *wanted* the card in my crapola hand? *No way.* "I'm just making sure Lucia knows what she's doing."

Lucia nodded, and this time her voice was stronger. "I do want to pass."

Allison passed too, meaning it was my decision if I wanted to call trump. I slapped the card face down on the blind. No way I wanted the responsibility of taking three tricks out of five with shit cards like these. Now China had the option of naming trump, but she passed again. I looked at Lucia, who smiled deviously. "I want to go alone. Trump is hearts."

My mouth dropped open. "Are you *sure?*"

China hissed.

"I'm not trying to table talk." I held my hands out to try to calm China Hellbeast Halloway. "But Luz, you know that means I don't play this hand, right? You're on your own."

"That is implied with the term 'alone,' yes." Her eyes glimmered.

Whoa. Her sudden confidence stoked a fire in my belly. I set my cards face down on the table and crossed my arms over my chest, grinning like an *idiota.*

China led with an ace of clubs, which Lucia promptly trumped with a ten of hearts. That put her in the lead, and she won the next three tricks. My heart pulsed with excitement as she held her last card in her hand, her eyes darting back and forth from China to Allison. If Lucia won the last trick, we earned four points and won the game. If she lost, we only earned one point.

Lucia closed her eyes, and I heard a muttered prayer in Spanish. Then she set down her king of spades. Allison frowned as she played her king of diamonds—Lucia's card beat hers. China's eyes narrowed before she shouted, "Shit!" Her queen of spades wasn't good enough to beat Lucia's king.

Lucia gasped as she looked up at me, her mouth open wide with joy.

"Hell, yeah!" I bolted out of my chair and initiated a victory dance. "We got a loner! We win ten-five, baby!" I sloped and shimmied my right shoulder, then my left, and snapped my fingers, mixing in some hip-hop moves Josh had taught me.

Lucia's giggle drew my attention back to the table. I ignored China's murderous scowl and grabbed Lucia's hand, yanking her up to dance with me.

"You got a loner your first time playing?" I marveled. "You're even better than Josh!" I jabbed my finger at the agents. "Eat that, Secret Service!"

Lucia's cheeks flushed as she laughed at my moves. "You're the worst winner, ever."

"Isn't it awesome?"

Her smile was so bright, so pretty. "I *guess*."

I drew her to me, my hand splayed across her back, and dipped her to one side then the other. As I gazed into her eyes, I wondered if she could feel my thumping heartbeat vibrate through her body, too.

She leaned in closer. *"Feliz Cumpleaños."*

"*Gracias*." I cocked my head toward the cake on the counter behind us. "Let's celebrate with a piece of cake?"

She bit her lower lip, then nodded.

"Cake for the losers, too," I said as I winked at Allison.

China pushed Allison toward their bedroom. "C'mon. I can't stand to be around that jerk right now."

I laughed as they walked out. I picked up the knife. "We'll just have a small piece, okay?"

"Okay." Lucia's voice trembled.

I cut a bite-sized piece and held it between us. It took her a second to realize I meant to feed it to her. "Oh!" She blinked.

"Sweets for the sweet." I smiled at her. When she nodded, I gently tucked the cake into her mouth. A stray blob of icing got trapped in the corner of her lips, which left me no choice but to lean in and lick her mouth. Her skin was honeyed satin.

I pulled back, and she beamed at me as she chewed. When she gestured for the knife, I handed it to her. She soon held a small piece for me in her hand, and I nudged in closer for her to feed it to me. As my tongue absorbed the sugar, she brushed her finger across my lip. Then she licked the icing from her finger, her lips molding and sucking it clean, her gaze fixated on me.

Christ.

I captured her face in my hands and kissed the hell out of her. *Best birthday ever.* We grinned at each other between kisses. "You taste delicious, Luz."

23

Lucia

★ ★ ★

"'Bout time you got here." The next afternoon Dane reached for my hand and guided me up the steps into the private jet for our flight to the presidential debate in Florida. I was still reeling from yesterday's roller coaster: the awful loss to Bridgetown, followed by a fantastic evening with Dane, and I barely had space in my brain for what lay ahead of us. Thankfully I remembered to stoop to enter the small space.

I rolled my eyes. "Sorry, but you know how Coach is." Still warm from practice and my hurried shower, I peeled off my jacket.

Dane laughed as he read my T-shirt:

Your Mom Called... You Left Your Game at Home

He sat and patted the seat next to him. We'd stopped hiding our feelings for each other from the agents, but it would be a different situation tonight with our families at the debate.

Allison and China sat in the row behind us, and I glanced at Frank ahead of me as I slid across the aisle from Dane. Although he leaned in by the cockpit, conferring with the pilot, he still had time to offer us a stern frown. His obvious disapproval of my relationship with Dane vexed me.

"Did Coach ask you about the match on election night?" Dane asked.

I winced. We were supposed to have beaten Bridgetown, thus earning a bye in the first round of the conference tournament. But our loss meant we had to play on November eighth—the same night my family expected me to be in Texas, waiting to find out if my dad would become leader of the free world. "Not yet. He was too mad about last night's match to worry about future games."

Dane reached across the aisle for my hand, and his touch felt warm and solid. "Have you decided what you'll do?"

"No." Either my team or my family would hate me that night. Considering my team was beginning to feel like a family, there was no doubt I'd have to let down people close to my heart. I swallowed the ball of stress climbing up my throat as his thumb stroked my palm. "In happier news, Nina's setting me again."

He let go of my hand as his mouth quirked. "Glad she got her head out of her ass."

"I guess Coach reamed her for last night."

"Hmm." Dane bent forward to rummage in his backpack.

I studied him. I was touched that he'd come to my match on his birthday, but he hadn't said much about our horrible loss. He was probably too busy gloating about our euchre win.

Brad lumbered into the plane and pulled the door shut behind him. He clapped his hands as he adopted a deep arena announcer's voice. "Let's get ready to rumbbbuuuuuuuuuullllllle!"

"It's a debate, not a monster truck rally," Dane said.

Brad's seat jostled as he collapsed into it. "The election *rides* on tonight, ladies and gentlemen."

I chewed on my lip as I glanced at Dane.

"I hope it's not boring," he continued. "At least the moderator's a hottie."

Dane scooted forward in his seat. "But I thought Molly Martins was a hopelessly biased liberal. You're attracted to her, Marine?"

"Hey." Brad shrugged as he looked at us over his shoulder. "Gettin' it on across the aisle seems to work for *you* two."

Dane grinned as he settled back in his seat—he seemed to like that answer. I started squirming, however. The odds of my family—my *father*—finding out about Dane and me appeared to increase by the second.

"Seatbelts on," Frank growled before sitting across from Brad.

As the plane taxied to the runway, I watched Dane slide his iPad out of his backpack.

"Playing a game?"

He grumbled, "Reading for class."

"Oh." My frown matched his. "I should read, too." I sighed as I opened my ebook for English class. I was behind in reading *The Immortal Life of Henrietta Lacks*, mostly because Dane was horribly distracting when we'd tried to study together the past week. He brought the same intensity to studying that he exhibited in volleyball and politics, and I hadn't been able to stop staring at his furrowed brow as he read and typed. I'd been mesmerized watching his huge brain sucking in information like a sleek, stealthy vacuum.

I read a few paragraphs once we were airborne and felt heaviness in my chest at Henrietta's sad story. She was a Black woman with cancer, and scientists had basically stolen her cells for research and medical advancements. The hospitals and research centers should have compensated her family after her death, but instead her family struggled with poverty.

As I thought about it, helping the poor was bound to be a topic at the debate tonight. My dad believed the best way to lift up the poor was to increase opportunity for all by improving the economy. *That sounds right to me, but how will it play to the debate audience?*

And I realized I was distracted once again—staring out the window instead of at my book. If it wasn't Dane, it was the man who would be horrified to discover my feelings for Dane. *Chingar.* How was I supposed to get any schoolwork done with so much going on in my life?

China's voice floated behind me. "Where'd you learn to cook? That cake you made for Dane was kickass." Her tone was quieter than normal, like she only wanted Allison to hear. But the government had spared no expense on this plane, and the smooth jets allowed me to overhear just fine. Maybe China thought I was actually reading.

"My last detail was protecting the First Lady," Allison said. "Uber-boring. I asked the chef to teach me some skills, just to pass the time."

"Well, I had to work out an extra hour today because of your skills, bitch."

Allison's gentle laugh drifted toward me.

"Are you nervous for tonight?" China asked.

I couldn't hear Allison's answer.

"Be careful, okay?" China's voice seemed softer, more vulnerable.

"You, too. Don't take unnecessary risks out there."

They're adorable! I glanced at Dane, expecting to find him absorbed in his reading, but he stared back at me with a wide smirk.

"I never intended for this to happen," Allison said. "Office romances aren't the best idea." She paused. "But I'm glad it did. I've had a crush on you since Glynco."

"You *have?* Damn it, I wish my gaydar had been more accurate back then."

Apparently Allison and I had more in common than I'd realized. No wonder she'd been so giddy about moving into the greenhouse—it was an opportunity to get closer to the object of her lust. I looked at *my* forever crush, whose dark eyes smoldered. *¡Hijole!*

Tonight portended to be a disaster.

I entered the green room with Frank and Allison tailing me. Though it had sucked to say goodbye to Dane—he was now with his family in their own space behind the stage—I bounced on my feet when I saw my entire family waiting for me. It had been too long since we'd all been together.

"*¡Hermanita!*" Alejandro bellowed before wrapping me in a hug and kissing me on the cheek. "'Bout time you made it."

"*¡Hola*, Alex!"

My mom scowled at my T-shirt and yoga pants. "You're not wearing *that*, are you?"

I scowled right back. "We rushed here from practice, Mom."

"I've got her change of clothes right here," Allison said, holding aloft my garment bag.

Mom held out her arms. "I meant to say, you look beautiful." Her brown eyes sparkled. "Forgive me?"

I rolled my eyes as I stepped into her hug. Thankfully she didn't smell like cigarette smoke.

Mateo raised his fist and bumped mine.

I jabbed him with a light punch. "What, no hug?"

He gave a shy grin and allowed me to embrace him. Jeez, the kid was only a few inches shorter than me now. I wondered if he would grow as tall as Dane.

"Sorry we missed your game." He looked down.

"I'm actually glad you guys couldn't make it…total slaughter."

"Yeah, what *happened?"* Alejandro asked.

I grimaced. *Nina happened.* "Long story. It'll be better the next time we play." *On election night.*

"Lucy!" My dad broke off from a small group seated around a conference table and came toward me. He looked quite handsome in his navy suit, crisp white shirt, and red tie. "I've missed you, *mija!"* His hug lifted me off my feet, reminding me of dizzy twirls in his strong hold, my giggles filling the living room of our childhood home.

"So how do you like college?"

I peeked around him to see his campaign manager drumming his fingers on the table, next to the vice presidential candidate and his wife, with a few Secret Service agents hovering nearby. And there was my Aunt Maricela as well. *Tía* Mari and I waved at each other, then I looked back at my dad. "I don't want to interrupt your last-minute prep for tonight."

"If I don't know it by now, the Republicans nominated the wrong guy."

"They definitely nominated the right guy." I grinned at him. "But we can catch up later."

"Darn election." He frowned. "Okay, but real quick…tell me your favorite thing about Highbanks."

Dane Monroe. My heartbeat kicked up as I imagined what would happen if I'd said that out loud. "Uh…um, well it's gotta be my teammate Maddie. She's super nice, and she's taught me a lot about hitting."

"Excellent. It's good to have somebody to push you—to make you better."

Like Dane.

"Adolfo?" Dad's manager had joined us. He gestured back to the table.

Dad kissed my forehead and returned to debate prep.

"Ms. Ramirez?"

I looked over at a chair set up in front of a mirror, where two women stood and smiled at me for some reason. "Yeah?"

"Time for hair and makeup!"

I snorted, but the makeup lady kept smiling and held out the chair for me. I inched back. "What?"

"If *I* had to get makeup, you do, too," Mateo said as he propelled me to the chair.

Now that I looked closer at his face, I detected some traces of foundation and blush. "No way!" I cradled his cheeks as he shoved me forward. "You look so *pretty!*"

"Shut it." He latched onto my shoulders and pushed me into the chair.

In the mirror, I watched Allison backpedal to the door. "We'll leave you to it," she said.

Frank shook his head. "I'll stay."

I watched him move to the conference table before tugs on my scalp diverted my attention. The thin, blond woman fanned out my hair. "Did you let this *air dry?*"

"Yeah?" She'd made it sound like a capital offense.

The makeup artist exhaled. "We have our work cut out for us."

Twenty minutes later, I zipped up a red and black block-color dress in a private bathroom off the green room and stepped closer to the mirror to check out my glam self. *Day-um*, as Brad would say. I shouldn't have been so disdainful of the beauty artists who'd gussied me up. The soft waves of my hair shone, and their smoky eye shadow and mascara made my eyes pop. I couldn't wait for Dane to see me.

Gazing at my happy face, it seemed like so long ago that I'd fantasized about hightailing it from Highbanks—though I always knew I couldn't. My first month had been miserable. But Maddie had mentored me in the art of getting the most out of our surly coach. Dr. Valentine and Whitney had helped me manage stress better so I could finally breathe. And the best mood booster of all had come from Dane admitting his feelings for me. *Squee!* My feet did a little tap dance just thinking about him. Regardless of whether my parents' address remained in Houston or relocated to 1600 Pennsylvania Avenue, I'd found a home at Highbanks.

"Lucia Maricela Ramirez!"

My smile vanished. That was my dad's voice.

I took a tentative step out of the bathroom to find my parents glaring at me. *"¿Sí?"*

A storm raged in my father's eyes. "You've been with *Dane Monroe?!?"*

My throat closed in on itself as my hand flew to my mouth. A glance to the right revealed the source of my father's information—he stood there with a righteous set to his jaw. "Frank!" I squeaked. I fought to suck in a breath. "How could you tell them?"

"So you're not denying it?" My father stepped forward and hissed, "You had *sex* with him?"

"What?" I shrieked. *Air, I need air.*

"*¡Ay*, Lucia!" my mother cried.

Our raised voices had drawn in my brothers from the other side of the room, and Alejandro's mouth dropped open. "I *knew* it! How could you be so stupid, Lucia?"

"What's happening?" asked Mateo.

Tremors started up my legs and into my torso, and I couldn't look at my family's horrified faces. The only words I could form were directed to my betrayer, Frank. "How *could* you?"

"Your parents had a right to know." Frank folded his arms across his chest. "Especially after Dane forced that girl to get an abortion."

"He did *what?"* If I thought my father had been angry before, that was nothing compared to the flash of hatred in his eyes, the violence in his voice. A tortilla could burn in the hot air huffed from his nostrils.

"¿Qué pasa?" Tía Mari asked as she approached us. She cupped my father's tense shoulder. "*Cálmate*, Adolfo."

My mother whimpered. *"¡Es el diablo!"*

"Dane's *not* the devil!" My family recoiled as I shouted. This was the first time I'd ever yelled like that.

"*Lucia*." My father's tone was the harshest I'd ever heard.

My cheeks warmed, and I took a deep breath. "Sorry, Dad, but you don't have your facts straight."

He paced for a moment, like a caged beast, then swallowed. "Then enlighten us."

"Well, first..." Flames of mortification licked my face. "Dane and I aren't having sex." *Thank Dios Dane stopped us.*

Mateo snickered. "This is epic." Alejandro cuffed his ear. "Ow!"

My father closed his eyes, seeming relieved. "I'm glad to hear that."

"Five minutes, everyone," a male agent interrupted.

"Adolfo, you need to focus on the debate," my father's campaign manager told him.

But nobody paid attention to either man. Not with the sordid details of my love life flayed wide open in front of my entire freaking family.

"Secondly..." I glowered at Frank. "Dane didn't know about the girl's pregnancy until *after* the abortion."

"Just how do you know that?" Frank challenged.

"Because he told me!"

"Yeah, *that's* reliable," Alejandro scoffed.

"And the girl in question admitted it, too," I added with a huff.

My mother shook her head. "You know her? Who is this girl?"

"I shouldn't say. I'll respect her privacy, unlike some people." Another hostile glance at Frank. "She felt like she had no other choice."

"There's *always* a choice!"

"I know, *Mamá.*" I sighed. "And I think she regrets it now. Dane too. The abortion...it crushed him."

Tia Mari's low laugh began to build. My father turned to his sister. "What could possibly be funny right now?"

"Lucy has it bad, bad, bad for this boy." She kept chuckling. "Your daughter's fallen for a liberal."

"Like hell she has!" He grabbed my wrists. "*Mija*, you've got a good head on your shoulders. How can you want anything to do with that corrupt family? They intend to destroy our country!"

I opened my mouth to respond, but nothing came out. I wasn't ready for this—I hadn't thought this through. Why had Frank snitched my secret? He'd ruined this entire night. I felt tears well up, and I tried to blink them away. Dad let go of my wrists and began pacing again.

Mateo shrugged. "I like Dane. He's cool."

I'd never loved my brother more. "Thank you, Matty." I turned to my parents. "Dad, Mom, this isn't about Dane's family, or his politics. It's about *him.* I'm not changing who I am, but I care about Dane. He's a good person...I hope you'll come to see that."

"No." My father's jaw flexed. "I won't. You don't know these people like I do, Lucy. They're *not* good people. They lie, they cheat."

"Don't you know that's exactly what Dane thought of you, at first? But then he got to know me, and…"

Whoops. Dad snorted fire again—clearly that hadn't been the best argument for winning him over. "I *won't* have my only daughter mixed up with that family."

"Governor?" His manager approached.

"One second!" Dad bellowed, then gave me the death stare. "Whatever you've started with Dane Monroe, you'll end it. Tonight, *mija.* We'll move you to another place. It's over."

No. My breath came in spasms, close to hyperventilation. Tears cascaded down my cheeks as agents herded my family toward the door.

"Governor," the manager said, "when she brings up global warming as scientific certainty—"

"No!" The word flew out of my mouth, and my father spun around. I swiped my cheeks. "I *won't* leave Dane. You don't know what you're talking about."

My mother gasped. "Lucia."

Dad's face colored to the shade of a hot red pepper. "You most certainly *will*—"

"Governor, I'm sorry, we must go." The manager hustled him out the door to the waiting area behind the stage as the agents lined us up.

My mother's hands shook as she pulled a cigarette out of her purse and attempted to light it.

Alejandro swooped in to yank it from her lips. "No time for that, *Mamá.*"

She frowned.

Tia Mari rubbed her back. "*Está bien,* Sylvia. It will be okay." She glanced at me, then back at my mother. "Have you *seen* that boy? Who wouldn't fall for him?" She winked at me. "Well done, Lucy. I think he's a hunk."

I somehow managed to smile at her through my tears. As we proceeded toward the auditorium, Frank sidled next to me and offered me some tissues.

"You know, Frank…" I yanked the tissues from his grasp. "I already have a father."

"I'm sorry, but—"

"Stay away from me." I dabbed beneath my eyes and marched away.

As we emerged from behind the stage and filed into the packed auditorium, the spectators clapped and hollered. Why did they celebrate my family's arrival? We hadn't done anything worth applauding. In fact, the bombshell Frank dropped on my father minutes before he took the stage would likely destroy his performance in this key debate.

On the other side of the auditorium, I noticed Dane and his family heading toward their seats, also in the front row. His sister walked in front of him and his father behind him, along with some agents and people I didn't know, and he looked as gloomy as I felt. He carried his body with a sense of tension I hadn't seen since Beergate. *Look at me*, I willed. *I need to see you*. Finally he lifted his head and glanced my way. When his dour expression brightened, the pressure in my chest evaporated. His smile was that dazzling. I noticed how his crisp black suit accentuated his height and the broadness of his shoulders. Unfortunately, once we sat, I couldn't see him without leaning forward in an obvious move.

My black clutch vibrated, and it took me a second to realize it was my phone. I never carried a purse—way too girly, but my heart soared once I read Dane's text:

You look stunning tonight.

He was obviously too far away to see my blotchy face. Alejandro whispered to our mother on my left, but Mateo grinned at me from the right. "Sexting?" He smirked.

I elbowed him, then furtively typed:

Gracias. U look guapo, like always. U ok?

As I waited for his response, cheers erupted and the candidates took the stage. I'd never realized Senator Monroe's beauty until I saw her in person. Of course, I should've known she had to be gorgeous to produce a son like Dane. Her lithe frame moved elegantly, and her eyes held a spark of intelligence and sass. Her dark purple business jacket and skirt must have cost a fortune, and I loved the floral scarf tied at her neck. My phone buzzed again.

My dad's a prick.

My lips parted. Dane had never discussed his father before. And though my father had his moments, I would never say something like that about him. I knew his freak-out about Dane was just because he loved me.

I looked up at my father as he stood behind the podium. His hard stare pulsed hostility across the stage, and I realized he likely aimed his fury at Dane. I gulped. Dane had a right to know what had happened.

Speaking of dads, mine knows.

The return text came seconds later:

Fuck ME.

Despite my prior meltdown over the situation, I stifled a giggle. His potty mouth was something to behold. Yet another thing my dad wouldn't like.

My dad looked straight at me as the moderator began to speak, and it seemed like he was barely holding it together. I mouthed, "*Te amo.*" His glare seemed to soften.

"Welcome to Florida State University, site of the last presidential debate. I'm Molly Martins, your moderator this evening." From her perch at a desk downstage, she paused as applause echoed through the auditorium. "We will start with an opening statement from each candidate, three minutes each. First, Governor Adolfo Ramirez."

My eyebrows arched. Perhaps letting Dad go first meant the moderator's liberal bias wouldn't show tonight. Or perhaps she could see how rattled he looked and wanted to pounce on that.

"Thank you, Ms. Martins. Good evening, Senator Monroe." He nodded at Dane's mother, then gripped the podium. "My father grew up in Mexico, and though he had a loving family, he wanted a better life: Economic opportunity. Safety. Autonomy. Freedom. Where could he find these treasures? What country did he pine for? America, of course…the beacon of light to so many around the world. When he was nineteen, my father legally emigrated to Texas, where he met my mother."

He smiled as he walked to the side of the stage, appearing relaxed and animated like his typical self.

I exhaled.

"The America my sister and I grew up in was a strong one. Education: top-notch. Innovation: fostered. Entrepreneurship: celebrated. Freedom: cherished.

"The America my three children grow up in..." He looked straight at me as he moved to the center of the stage. "Sadly, it has weakened under eight years of liberal leadership. Our government fosters dependency, paying citizens more to stay at home than to work. For those who are able, work is *crucial* for well-being, yet we deny them that key sense of self-worth. Excessive regulations have produced a stranglehold on innovation and freedom. And our economy? Well, our economy *sucks*."

What sounded like surprised laughter bubbled up from the audience.

"My administration will restore strength to our great country. We will surge forward with vibrant success, leveraging the untapped talents of our diverse population. We will achieve excellence once again!"

Did he honestly just pump his fist? The crowd erupted into thunderous applause, and I looked over my shoulder with awe at the clapping spectators behind me. A few shouts of "Rez for Pres!" rang out. Maybe he did have a chance to win. Clearly jazzed, Alejandro tapped my thigh with his fist.

"Thank you!" the moderator shouted, barely heard over the volume of cheers. "His time is up," she repeated, until finally the crowd quieted. My phone buzzed in my hand.

Not bad. He's dead wrong, but at least he's passionate.

Jerk. I typed back immediately:

Should've seen his passion when he found out about us.

"Senator Monroe, your three minutes begin now."

"Thank you, Molly." Dane's mother smiled warmly. "I started my career as a psychologist, where I first learned about the resilience and strength of Americans. For the past eleven years, it's been an honor serving in the US Senate, representing the good people of our country. Most recently, I've cherished the opportunity to learn even more about Americans on the campaign trail—to listen to their hopes and dreams. People like José Almada, a migrant farm worker in California who battled for over ten years to gain citizenship."

Alejandro leaned in and whispered, "Taking it right to us on immigration."

"People like Alice Briggs and Jeanie Young, who now have the right to express their love via legal marriage."

A few cheers erupted, and I thought of Allison and China.

"People like Bill Compton, whose medical bills would have bankrupted his family before Democrats insisted on affordable health care." She placed her hand over her heart. "These are my people. I will fight for their dreams. I care about each and every American, and I will fight for *all* of us, not just wealthy business owners. I will fight for equality!"

The applause seemed even louder this time. I typed another quick text:

Game on.

24

Dane

"I disagree with the governor that our military is the first line of attack." From behind the podium, my mother scanned the audience. Both candidates had responded to a question about education, and it now was her turn to discuss national security. "Diplomacy and negotiation are fine arts that have been lost by war-hungry Republicans. We need to bring back the ability to *listen* to our neighbors, instead of foisting our agenda upon them."

My smile broadened as the applause rained down.

Dad leaned across Jessica and nudged me. "She sure schooled *him* on foreign policy."

Like you care. I wished he'd stop talking to me. His arm draped across Jessica's shoulders made me want to barf.

"Listening *is* important," Governor Ramirez said when it was his turn for rebuttal. "For years we've listened to terrorists call us infidels. We've listened to their deep desire to destroy us. But listening is a two-way street. The only way our *enemies* listen is through force, through strength. Senator Monroe, the past regime has been all talk, no action, and it sounds like you want more of the same. Terrorists ignore us when we speak loudly but carry a small stick. A *tiny* stick."

When he held up his index fingers an inch apart, I almost laughed along with others in the audience. Who knew Adolf could pull off sexual innuendo on national TV? Standing at the end of the row, Brad gave me a thumbs-up. But I scowled back at him, refusing to succumb to Adolf's charm. He would likely have none of that charm for me.

"Next," the moderator said, "we turn to the pressing problem of climate change. How will you keep America safe from the threats of global warming? Senator Monroe, you're up first."

"Thanks, Molly." Mom aimed a smile over my shoulder. "And thanks to Dr. James Thompson for his seminal work alerting us all about the dangers we face..." She extended her arm to gesture to the same spot behind me, and I craned my neck to find him sitting a few rows back.

Yes, thank you, Dr. Thompson, for the house that brought Lucia and me together. It hit me with a thud that Adolf probably wouldn't let Luz live with me ever again. I swiveled back around to find the governor staring at me with angry eyes. *Yikes.* I wondered if Mom's mention of Dr. Thompson had sparked thoughts of our living arrangement for him too.

"Why is he staring at me?" Jessica whispered.

"He's not." I gulped. "He's glaring at *me*."

"Why? It's creepy."

I glanced at my sister, feeling guilty for keeping yet another secret from her. But I hadn't had a moment alone with her all night. She'd been so thrilled to see our absentee father that she'd clung to his side in the green room, and of course the fucker had only fostered her adoration of him. *Narcissistic nutsack.* Jess had no idea Dad would break her heart once the election ended.

"He's staring because he's a d-bag," I told my sister as I tuned back in to my mother's voice.

"We have a moral *imperative* to fight climate change!"

Applause erupted, and I realized I'd missed most of my mother's response. But I already knew the science she'd likely cited: human pollution was destroying the world. When the moderator invited Adolf to chime in, I braced myself.

He gave a shitty half-smile, clearly full of sarcasm. "I find it interesting you bring up morals, Senator, when you and your cronies make millions off environmental lobbyists. And you cost our country billions with failed green energy investments. This isn't about science—it's about money."

He'd definitely slipped a cog. How could this twat have produced a sweetheart like Lucia?

"Yes, there is climate change, as there has always been. In fact, we've seen a *cooling* trend the past seventeen years. But we are decidedly uncertain about its causes and effects. Methane gas from cows and volcanoes contributes far more to climate change than human carbon monoxide emissions."

What a fucking farce! What kind of pea-brain 'scientists' did he have on his payroll?

"The moral imperative here is *not* to limit American productivity based on unverified, incomplete information. The moral imperative—and the right thing to do for national security—is to break free of the Middle East by utilizing our vast resources..."

Thank God the moderator cut him off for going over his time. She asked Mom for her rebuttal.

"More than ninety-seven percent of climatologists believe human activities cause global warming. That, my friends, is called scientific consensus."

Hells yeah! My feet jiggled with the desire to jump up and cheer.

Forty minutes later, Adolf finished the debate with his closing argument. I joined the applause, not because I agreed with a word he'd said, but because I was so damn relieved never to have to listen to his asinine arguments again.

"Let's go, Dane," Grandfather Monroe said as he stood. He was pretty spry for an old guy. "Time to join your mother on stage."

Ugh, time to get closer to Adolf. I followed Jessica around to the left, and as I climbed the stairs under the watchful eye of Secret Service, I glanced across the stage. The Ramirez family had also joined their candidate onstage, and Lucia's alluring smile floored me. She looked so gorgeous that I longed to take her in my arms. But then she turned to hug her father, and I had to look away.

My mother waved to the crowd as she stood stiffly next to my father, and I stepped between them to wrap her in a hug. "You did so great, Mom."

"Really?" She looked up at me, and I noticed worry lines around her eyes. Had those been there before the campaign started? I could only imagine how tired she must feel after word-wrestling with that Nazi. It was probably like a bitter, five-game match with Bridgetown that came right down to the wire.

The applause continued, competing with some cheesy music they'd piped in, and hundreds of flashes lit up the auditorium like fireworks in a night sky. Steve, my mother's campaign manager, gestured from the front row of seats for us to stand together to wave to the crowd. I suppressed an eye roll when I ended up next to my father, but I couldn't hide my disdain when Dad grabbed my right hand.

"Hold your sister's hand," he ordered, pointing to my left.

One fat, fucktastically happy family. I plastered on a fake smile as I scooped up Jessica's hand, completing a line of Monroes: Grandfather, Mom, Dad, me, Jess. A glance to my left revealed the Ramirez clan in the same formation. At the end of their line, closest to Jessica, Mateo seemed to be watching us. I nodded at him but he didn't respond. As Jessica waved at the audience, looking from left to right, I noticed a curious blush on her fair cheeks when she turned my way. I looked again at Mateo and caught his eyes roaming down her body. *Oh. Caught ya.*

That was when I remembered I'd promised to introduce Lucia to Jessica, and this was probably our only chance. But I didn't know how Adolf would respond if I approached his daughter. *Screw it.* I wasn't going to live in fear of that man.

I leaned in toward Jessica's ear. "I want to introduce you to the enemy."

She nodded vigorously. "Sure!"

I shook my head at her exuberant response. She probably thought I'd meant Mateo. Well, maybe I could introduce her to him as well—at least *this* crush would be more age-appropriate than her infatuation with the Secret Service agent John.

When Governor Ramirez turned to his left, pointing and schmoozing with some guy in the audience, I led my sister toward Lucia. It seemed like the camera flashes picked up speed, blinding me for a moment...or was it Lucia's exquisite face that almost knocked me over? She didn't typically wear makeup—someone with her luminescence didn't need it—but I loved how seductive her eyes looked, lined in charcoal. It was like she'd matured into a woman in the hours we'd been apart.

I fended off the urge to touch her. "Lucia, this is Jessica."

"I hear you're an awesome swimmer!" Lucia grinned as she pumped her hand.

Jessica blinked, wide-eyed. "You're tall."

"Ugh, these stupid heels." Her hand flapped toward her feet.

It's not the heels making you tall, sweetheart. I smiled and noticed Mateo hovering like a curious hummingbird feigning disinterest. "Teo." I waved him over. "This is my sister."

"Hey." He shrugged.

Jess twisted her hands together, her expression grave. "Hey."

I glanced at Lucia, whose shoulders shook with suppressed laughter. She'd noticed our siblings crushing on each other, too.

Alejandro didn't look so amused as he stepped into our foursome. When his dark eyes met mine, I realized Adolf wasn't the only one who'd learned about Lucia and me. What the hell had happened in that green room? He looked at me scornfully and spoke in a tight voice. "Lucy, say goodbye to Dane."

My heart fluttered with sudden dread that I wouldn't see her again. My eyes darted to hers, and fear flashed in her expression, too.

"I'll see you *soon*, GD," she said with a firm nod, then turned toward Allison.

I exhaled. I would hold her to that promise. China had materialized behind us, and she gestured to the stairs.

As Secret Service herded us off the stage, I put distance between Dad and myself. We returned to the green room, where I collapsed on the sofa. Way too much drama for one night—I didn't know how my mother did it. And she and her advisors were still going, huddled around a TV showing debate analysis. At times Steve patted her on the back and at times he shouted at the screen.

Brad tossed me a bottled water, which I caught one-handed and offered to my sister. She unscrewed the cap as she sat next to me. Dad went to sit on the other side of Jess, but after my warning glare he walked away. *Good riddance.* I watched him take his cell phone out of his pocket and dial a call. Swear to God, he'd better not call his floozy with my mother in the same room.

"So, are you going to tell me why that Ramirez guy doesn't like you?" Jessica asked.

Only a teenage girl could refer to a man that powerful as "that guy." I glanced at Mom, but she was engrossed in conversation with Steve. I lowered my voice. "Tell me about you and Mateo first."

She sputtered her sip of water. "What're you talking about?"

"I saw him checking you out."

"He did?" The sofa bounced.

"And you *liked* it."

That same blush reappeared. "Well, he's no Johnnie, but…he's tall, dark, and *caliente*." Her eyes took on a far-away gaze.

"You like his Latino looks?"

"*Sí, señor.*"

"I know what you mean—I like them too."

Her eyebrows hit the ceiling. "Are you coming out to me, brother?"

"Am I…?" After a moment I laughed. "No, I'm not attracted to Mateo." I shook my head. "I'm attracted to a Latina." I swallowed as I searched her eyes for judgment. "Lucia."

It took a second for the news to sink in. "Whoa…I *knew* it!"

"We're dating. I know it's crazy."

"What…What'd Mom say?"

"Mom doesn't know."

"*What* don't I know?" Mom asked.

Where the hell had she come from? She tilted her head as she stood over us, and I saw Steve about ten feet behind her, his finger still poised in the air like he'd just been taking to her. Mom untied her scarf and slid it off her neck. "Steve." She glanced over her shoulder. "Give us a minute."

He frowned, but turned to walk back to the TV. Mom sat next to me, letting the back of her head rest on the sofa cushion. "What a long day." She closed her eyes. "What a long election."

"It's almost over," I said.

She sighed. "So, what don't I know, Dane?"

I peeked at Jessica, who winced, then back at Mom. "Don't get upset, okay?"

"You don't want me to feel upset," she echoed, her eyes still closed, "that you've fallen for Lucia Ramirez?"

I bolted upright. "Secret Service told you?"

Her eyes opened. "No, honey." She reached up to pat my hair. "A mother just knows these things." She sat up. "You've been avoiding me, and I saw you with her on stage. I saw the way she looks at you."

"Are you…mad at me?"

"No, I'm not angry." She frowned. "More like concerned. Loving someone is hard enough when you have the same values…" Her gaze flitted over to my father, who stood across the room with his phone tucked to his ear. Watching her look at him, my throat tightened with sadness. She sighed as she turned to me again. "And I'm worried how hard this will be for you both. Her world view is so different from yours."

"I know." My hands curled into fists. "I can't believe the bullshit her dad spouted tonight."

China approached the sofa. "Uh…" She nodded at my mother, then looked at me. "Governor Ramirez wants to talk to you, Dane."

Holy shitcakes. I'd thought something like this might happen.

"He knows, too?" asked Mom.

I nodded. "Lucia texted me that he found out about us. But I doubt he's taking it as well as you are."

Mom snorted.

China said, "Want me to tell him no way, José?"

I looked to my mother, who smiled at me. "This is your decision. You're an adult now, Mr. Twenty-Years-Old."

My stomach twisted as I imagined Adolf's scowl, but when I pictured Lucia's soft smile, I knew what I had to do. "I'll talk to him." Lucia was worth fighting for. "Let's do it."

As I scooted forward, Jessica grasped my forearm. "Are you sure? He's kind of *loco*."

"*Completamente loco.*" I winked at her, then followed China to my castration. I gave my joystick a fond goodbye squeeze in the hallway.

"Wait here—Frank's bringing the governor." China let me into a smaller room with two loveseats and a bucket of iced waters on the coffee table between them. My throat now dry, I lunged for one and had downed half of the bottle by the time the door opened again.

Though Lucia's father was a few inches shorter than me, he seemed to fill the space. His gaze was sharp, incisive; his dark suit neat. In a word, he had *presence.* I could see why he'd beaten a more moderate candidate in the primaries. He just seemed more presidential than that wussy guy.

His eyes stayed on mine. "Please leave us, Frank."

"My pleasure, sir."

I took in Frank's departing smile with interest. *They* seemed rather chummy.

He sized me up as he extended his hand. "Adolfo Ramirez."

"Dane Monroe." His handshake was firm, as expected.

"Your mother did a fine job in the debate."

I hadn't expected him to say something like that. "I agree."

"Obviously, it helps…" He paused, appeared uncertain for a moment, then shook his head. "Never mind."

"What?"

He puffed air out his nose. "It helps when the moderator's on your side."

I took a deep breath. "I thought Ms. Martins was fair."

"Of course you did."

I didn't appreciate his patronizing tone. "Just how was she biased, then?"

"One measly question on the economy, tucked in near the end. The economy's the number-one issue for American voters, but she avoided it because she knows it's a weakness of your mother's platform."

Huh. I hadn't noticed, but he was right that my mother's economic plan wasn't her strongest answer of the night. *Was* there media bias? I thought about that horrid photo of Lucia in the newspaper and her panicked gasps over the phone. I shook my head to clear that memory. "But the moderator did allow you to start and finish the debate."

"Big deal."

"It *is* a big deal, with primacy and recency effects."

A crease wizened his forehead.

"Psychology," I said. "People remember the first thing and the last thing the best."

The corner of his mouth twitched. He reached for a bottle of water and took a swig. Then he gestured to the loveseat across from him. "Take a seat, Dane."

I didn't like him ordering me around, and I felt the words *Fuck off* on my tongue. But then I thought of Luz and reminded myself to take a deep breath or two. Or ten. Once I sat, he sat across from me.

He recomposed his stern mask. "I told Lucia it's over between you two."

I recoiled as if he'd punched me. Why hadn't she shared that with me? My heart rocketed, and my mouth felt dry again. Was she trying to let me down easy? Would she break up with me on the plane ride home?

"That bothers you?" He studied me.

I realized my mouth hung open, and I snapped it shut. "Of course it does! You…you have no right."

"I most certainly do. She's my only daughter."

"And I'm my mother's only son."

He nodded. "Your mother knows about you and Lucia."

"I just told her, and she was much more reasonable than you."

"Right." There was that shitty, sarcastic grin again.

What exactly was his agenda here? "Why are you talking to me? You told Lucia to end it, and she always obeys *Daddy*. So why this conversation?"

"Lucia plans to defy me because she has the wrong idea about you. I need you to help her see reality."

I massaged my forehead. "And what is this supposed reality?"

"You started this relationship to get to me, to my campaign. To learn insider secrets. That's why your mother invited Lucy to live there in the first place—to set me up."

And I'd thought *Lucia* was paranoid. *Jesus!* "How dare you cheapen what Luz and I have. *You're* the politician, not me. I care for her."

"What'd you call my daughter?" His eyebrows pinched together.

I paused. "Luz."

"You know the meaning of the word?"

I stared at him, trying to figure out his angle. What was he accusing me of now?

"Luz means light," he finally said.

"I know." I nodded. "*Su hija es…brillante.*"

His face changed, either from surprise that I spoke Spanish or that I'd called his daughter brilliant.

"Yes, *espléndida*," I added. *She's splendid. Stunning.* Adolf didn't speak, so I soldiered ahead. "Listen, believe what you want, but Luz and I know what's between us. And it's not some bullshit political maneuver. She's the only reason I'm surviving this damn election, and I think she'd say the same about me. Our relationship isn't something you can make disappear with a unilateral snap of your fingers. She deserves better than that. We're both adults now—free to make our own decisions, maybe our own mistakes—but that's our call, as adults."

When he finally spoke, his voice had lost its edge. "Your mother approves of your relationship with Lucia?"

I sighed. "She's concerned we're too different to make it work."

He chuckled as he shook his head. "Finally something the senator and I agree on." He hesitated. "And your father? What does he think of this?"

I looked at my shoes, wanting to hide my reaction to the mention of my father. "He doesn't know."

"Where was he when your mother found out?"

I said nothing, just listened to the tick of the clock as I rubbed a scuff on my dress shoes.

"Off talking to his mistress?"

My head shot up as I sucked in a gasp. *Fuck!* Realizing I'd just confirmed Adolf's suspicions, I closed my mouth and swallowed. "I-I-I don't know what you're talking about."

"You're a worse liar than your mother." He looked away and scoffed. "And I guess that makes you slightly more trustworthy." When he looked at me again, there seemed to be a hint of kindness in his eyes. "Don't worry. I won't say anything to the press."

"Why not?"

"I don't want to win that way, Dane. That's not the campaign I want to run. I love this country, and I want to help, but I promised my wife I wouldn't lose my soul to win office. My integrity's not for sale."

Whoa. His expression was so fierce that I believed every word. "Where'd you find out about my dad?"

"I hear things." He shrugged. "I make sure to get the information I need. It's why I asked Agent Vanderberg to look after Lucy."

Ah. That's how he'd found out about us—Frank had snitched. *Asshole.*

"It's unfortunate how your father has treated your family," he continued. "But this is yet another reason I don't want my daughter with you. What kind of values have you learned in your family, given what your father has done?"

I saw red. "It's not fair to compare me to my father!"

"That's not my goal here. My goal's to protect Lucy."

"But you think I'm not good enough."

His mouth pressed into a line. "*Nobody's* good enough for my *brillante* daughter. You should know that already."

He had a point.

"I need to talk to Lucia's mother, think this through some more. You and Lucy together…well, it's shocked me, and I need to give this time to settle." He shook his head. "One thing I *do* know: I'm moving Lucia out of that house. I should've known better than to let her live there with a college boy. I was your age once—I know where your brain is."

When he glared at my crotch, my penis twitched.

"Keep that thing away from my daughter, Mr. Monroe."

His exit was swift, and my mortification complete. Why oh why did I have to fall for a crazy man's daughter?

25

Lucia

Should Henrietta Lacks's family be compensated for the use of her cells in science? Why or why not? Do you believe the Lackses deserve health insurance even if they can't afford it? How would you respond if you were in their situation?

This English paper prompt was killing me. The blank document on my laptop stared up at me, glaring white in the soft lamplight of Dane's bedroom. Darkness encroached earlier now that it was November, and the mornings were already colder than Texas winters. It had even threatened to snow on Halloween, which had (of course) been another non-event in our frantic lives. I'd dressed as a volleyball player. Ha ha.

My paper was due on Election Day—just two days away—and I'd barely recovered from the debate a few days ago. Just to get something on paper, I typed:

> I hope the Lackses feel proud that Henrietta's cells have helped so many. If it's possible for hospitals or researchers to compensate her family monetarily, I support that. But I don't believe people deserve health insurance or other benefits simply for living in America. I believe we have to work for health insurance. For example, I'm writing this stupid paper to further my stupid education so that I can get a stupid job with stupid health insurance.

Somehow I didn't think my TA would give this an A.

From where I sat on Dane's bed, my back leaning against the wall, I had merely to raise my eyes from the blank screen and I could rest them on a more welcome sight: six-foot-eight of muscle and sexy folded into an office chair. The only time he stilled was when he studied, and I could watch him for hours. Realizing my dad would follow through soon on his threat to move me out of the greenhouse, I figured I'd better take advantage of Dane Time right now. The assignment could wait.

He'd angled his chair catty-corner to the desk so he could extend his mile-long legs, and the black chair tilted back as he curled his socked feet over the bar connecting the legs of his computer desk. He frowned as he drew the iPad closer to his face, then a smile broke through. "*Cooool.*"

"What?"

He set his feet down and spun his chair toward me, his eyes alight. "We're learning about booze in my psychopharm class. Did you know there's nothing you can do to speed up getting sober?"

"I thought coffee was supposed to help."

"Nope—all that'll give you is a hyper drunk person." He grinned. "Your blood alcohol concentration increases with each drink, depending on various factors. But alcohol leaves your system at a constant rate—point zero one five each hour—regardless of coffee, showering, exercising, whatever. It takes a really long time for your body to process the alcohol." He pointed to a colorful electronic chart. "You see this? You could go to bed with a BAC of point two and think you're hungover the next morning, when in fact you're still drunk!"

He was so cute when something excited him. "You should share your newfound knowledge with Dr. Valentine. Maybe she'd give you extra credit."

"Ugh." He wrinkled his nose as he jettisoned the iPad to his desk. "This just became uncool."

I laughed.

"You had your session yesterday with her, right?" When I nodded, he asked, "How'd it go?"

"Um..." I sighed. "We discussed election night—playing the match or being with my family in Texas."

"Haven't decided yet?"

"Nope." A knot tightened in my stomach.

"Your family expects you to be there?"

"Yep."

"But your team expects you to be here."

"That about sums it up." I clutched fistfuls of my hair as my body tensed.

"Sounds like an impossible decision." His foot extended to rub my knee. "But I know you'll do the right thing."

"Which is?"

His mouth curled into a condescending smile. "If Valentine won't tell you, I won't either."

I shoved his foot off the bed. "So how did *your* session go?"

His smile faded, and he looked down. "Nothing too exciting." He shrugged. "Family stuff."

Why had he become evasive? And not just about therapy—there was something else he'd been hiding, too. "You're keeping secrets from me."

He looked up. "What's that?"

"Nina talked to me in the locker room after practice tonight."

He blinked as he drew back from me.

"Now I know why she's setting me again. You spoke to her. Smoothed things over."

He nodded.

"Why didn't you tell me?"

"I didn't want to drag you into this mess more than I already have. It was my problem, so I had to fix it." His jaw tightened. "I'm sorry my stupidity affected your volleyball career."

"It's not your fault Nina's unstable."

A scoffing sound erupted from his throat.

"Did you know she actually apologized to me?"

His chin dipped. "No way."

"Not only that, but she said we're kind of cute together."

"*Nina* said that?"

"I know." I grinned. "I couldn't believe it either."

"Cute, huh?" He glanced at the open bedroom door—a rule my father had established, and Frank had enforced. Then he leaned forward, and I inhaled a little puff of air when his hand brushed my hair behind my ear. "You *are* damn cute, that's for sure."

My heart jumped a beat at his warm touch. "One thing Nina said was kind of strange. You, ah, you told her I was praying for her?"

He stole his hand back. "Does that bother you?"

"No." I shrugged. "It's true—I was. I am. It's just...I guess I'm kind of surprised you told her that. Were you guys...?" I bit my lower lip as my cheeks warmed. "Were you making fun of me?"

"No!" His eyes opened wide, and he lunged for my hands. "I may not understand your beliefs, your faith, but I won't mock them anymore, I promise." He swallowed as he stroked my fingers. "I told Nina you were praying for us because I thought it was such a sweet, forgiving thing to do—so like you. I guess I wanted to show Nina all that you are, and all that she's not."

I nodded, though it was difficult to believe I was better than Nina at anything.

"I'm *grateful* you pray for us, Luz. Your faith is so strong...it's, it's kind of beautiful, really. I wish I could feel that way about something."

Wow. I just fell for him a little bit more.

He lured me forward, and he kept holding my hands while his thumb swirled circles on the inside of my knee. Sparks of delight traveled up my thigh. "I'm not the only one keeping secrets, Luz."

"*¿Qué?*" My mind didn't function well at the moment.

"I've been trying to work out why you didn't tell me this, but I got nothing. You asked Phil to keep me on the team?"

"Oh." I came back to earth. "He told you about that." I hoped Dane didn't think I'd interfered with his life.

"Yes. Why'd you do it?"

"I wanted to thank you for helping me, you know, after the photo in the paper." His eyes clouded over with apparent anger, probably remembering my she-beast photo. "And because..." I waited until his gaze cleared. "Because you're such a talented setter—I didn't want that to go to waste. I've never hit better than the night we played. You brought out the best in me."

His eyes glittered as he rolled his chair to the edge of the bed and tugged me forward, away from the wall. He drew our hands together, close to his heart, and his face came inches from mine. "That's the kindest thing anyone's ever done for me. Why didn't you tell me?"

"I thought you'd be mad." When his eyebrows lowered, I added, "It seemed like no matter what I did, you got mad at me."

He groaned. "Asshole, party of one."

"Stop beating yourself up. You eventually saw the light."

The corner of his mouth perked up. "Yes, I did, *Luz*."

And I did, too.

His face nudged in, and I closed the distance by touching my lips to his. His hard mouth molded over mine, and he let go of my hands to cradle my head. With my chest folded over my legs and the excitement pulsing through my bloodstream, I felt breathless. Our position must not have been to his liking, either, because he launched himself from his chair to the bed with one swift push off his feet.

We found our way into each other's arms so easily that it felt like we'd been together for years. But I didn't feel good about the possibility of Frank walking in on us. "This open-door policy's stupid." I scooted down the bed and extended my foot to shove the door shut.

"*Very* naughty, Luz." His grin stretched wide. "GD approves."

But Governor Ramirez doesn't. I pushed down my concern as I slid my way back up the bed. We lay on our sides, facing each other. His hand lowered to my thigh and rubbed from my hip to my knee in long strokes. He watched me shiver, and his eyes darkened. His face had lost some of its tan since August, making him look even more like the All-American boy he was. He was my gringo. I felt so warm and loved in his arms.

I traced the raised ridge of skin above his right eye. "How'd you get this scar?"

"Guatemala." He shook his head. "I never told you that story?"

"When were *you* in Guatemala?"

"One summer in high school. My family went there on a cross-cultural trip—a humanitarian mission. We helped build a well, some houses, that kind of thing."

I smiled. "That's where you learned to speak *español*."

"*Sí, cariña*." He smiled back.

"So..." The bumpy scar fascinated my fingers. "You were building a house, and got hit by a *dos-por-quatro?*"

He chuckled as he grazed his fingertips up the inside of my arm. I closed my eyes to savor his touch. "No two-by-fours were involved. But a piece of pipe, yeah."

My eyes flew open. "What *happened?*"

"I was being a hothead, as usual." He grimaced. "Jess was only twelve, maybe thirteen, and the creepy locals kept staring at her."

"The first *rubia* they'd seen?"

He pointed to his short blond hair. "Yeah. They stared at me, too, but not in the same lecherous way. I confronted one villager about it—we'd only been there a few days and my Spanish sucked—and I inadvertently insulted his mother or something. He came at me with a busted pipe."

I gasped.

"Do you know how much a cut on your face bleeds?"

I shuddered as I pictured blood dripping down his face. "One time, a club teammate broke her nose when the ball smashed her face." I cringed. "Blood everywhere."

"Exactly. My dad was off painting in the mountains, and my mom freaked when she saw all that blood. At first she was screaming for the guy to be arrested, but then our translator got involved and explained I'd insulted the villager in the worst way possible—basically, I was lucky to be alive. Upside of the story: I became motivated to learn Spanish like never before."

His eyes smiled at me, and I kissed the jagged skin on his forehead.

"Then I love this scar," I said. "It represents your love for your sister. You were just trying to protect her. You were helping people."

"Sure botched that one. I bet the villagers were happy to see us go."

I gazed into his eyes. "I would *never* be happy to see you go." *And I'm praying I don't have to.* "You said you wished you felt deep faith in something. Don't you see? You have deep convictions. You help people. You love your family."

His head dipped. "My family's not...close like yours."

He looked so sad! "Maybe that's a good thing? Your mom isn't trying to break us up like my dad is."

"Your dad's a good man, though."

I pulled back with shock. "Dane Monroe." I pressed the back of my hand to his forehead. "Are you feeling okay?" When he didn't smile, I dropped my attempt to joke with him. "Hey." I skimmed my fingertips over his collarbone. "*Are* you okay?"

"You asked me what I talk about with Dr. Valentine." He closed his eyes as he let out a long breath. Then he rolled onto his back and covered his face with his palms. "My parents don't love each other. My dad's having an affair."

¡Dios mio! That would destroy me. I didn't know what to say, but when Dane's big hands slid down his face so he could see my reaction, I knew I had to come up with something. "That's awful. I'm so sorry." I inched closer, and when he nodded, I climbed onto him and snuggled in so that my ear rested on his chest. "When did you find out?"

"Right before Beergate."

Ah. That made a lot more sense.

"I couldn't tell anyone, 'cause of the election."

I lifted my head. "I won't tell, I promise. I won't tell my dad."

Dane stroked my hair. "He already knows."

"What?"

"He found out from Secret Service or something. He said he would keep it private because he didn't want to run a dirty campaign."

Pride swelled in my heart. But Dane's expression seemed more like one of shame than pride.

"Your dad said I'm not good for you—I haven't had proper role models."

"Well, *that* was mean."

"He's right." Dane grimaced. "Dr. Valentine said I have a fear of intimacy because of my parents' relationship. It's probably why I pushed you away so much."

"You're not pushing me away now." I kissed his cheek. "And my parents' marriage might be fine, but Alex drives me and Matty nuts with his bossiness. No family's perfect."

He blinked up at me, seeming to weigh my words. "My dad has really hurt my mom with all of this. I just worry about her, you know?"

"I don't. She's a badass." He arched his eyebrows, and I laughed. "It's true! Running for president as a woman? That's amazing. And she's so beautiful, I'm sure she'll find another guy who's even better—"

A knock on the door interrupted me. I pushed back from Dane but he clutched me to his body. "It's okay." He nodded. "Come in!"

Please, don't be Frank. I exhaled when I saw Allison in the doorway.

"Guess who's on his way from the airport?" she asked.

"Adolf," Dane moaned.

This time he let me scramble off of him. I scooped my hair up as I hunted for my shoes on the floor. "When's he getting here?"

"Two minutes."

Where was my other darn shoe? As my eyes scanned the floor, I dug in the pocket of my hoodie for a hair band while my other held my hair aloft. Was my room clean? Would Dad make me move out tonight? "I can't find my shoe!" My heart pounded, and I felt close to tears.

"Hey." Dane extracted my hand from my pocket and nudged me to let my hair fall before he clasped my hands in his. "Breathe."

I nodded and tried to calm down.

"It's going to be okay."

"What if he makes us break up?" My voice was shrill.

"We talked about this. We won't let that happen right?"

I gazed into his deep, blue eyes. "Right."

"He told me he needed some time to think. So I guess he's done with that now. Whatever he tells you, it'll be good to know what he's thinking."

I took a deep breath. Dane was right. And truthfully, I wanted to see my dad. It was pretty awesome he was visiting me right before the biggest night of his life.

"Now, first step." He grinned as he kneeled down to slide on my wayward shoe, then stood and spun my body to face the door. "Get the hell out of my bedroom."

I laughed as I jogged out the door and headed for the foyer. It felt so good to laugh. His sense of humor was one thing of many I loved about Dane. As I passed by the TV room, I noticed Brad tidying up the oversize pillows on the sofa. Allison and China waited for me by the video monitors.

"Do you think we should set out drinks for the governor?" asked Allison.

"Yeah, get him some booze," Dane said as he swooped in. "He'll love that." He'd exchanged his sweatpants for khakis and had pulled a royal blue sweater over his long-sleeve T-shirt. I loved how that sweater matched his eyes.

I glanced down at my typical post-practice uniform of T-shirt, hoodie, and yoga pants and wondered if I should have changed clothes too. I was about to bolt back to my room when Dane clasped my wrist.

"You look fine. Your dad will like you wearing the shirt he got you."

I unzipped my hoodie another inch so the T-shirt saying was visible:

I spiked your dink

China scrunched her nose. "What's a dink?"

"It's a tiny tap of the ball over the net," Dane explained. "The defense expects a big hit, but you trick 'em with a dink. Unless they spike it straight back at you."

"Volleyball humor," China scoffed.

I tensed as Frank and Brad swept into the hallway. "They're almost here," Frank said. He glanced at me, but I kept up my silent treatment, so he disarmed the alarm and stepped outside to wait for my dad's convoy.

Dane's elbow tapped mine. "Frank was only doing what your dad asked."

"So you think Frank was right to tell him about us?"

"No. I think he should've butted out." He gestured to the five of us standing there with expectant, nervous energy. "But then we wouldn't have fun times like this."

"Yeah, good times," I said, and the front door opened.

There were no fewer than four Secret Service agents with my dad. And I was betting there were more back in the vehicles now in our driveway.

"What a great house," my dad said as his tired eyes took in his surroundings, and then me. "*Mija.*"

I stepped forward, and he gathered me in a hug. "Thanks for visiting, Dad."

He let me go. "I wanted to check out the famous greenhouse for myself. And, I have a belated birthday gift for you. I meant to give it to you after the debate, but..." He looked at Dane.

But the Dane bombshell blew that night to hell.

One of his agents handed me a box with a bow, which I untied to reveal a volleyball T-shirt. *If you wanted a soft serve, you should've gone to Dairy Queen,* I read. "Thanks, Dad." I smiled and gave him another hug.

"Want a drink?" I gestured behind me.

"How 'bout a beer?" Dad asked Dane. "You can set me up with a quality brew, right, Dane? You *love* beer, as I recall."

I glanced at Dane, who rolled his eyes, but he did sport a hint of a smile.

"There's no alcohol in the house, sir," Brad said. "Not with minors on the premises."

Dad grinned. "Just kidding. Why don't you show me around, Lucy?"

We left Dane and the agents in the kitchen as I showed him the rest of the house. The tour ended in my bedroom. "Let's talk, *mija*."

I nodded—I'd expected this talk was the purpose of his trip—and shut the door. He sat in my desk chair while I reclined on my bed with my back against the wall. *Dane's wall.*

"What're the latest numbers, Dad?"

"It's a barnburner. The closest election since Bush-Gore in two thousand." He shuddered. "I hope *this* election doesn't last for weeks, like that one did." He loosened his tie as he looked at me. "So, I thought about things, and it doesn't make sense to move you out of here before the election."

Phew. At least two more days with Dane.

"If we lose, I don't know if you'll need protection after that, so we'll have a bigger selection of places."

I winced. "I might *still* have agents if we lose?"

"Maybe. They'll have to analyze the security parameters. They're investigating some racist threats."

My stomach twisted. "Racist threats?"

"Some people don't like the idea of a Mexican American president." He shrugged. "Comes with the territory—forging a new path isn't easy."

I gulped.

He leaned forward and rested his elbows on his knees. "When were you going to tell me about your match on election night?"

"Oh. I…I was trying to decide where I'll be first."

"Decide? Of course you'll be here, with your team. You made a commitment."

"But I have a commitment to my family, too."

"We *know* that. You demonstrate your love for us all the time, sweetheart. You babysat Mateo when we traveled to Alejandro's baseball games. You play referee between your brothers. You helped your mother with the cooking. You..." He looked away and his Adam's apple bobbed as he swallowed. When he looked back at me, his eyes shone. "You starved yourself as a sacrifice for the family."

I'd never seen my dad anywhere close to crying, and my nose burned with impending tears. "What do you mean?" My voice shook.

"Your collapse at practice—God, that terrified me. I've done some reading about eating disorders, and I don't want to oversimplify things, but when I read about individuals who take care of others so much that they neglect caring for themselves..." He exhaled. "That's *you*, Lucia."

It was like two months of stress bubbled up and over when he said that. Tears spilled down my cheeks, and he reached out to wipe under my eye. "My sweet girl. How're you doing? Your mother tells me you're seeing a psychologist and a dietitian?"

I nodded. "I'm getting better. They're helping me...I think you'd like them." I sniffed.

"I'm sorry I haven't been here for you."

I smiled through my tears. "You've been kind of busy. How in the world are you here tonight?"

"How in the world haven't I been here before?" He shook his head. "I haven't seen you play one game as a Cougar."

"It's okay. I understand." I swiped at my cheek. *Get it together.*

"I *will* be there, for every postseason match after election night, hopefully all the way to the NCAA finals. Okay?"

I nodded.

"So here's what I need to know." His mouth tightened, and I braced myself. "I've spoken to your mother extensively about this thing with Dane. You said you're recovering from the eating disorder. Is that *with* Dane's support, or in *spite* of him? Does being with Dane make you stronger or weaker?"

"*Stronger*, Dad!"

He frowned as he patted his thigh. "You've always been honest with me. Think about this for a second. This is important."

I counted a few of my breaths. "Okay," I admitted, "at first Dane was kind of...*angry* about Republican beliefs." Angry was probably an understatement. I remembered Dane's enticing smirk as he insulted my dad, and my cheeks flamed. "I've sort of had a crush on him for a while—"

"You have?" His eyes seemed to flicker with amusement. "I didn't know that."

"I wasn't about to tell you guys I had a thing for your opponent's son."

He nodded. "Good point."

"But he…he seemed to hate me, and he said some mean things…"

My dad's eyes narrowed, and he looked toward my bedroom door. I looked down to see his feet jiggling, like he was about to go find Dane and kill him. I rushed ahead with a twinge of desperation in my voice.

"And I thought I wasn't pretty enough for him, and then Coach told me to lose weight…" I stopped babbling when Dad stared at me with wide eyes.

"How could you believe you're not *pretty?* That's the most ridiculous thing I've ever heard!" He pointed at the door. "Dane thinks you're *brillante!* He called you *espléndida* ."

"He *did?"* Warmth zinged up my spine, filling my body with buzzing joy. I realized I grinned like an idiot.

Dad watched me for a few moments before he chuckled. "This isn't just a crush anymore, is it?"

I chewed the inside of my mouth as I shook my head. "Sorry."

"Well, at least he's better looking than that idiot James Carville."

"Who?"

"Never mind."

"Dad, Dane really does support me…he helps me with my meal plan, and he helps me with my panic attacks. Dr. Valentine said I have high anxiety."

"You don't need to be a psychologist to know that, my little worry bug. You probably get that from your mother."

"Right." I shrugged. "But you know how Dane helps me the most? He makes me *excited* to wake up every morning. It's been tough here some days, but he makes everything brighter."

Dad gazed at me for a few moments, then gave me an earnest smile. "*Mija's* growing up. My baby girl's turning into a strong, *magnífica* woman." He took my hands in his. "And I couldn't be prouder."

26

Dane

"Don't *you* look handsome," China purred as we drove past the throng of reporters outside the greenhouse.

I glanced down at the navy blue suit Mom had ordered for me. "It's not every day your mother gets elected president."

"Feeling confident, huh?" China winked from the seat next to me.

I studied her form-fitting, sequined evening gown. "Where exactly do you hide a gun in there?"

She smirked. "A place only Allie can find."

"TMI," Brad groaned from the driver seat.

"I hear ya, brother." I reached forward to tap my fist on his shoulder. My jacket sleeve hiked up to reveal my watch, and I noticed the time. Lucia was warming up for her match by now, and I wished I could be there with her.

"So…" China's smirk faded. "This might be our last night together."

They'd told me if my mom won, I'd likely get another security detail. If she lost, I might not have any protection at all.

I watched Brad bite his fist. "I'm getting *verklempt* up here… crying so hard I can't see the road."

I laughed and smacked the back of his head, then turned to China. We stared at each other for a minute or so before I offered, "I never thought I'd say this, but I'll miss you guys."

"You've been a challenging protectee, Mr. Monroe," China said with a stern voice. Then her face softened. "The best kind."

Twenty minutes later, we entered through the back hallway of a swanky downtown hotel. Attending a university in the capital of my mother's home state made it easy to hop over to the victory bash—and easy to slink away if it turned into Loserville with my mother conceding the election to President-elect Ramirez. Adolf as president would be so weird. I'd never considered the possibility, but since the pollsters still couldn't predict the outcome of an election wrapping up this very evening, I had to entertain the idea of a Republican win.

I heard the party halfway down the hall, and by the time we entered the ballroom, hip-hop music blasted my ears. A voice boomed, "Welcome to Senator Monroe's son, Dane!" I peered through the darkness, illuminated only by blue lights and a massive TV screen in one corner, to find Steve on the spotlighted stage, a microphone in his hand. Shouts and cheers rang out, and lighted TV cameras swiveled my direction. Brad maintained his hold on my elbow as he scanned the throngs of people, his face a mask of stone.

"Your family's this way," China shouted in my ear, and we made a Secret Service sandwich as we weaved through the crowd. Though it was early evening, most of the guests already held beer bottles and wine glasses. I knew everyone had entered the party through a metal detector, with their belongings searched, but I still felt nervous.

"Dane!" My sister waved at me when we reached a side room off the ballroom. I let out a breath in the quieter, calmer space. Jessica wore a light blue dress that came to her knees, and with her curly hair swept up into a bow, I swore she looked like a princess.

"*Hermanita.*" I gathered her into a hug. "How was the flight from DC?"

"Fine. My coach is mad I'm missing practice."

"He'll get over it. This is a big night for the Monroe family." I looked up to see my dad approach.

He paused when he reached us. "A hug for your old man?"

What the hell—I was feeling generous. When I stepped into his arms, I could smell booze. So *he'd* started early too. With the tension of impending election results in the air, I wouldn't mind a drink myself. Once Dad let me go, he hugged Jessica and kept her by his side.

Jessica asked, "Did Lucia decide to go to Texas or play her game?"

I silently cursed as I watched the question on my dad's face. "Lucia?" He nodded. "Oh, the Ramirez girl. You're living with her."

"Dane and Lucia— "

I cut Jessica short with a glare. If Dad didn't care to show interest in my life, I refused to share it with him.

"What were you saying, Jessie?" Dad asked.

"Dane's glad Lucia will be moving out soon," I supplied as I watched my sister to make sure she didn't open her mouth. *Time for redirection.* "So, Dad, how's the painting coming along?"

"Exquisitely. I'd love to show you my latest piece, if that's okay." He extracted his phone from his pocket, scrolled through photos, and handed it to me before obtaining my permission. Shades of red blasted off the screen, and I couldn't take my eyes off the photographed canvas.

"What do you think?"

I glanced up to find my dad sporting an easy smile, but his fidgeting hands belied his nervousness about my appraisal. *Huh.* I'd never thought he cared about my opinion. I looked back down. The painting had movement and vitality, visible even in a photo, and the undulating crimson waves made me think of geysers of lava. "It looks...pissed off."

"Yes, I suppose so." He shrugged. "I just painted what I felt. My agent thinks it's my best work in years."

"It's a powerful work," I admitted. "Quite evocative."

"Let *me* see." Jessica reached for the phone.

Dad's eyes held mine for a moment, and it felt like he was paying attention to me for the first time in years. He seemed weary, sort of sad. He cupped my shoulder. "How's school going?"

I didn't know how to respond at first. "Fine."

"Sophomore year." He smiled. "That was a big party year for me in college. In fact, why're you empty handed? It's a celebration—let's get you a drink."

Before I could protest, he'd disappeared to the main ballroom, undoubtedly headed for the cash bar. I shoved my hands in the pockets of my dress pants.

"I have to say I don't *get* this painting," Jessica said as she looked up from Dad's phone. Her cheeks pinked.

I chuckled as I took the phone. "I think that's a good thing. It means you haven't been to hell and back, like some of us." Just then Dad's phone vibrated, and I held my breath. *Should I read the text?* I looked around the room, but the agents chatted or guarded the doors, not really paying attention to me. I couldn't help myself:

Self-absorbed prick. I can't BELIEVE you're with her.

I gasped—that *had* to be Dad's mistress.

"What's wrong?" Jessica grabbed for the phone, but I yanked it out of her reach.

"Nothing." My stomach twisted with revulsion. It was *her*. Fucking floozy ho-bag. But she was furious with my dad? Did that mean my parents' marriage still had a chance?

I froze when my mother entered the room, trailed by Steve. She made a beeline for us. After she hugged my sister, she turned to me and cocked her head. "You look like you've seen a ghost."

Maybe a ghost of affairs past. I gulped as I slipped his phone into my pocket. "Nah, I'm cool." I forced a smile. "I'm just stoked for your big win!"

She blinked at me for a moment, her psychologist brain seeming to work overtime, but then she shook her head. "Steve says Florida's going to Ramirez." She gestured over her shoulder, and I saw Steve about twenty feet away, scowling at a piece of paper in his hands. "So it's not over yet."

"But you expected the Latino vote would swing to them, right?"

"Florida was still up in the air, though. It'll be tight. But thank you both for being here." She reached out for me, and I held on to her for an extra-long hug. She'd been through so much.

"Of course we're here," I said.

"Here we are." Dad arrived and stretched a beer bottle my direction, but Mom spun around.

"What're you *doing?"* she hissed.

Dad's bewildered gaze darted back and forth between Mom and me, and he slowly retracted the offered brew. It looked delicious. "Getting our son a drink. What's the big deal, Lois?"

"For one thing, it's a media disaster. He's underage! And he can't have alcohol anyway. If you were involved at *all* in his life, you'd know why."

"Like *you've* been mother of the year," Dad spat.

Her eyes blazed. "How *dare* you."

"Mom?" Jessica's voice quivered, and when I peeled my eyes away from the clusterfuck that was my parents' marriage, I saw tears in her eyes. I stepped around Mom and draped my arm across Jessica's shoulders.

"It's okay," I whispered, with a squeeze. On the other side of me, Mom seemed to shake from anger, so I cradled her elbow in my free arm.

Dad looked at the three of us standing together, in obvious distress, and he took a step back. "I'm sorry." He swallowed. "I'm so sorry. I've been such an idiot." He gazed at Mom. "I hope what I told you tonight means something. For you. For us. But now I realize I can't make this all better in an hour. You're too hurt for that."

I glanced to my right and saw her mouth tremble. She nodded.

"Of course you're hurt. I've made a proper mess of things." Dad shook his head.

"What're you guys talking about?" asked Jessica.

When Dad met my eyes, I told him, "She deserves to know." I looked at my mom. "Jess is stronger than you think."

Steve swooped in next to my mom. "Mr. DuPont, how 'bout you head back to the party? We're pretty busy back here."

Dad hung his head for a moment before he nodded. "Jessie, let's talk." He looked to my mom, and she must have given her approval because his fingers curled as he beckoned my sister. I nudged her toward him.

"Wait—here's your phone." I handed it to Dad and watched him lead Jessica to a corner of the room.

Mom let out a rush of air, and Steve clasped her forearm. "You okay, Lo?"

She gave him a wobbly smile and nodded. "Thanks for getting rid of him." She patted his hand. "Find out the latest Colorado numbers, okay?"

As I watched their exchange, something felt strange. They seemed curiously intimate. I studied Steve as if seeing him for the first time, with his compact build and shrewd brown eyes. He smiled at my mom before he left, and then she turned to me.

Her voice wavered. "Why'd you have Patrick's phone?"

I wasn't sure if my heartbeat kicked up from seeing her so shaken or at the thought of her possibly finding out about the text. "He showed me his latest painting."

"Ah." She blinked. "*Homage to Fuck Off.*"

I suppressed a laugh.

"Evidently he's working through his anger toward my father."

Maybe I *should pick up painting too, then.* "Mom, what did Dad tell you tonight?"

Her eyes flickered. "He wants me back." She huffed out a breath. "He said he made a huge mistake. He wants to go to couples counseling, work it out."

"Wow. That's some kind of timing he has, huh?"

"Honestly, it's been a good distraction. There was always more I could do during the campaign, but tonight...well, now I've done all I can. It's out of my control, and I'm incredibly nervous."

"But it feels good to put it all out there, whatever the outcome."

She smiled at me. "Exactly, Mr. Volleyball Player. You know what that's like." Her smile faded. "I'm glad he told me. It feels validating to know he still wants me, even if I'm not sure we can work this out."

"Because of your feelings for Steve?"

She flinched, then gaped at me for a long minute. "Steve and I are friends, and that's all...even though he wants more."

"And you?" I looked into her eyes. "What do you want?"

"I want things to be simpler." Her grin seemed cheeky. "I want to be President of the United States."

This time I did laugh. "Yeah, 'cause those things go together *real* well."

She shook her head. "I can't believe you saw through Steve's feelings." She straightened my shirt collar and gazed up at me. "You're becoming quite the psychologist, hmm?"

I shrugged.

"Of course, this is familiar territory to you—forbidden romance and all."

I looked at my watch. Lucia's match had started fifteen minutes ago.

"Go to Lucia, Dane." When I inhaled sharply, she patted my chest. "This election will last late into the night, and you being here won't affect the outcome. We'll be okay." I looked over to Jessica and Dad in the corner, but Mom cupped my face and turned my attention back to her. "Jessie will take the news better than you, because now there's hope for reconciliation. You didn't have that. And unlike your situation, I'll be here for her. I'll make sure John keeps her away from the cash bar."

When my mom's eyes twinkled, I chuckled. "But, Mom—"

"I'll be fine, honey. I've got two men who love me, and soon I'll be president. *Go*, Dane. Go to her."

I kissed her cheek. "Will you tell Jess I'll be there for her meet next weekend?" When Mom nodded, I hustled over to Brad. "Hey, I want—"

"China's already got the SUV fired up, Maverick," he said with a grin. "Let's roll."

After China broke all kinds of traffic laws, we lurched to the curb near the gym. I could hear the cheerleaders from outside: *Cou, cou, cou, cou-gars!* Inside the gym, it was a wall of sound. A glance at the scoreboard told me Highbanks was up seven to two over Indiana University in the second game. China veered toward Allison, who stood on the gym's upper level, and Brad led me to the bleachers behind the Highbanks bench. Frank must have been somewhere here too.

Focused on the game, Lucia didn't see me come in, but the one TV camera on the floor did. I ignored it as it swiveled to point at me and watched my girl play our favorite game. Lucia and Maddie went up for the block, but the Indiana hitter managed to hit through them. Kaitlyn's missed dig made it side-out to IU, and I turned to a motherly type sitting next to me. "Who won the first game?"

"Cougars!" She grinned.

Phew. Hopefully Nina was playing better this match. But then the Indiana server rattled off four zingers that stymied the Highbanks defense and tied the game, and Coach Holter called a time out. When Lucia jogged over to the huddle, she happened to scan the stands, and she jumped when she saw me. Her mouth formed the cutest O as her eyes grew big. My heart thrummed and her huge smile undoubtedly matched mine.

"You okay?" she mouthed.

I nodded and tapped the big metal button on my lapel that read GO MONROE.

Her eyes sparkled as she shook her head.

I worried Coach would have a hissy fit that her focus wasn't on the team, but he funneled his rage on the defense, jabbing his finger at Kaitlyn and Lynette. The referee blew his whistle, and the teams took the court again. Another serve screamed across the net, but this time Kaitlyn executed a clean pass to Nina, who set a good ball. Lucia flew like an angel—*damn*, her vertical leap was impressive—and slammed the ball at a vicious angle. The IU libero didn't have a chance in hell to dig that heat-seeking missile. *Point, Highbanks.*

Lucia high-fived Nina, then snuck a quick wink in my direction. That wink did all kinds of dirty things to my body. A tingle in my toes jolted up my legs and made me hard in an instant. The racing thud of my heartbeat, the burn in my hands, desiring her hair in my clutches, craving the touch of her sweet, smooth skin…I swallowed. I hadn't noticed how warm it was in the gym, and I loosened my tie.

When Lucia's next block stuffed the opponent, she fist-pumped as she hopped up and down, then wrapped Maddie in a hug. A bead of sweat trickled down my back, and I peeled off my suit jacket. I draped it over my lap to hide my growing problem. After a few more kills by Lucia, the nape of my neck felt wet. I folded up my shirtsleeves to my elbows.

"You gonna strip it all off?" Brad leered as he leaned in.

"Wish I could. It's *hot* in here." And she was undoing me with her astounding play.

There was often a time late in the season when underclassmen stepped up their game, confidently filling the holes left by graduating seniors. A changing of the guard, so to speak. It had happened for me when our starting setter's old knee injury acted up in our home game against Bridgetown last spring. When Phil had put me in, at first I'd thought I would hurl, but I'd been ready. I'd run the offense like a Tesla Roadster—smooth, precise, and confident—just like Lucia's play at the moment. There was no need for Nina to set Maddie because Lucia crushed every ball sent her way. It was a thing of beauty.

After the match, which Highbanks won three games to zero, I headed to the hallway outside the locker room with my agents behind me. Hanging by the wall was a muscular guy, almost my height, and when I got closer I recognized him immediately. But he was the one who first spoke. "Dane Monroe, right?"

I stuck out my hand. "Hey, TJ." The starting football quarterback at a volleyball game?

"Um..." He cocked his head. "This is election night, right? And... you're *here?*"

Before I had a chance to explain, the locker room door swung open, and I wondered if Lucia's arrival would explain my presence. But it turned out the player who emerged explained *TJ's* presence.

"Hey, gorgeous," he said, and Nina shimmied right up to him. She'd planted a kiss on his lips before she realized I was there.

"Dane!" Her eyes widened.

"That was one hell of a match, Nina."

It was the first genuine smile I'd seen from her. "Thanks." She leaned into the big man behind her. "You know TJ?"

"Of course." I nodded at him. "I go to Highbanks, after all."

He groaned. "No going anonymous around here, that's for sure."

It struck me that maybe TJ would be a good friend—he certainly understood the burdens of celebrity. I shrugged. "If it weren't for my mom, I could go incognito as a volleyball player. It's a little different for a star football player."

"Well, a volleyball setter's like a quarterback," Nina said. "The leader of the team."

"And you did a great job leading tonight," I said.

She beamed. "Thanks. See ya, Dane."

I nodded at them as they left, and hoped the pain I'd caused Nina was in the past. Then the girl of my present walked out of the locker room and bounded into my arms.

"I can't believe you're here!" she gushed.

"*I* can't believe I almost missed that performance. You were incredible."

A giddy grin lit up her face. "It was so fun! But why aren't you with your mom?"

"You know what, my mom's going to be fine, win or lose." It was the first time in recent memory that I didn't feel a knot of worry in my belly when I thought of Mom. "She saw that I wanted to be with you, so she told me to go."

"Wow. Your mom is so cool." She turned to the agents. "What's the latest with the election? Alex texted me that it's still too close to call."

China stepped closer. "Want to know what happened with Colorado?" When Lucia nodded, she said, "Senator Monroe carried the state."

Lucia seemed to take the news well. "What's the electoral vote count?"

"Tied at two-thirty-six," Frank said.

Lucia looked at me with big eyes. "*¡Híjole!*"

"So California's still up in the air?" I asked.

"And Arizona," Brad said.

I cradled her head. "Let's go home and watch the results. Together."

"Great idea." She smiled.

We walked arm in arm out of the gym, and I tucked Lucia closer to protect her from the icy November wind. That's when I heard a woman call my name. I turned to see a reporter rush toward us with her camera guy in tow. I felt Lucia tense next to me, but she didn't pull away. When the reporter got closer, my jaw dropped. I'd met her before. *Beergate.*

"Beverly Jackson," I said. I snuck a glance at her microphone and camera but didn't see any Fox logo. "You got your job back?"

"You think I'd work a volleyball game on *election* night if I got my job back?"

"Good point." I winced. "Were there criminal charges?"

"I had a good lawyer." She frowned. "Now I'm stuck doing freelance work, trying to claw my way back."

Guilt stirred in my gut. "I feel bad you never got the inside scoop I promised you."

"You can still make it up to me." Her eyes took in Lucia and me. "It appears you've got quite the scoop right there."

Lucia shot me a questioning look. I grinned at her, then turned to Beverly. "You're right." I took a deep breath as I looked straight into the camera. "I love Lucia Ramirez."

The cutest gasp lifted the air next to me. I turned to see her mouth hanging open, a full-on blush coloring her pretty cheeks. Her lips gradually pulled together and slid into a grin as wide as Texas. Her eyes danced as she gazed up at me. "And I love Dane Monroe."

"How 'bout a kiss—"

But Lucia's mouth was on mine before Beverly had a chance to finish her suggestion. Her warm lips and floral shampoo filled my senses, and I massaged my hands through her thick, wet hair to release more of the heavenly scent.

Somewhere a man cleared his throat, then a moment later I heard Brad say, "*Jesus*, horndogs! Get a room."

I unlatched my lips and looked over Lucia's shoulder to find Brad cackling and Frank shaking his head. I looked back at Beverly. "Will that work for you?"

"Who do you predict will win the election?" she asked.

How will I answer that?

Lucia looked at me, then at the camera. "One of our parents will win, of course."

Beverly shook her head and opened her mouth as if to question us again, but then she tapped the camera operator's shoulder. "That's a wrap."

I know I sighed with relief.

Sometime later, we cuddled on the TV room sofa and watched political commentators argue. The anchor touched her earpiece. "Well, what do you know. In this bitterly contested election between two very different candidates, it appears there *is* some common ground to be found." The video of Lucia kissing me flashed on the screen, and I bolted upright as she squeaked. That reporter was *fast*.

"I've never seen myself kiss a girl on TV before."

"It's kind of weird." She nodded. Then her mouth curled into a devious smile. "And kind of sexy."

My lower body stirred. "Kind of a turn on."

I leaned down to kiss her and tasted fajita from our takeout after the match. Spicy and delicious, just like her. We stretched down toward one end of the sofa, her on top of me and our legs tangled together. She skated her fingertips underneath my shirt, springing goose bumps up the midline of my torso, and my hands wandered down her back until they cradled her fine butt cheeks, soft and muscular through the Spandex.

I barely heard the reporter say that Arizona had gone to Governor Ramirez, but it seemed neither of us cared. The real decider would be the massive number of electoral votes in California, and it was still too close to call.

My breath caught when she unbuttoned my shirt and yanked it open.

"Gotta see this gorgeous chest." Her brown eyes flared with heat as they roved down my body, and her lips soon followed the scorching trail her eyes had left. Her sweet mouth on my belly ignited a fire in my core, and my hips bucked off the sofa.

She grinned up at me. "You like that?"

My fingers played with her hair as I tried to catch my breath. "I've got no words for how much I like that."

She pressed lingering kisses up my chest, and the flames licked higher. Her warm breath tickled my collarbone. Just as her face hovered over mine, an involuntary yawn stretched her mouth. Her eyes widened as her hand flew to cover her mouth. "Sorry!"

I chuckled. "My little studette is tired after her stellar match."

"No, I'm not."

I touched my finger to her lips. "We've got time. It's okay." Then I drew her into me, and she snuggled in so her head rested on my chest. My fingers wove into her damp hair, and I breathed in her beguiling scent. A commentator said something about California typically being a lockdown for Democrats, but the Latino vote made that less certain.

I curled a strand around my finger. "What if your dad loses?"

"What if he wins?" She lifted her head. "That's a lot of pressure."

I laughed. "I was thinking the same thing. I wouldn't mind if Mom lost the election. Maybe my life could return to normal."

She twisted her mouth to one side. "That's not very nice of us to hope our parent loses."

"I think it's normal, in our situation." I pressed a kiss to her lips. "Whatever happens, I'm glad I found you."

She looked into my eyes. "*Te amo*."

"I love you, too, Luz."

I'm not sure what time it was later when the TV anchor said, "*California votes are in for over ninety percent of the precincts, and we're finally ready to announce the winner*." I looked down to find Lucia sleeping in my arms, so sweet and yummy. I nudged her awake. "Luz, there's a winner."

She gasped and turned her blinking eyes to the screen. We joined hands just as the reporter began to speak.

"*The next President of the United States is...*"

ACKNOWLEDGMENTS

Gratitude and blessings to:

Nicki Elson, critique partner. Thank you for warm fuzzies, raucous political commentary, and non-stop laughs.

Jessica Royer Ocken, editor extraordinaire. We've plowed through five novels together, and I look forward to many more. Thanks for articulating my ideas better than I do!

Coreen Montagna, book designer to the stars. Dane and I appreciate your talent.

Yelania Velasco, Spanish consultant. *Gracias* for your detailed and *rápido* assistance. (Any remaining errors are mine.)

Julie from AToMR Tours. Thank you for your intelligence and kindness, and for spreading the word about *Blocked.*

My volleyball teammates at Kenyon College, particularly the woman who shares my brain: Gwynn Evans Harrison. We had a blast together!

Supportive authors Carol, Elisa, Debra, Beck, Cherie, Susan, Colleen, Hannah, Jen, Judy, Trish, Robin, Darcia, Lisette, Alex.

Encouraging readers Mitsy, Grace, Roche, Leisha, Victoria, Jaime, Lorne, Janine, Cécile, Ina, Vishal.

My friends and family for putting up with this crazy writing gig of mine.

ABOUT THE AUTHOR

Get psyched for romance with psychologist/author (psycho author) Jennifer Lane! By day she witnesses tremendous growth in her psychotherapy clients, and by night she wrangles misbehaving fictional characters as she writes sports romance and romantic suspense with a psychological twist. She can't decide which is more fun.

A swimmer and volleyball player in college, Jen wove some of her own experiences into *Streamline*—a military mystery about swimmers. Dani at Refracted Light Reviews called *Streamline* "an emotionally complex story about the ones we love, the ones we hurt, the mistakes that break the human heart, and the love that puts the pieces back together." But you don't have to take her word for it. Readers can dip their toes into Jen's world of swimming romance by sampling her free New Adult novella *Swim Recruit*.

College volleyball romance *Blocked* is Jen's newest release. Peek inside big-time college sports and even bigger national politics when the offspring of two presidential candidates find out whether opposites really do attract, or their match is blocked from the start.

Stories of redemption interest Jen the most, especially the healing power of love. She is also the author of The Conduct Series, a romantic suspense trilogy that includes *With Good Behavior*, *Bad Behavior*, and *On Best Behavior*. "In a story of betrayal, responsibility, treachery, and honor, Lane does an excellent job portraying the intricate intersection of two lives connected by love...and lies," said reviewer Susan Swiderski.

Ultimately, whether writing or reading, Jen loves stories that make her laugh and cry. In her spare time she enjoys exercising, attending book club, hanging out with her plus-size, "I'm not fat, I'm big-boned" Izzie cat, and visiting her sisters and their families in Chicago and Hilton Head.

Made in the USA
Las Vegas, NV
28 November 2025

35275982R00167